UNDERSTANDING U S POLITICS

UNDERSTANDING U S POLITICS:
A PRIMER FOR NONVOTERS

Jack Vast-Binder

© 2015 Jack Vast-Binder

All Rights Reserved

ISBN – 978-0-692-59837-5

Cover design by Emily VastBinder and Joshua Kern

Contents

Author's Preface vii

Introduction: A Primer on US Politics; for whom? Why? ix

Part I: Preliminary Approaches

Chapter 1 What's Political & How do we Know it When we See it? ... 3

Chapter 2 The Story Behind the Left and the Right 17

Chapter 3 What's the Difference? 41

Part II: Economy and Politics

Chapter 4 Some Basics of Free Market Economics 77

Chapter 5 The Politics of Economics 109

Part III: The Politics of Morality

Chapter 6 Moral Beliefs: Some Background 153

Chapter 7 The Moral Divide in Contemporary Politics 175

Chapter 8 Beyond the Divide 201

Part IV: The Contemporary Political Scene

Chapter 9 The Facts   229

Chapter 10 The Script: Creating the Political Messages   253

Chapter 11 The Audience and the Actors: How do we Know the Politicians?   275

Concluding Thoughts

Chapter 12 Where Are We Going From Here?   309

Notes   331

Author's Preface

If you are reading this with the nagging feeling that you might be making a mistake, I'd say, that's a good start. You might be just the kind of person I am writing this book for. Because the audience I have had in mind from the start is made up of folks who would be very unlikely to pick up a book like this. It is about politics but it is intended for people who either hate politics or at very least don't give a damn about it. A book about politics written for people who aren't interested in politics, I obviously never set out to write a best seller.

Here's where I'm coming from. There was a time when things were different. In courses in high school and after high school a lot of people used to learn about the workings of politics. Maybe it was one of those non-elective classes that everybody had to sit through, but they got a basic start. In recent years, general political education has given way to the scramble for very focused career based training that promises to deliver only marketable skills. Civics and political science classes have lost out in this career training rush.

Let me make the case a little differently. Politics is a kind of world onto itself; like the art world, the sports world or the fashion world. These worlds are separate from one another. Each has its history, its common knowledge, its star players its scandals, and its great collaborations. For individuals like us, worlds like these can seem strange enough and confusing enough to outsiders to keep them out.

But what if there was a short cut; a quick way to get up to speed and get inside one of these worlds and check it out? What if you could get your hands on a thin book that would allow you to get inside the world of baseball, or opera, or movie directing, or comic books sufficiently so that you could not only follow what was going on in one of these worlds, but more than that, appreciate what people in that world are thinking.

I can't offer you such a book on baseball or opera, or movie directing or comics, but I think I can give you 200 pages or so that will really get you inside the world of politics. What's more, I think I can do it without pitching you some party line. Although my training has been in the social sciences, advanced degrees (or even I.Q.) don't necessarily seem to provide people much protection, when it comes to developing intolerant political biases. But in my case it might be, at least, a part of what has brought me to this subject with the kind of "outside looking in" perspective which lets me better understand those things that folks take for granted as their personal supply of common sense. If you have reactions or comments there is a website that I am about to get up, metapolitical.net, where you will be able to put them. I am indebted to the hundreds of political activists of every imaginable persuasion who I have engaged with and observed over a number of years in several states in preparation for this book. I am indebted even more to Sher, without whom this project would never have been completed. Special thanks to Olivia and Alexander for their timely reminder that our political situation is always only temporary. But whether sensible or foolish, the observations which follow are mine.

My aim has been to introduce you to politics so that you can better appreciate it. But our success in this venture will be to understand our politics beyond the take-it-or-leave-it basis. If we succeed, you should be prepared to easily take your place and make a difference among the politically active and motivated people who, at this point in time, define what self-government means in the United States.

Jack Vast-Binder
Kerrville ,TX
December, 2015

UNDERSTANDING U S POLITICS

Introduction: A Primer on US Politics; for whom? Why?

"I believe there is something out there watching us. Unfortunately it's the government."

Woody Allen [1]

"Political language--and with variations this is true of all political parties, from Conservatives to Anarchists--is designed to make lies sound truthful and murder respectable, and to give an appearance of solidity to pure wind."

George Orwell(1903-1950) [2]

"I never vote. It only encourages them."

Anonymous

"A zeal for different opinions concerning religion, concerning government, and many other points, as well of speculation as of practice; an attachment to different leaders ambitiously contending for pre-eminence and power; or to persons of other descriptions whose fortunes have been interesting to the human passions, have, in turn, divided mankind into parties, inflamed them with mutual animosity, and rendered them much more disposed to vex and oppress each other than to co-operate for their common good."

James Madison(1751-1836)[3]

UNDERSTANDING U S POLITICS

As it happened, September 11, 2001 was mayoral primary election day in New York City. For obvious reasons the election had to be rescheduled. To help bring out the voters when the primary was finally held, the City election Board had put up a banner saying "Vote or Liberty is History". According to the Boston Globe, only 13% of voting age New Yorkers turned out.[4] This might have been expected. From primaries to presidential elections, low turnouts in elections continue to be a staple of our politics. More recently, in the 2014 election cycle, when candidates for Federal, state and local offices were running, almost two thirds of those eligible to vote, stayed away. This was hailed by the press as a 70 year low for the elections we hold mid-term between presidential elections. But 70 years before, we had an excuse. It was 1942, and World War II made it a little harder for some people to vote. In national elections between 1960 and 2012, on an average, just over 47% of voting age people actually voted.

We Americans are fortunate enough to live in what is perhaps the grandest and most powerful country that has ever existed. We call our representative governing system democracy and yet more than half of us consistently opt out of participating in the process. Those who are really hooked on politics may be a vanishing breed. Take for example those two rock'em-sock'em cable news networks that cater to the political faithful on the left and the right. The conservative oriented and more popular of the two, Fox News Network boasts an audience whose average age is 68 years old. At the progressive oriented MSNBC, viewers are reported to have an average age of 60. The average ages of viewers of the traditional network news shows on ABC, CBS, NBC, and PBS fall between 62 and 64.[5] If these age stats are revealing a trend, we could be on the verge of an extinction of interest in politics within the next few decades.

It's a fact that for many of the rest of us, our country's politics has stopped making sense. This book is for those people. It is about the two sides that dominate our politics: the right and the left, the conservatives and the progressives. It traces their history and explains how their political battle is being waged. I've called this little book a primer. The dictionary tells us a primer is a "small introductory book on any topic." So why should anybody want to read a small introductory book about politics? The answer for me is easy. It is because politics is not just important in our lives, it is also endlessly fascinating. If you do not agree with me, you are certainly not alone. But what is more, if you don't agree with me, you just might be someone who'd like my little book. It is not intended for people who are into politics. It is intended for you.

I know from my own experience with picking up all kinds of primers and manuals that when they promise "the fundamentals," most of them fall short. I think I know why. They start simple and soon slip onto incomprehensible jargon. Then, half-apologetically, they tack on a glossary of terms to which they give head-scratching definitions. I think that I can do better if I try to give you important political concepts along with some history and tradition of where they come from. Politics is not like geometry, some logical system unrelated to anything else. In fact, as we proceed I hope that I can show you that the thing about politics that is most confusing is that politics is hardly ever just about politics. It is easier to understand if you think of it as an arena where people work out their differences about things like what's right and wrong, what's fair and unfair, and what we as humans need to do to survive and ever prosper. So as we proceed, you shouldn't be surprised when we seem to get off topic and into subjects like the media, culture, economics, marketing, and even philosophy and religion. It is just not realistic to think we could reach any understanding of politics without digging into the beliefs and desires people carry around with them. Think of this part as getting into the background where the content of politics comes from. The part about campaigns and lawmaking and the courts only looks at the strategies and tactics that the political practitioners are using to pursue that content.

There are lots of reasons why so many people don't participate in our politics. Thinking about what keeps you and the rest of that half or more of our citizens out of politics is as good a place as any to begin.

The Other Half

Let's first reflect a bit more on the nonvoters (this other half you are a part of). Of course there are a lot of other reasons, besides disinterest, that people have for not getting involved in politics. There are many adults who for one legal reason or another cannot vote. Past and present, many people have been prevented from voting. Former slaves got the vote in 1867; women in 1920. State laws have sometimes made it difficult and other times outright impossible for poor people and minorities to vote. For example, in the 1938 presidential elections, only 35,000 citizens overcame the hurdles of poll taxes and other regulations to vote in Mississippi, a state with over 2,000,000 people.[6] A recent Supreme Court decision on the right to vote, and a number of new state laws that have followed it, signal trends that will likely prevent many people from voting, even though they voted in the past. But in contemporary elections those prevented from voting represent only a small fraction of the nonvoters when compared to those who could vote but don't. This book will not do anything for people who can't vote. It is for a much bigger category of people, the ones who can participate legally, and relatively easily, but just don't.

Commentators are forever questioning what is going on with folks like you who are choosing to stay away from the polls. Let me mention some of the reasons they come up with. For some, it might be the sheer number of elections and candidates out there. Compared to other countries with representative governments, we might be over-doing it. There are over 90,000 different government entities in the United States, and most of them depend, at least in part, upon elections to staff themselves. Then there is the "why bother?" argument. Should I vote for Tweet-el-dee or his identical twin, Tweet-el-dum? There is a separate issue that pushes people away in many jurisdictions. Surveys are now telling us that many of our elections are in jurisdictions that are so dominated by one party or the other that elections are a foregone conclusion. Again, why bother? There is another problem that really puts some people off. It happens when state legislatures pass off their duties to voters. Interest groups then can put long, deliberately confusing questions written in legalese on ballots. Voters reading these ballot "initiatives" walk away, talking to themselves. Then there is the inconvenience of voting, though there has been some improvement in early voting in recent years, when asked, many nonvoters say they don't have the time. For a lot of people, getting to the polls on a workday presents a challenge. In a rough economy, just surviving takes real effort and time. Even when the economy is good, we now live in a country where just about every adult in every stable household needs to get and keep jobs. Finding out about the candidates and the issues you need to know about and then getting to the polling place can make unreasonable demands on a person's time. Besides all these reasons, you might agree with those who are convinced that the game is fixed!

The Dysfunctional Shouting Match

In recent years, along with all other reasons for opting out, there is another even more important reason that is motivating folks to avoid politics. Nowadays a lot of people find the uncivil, polarized arguing of politicians, TV personalities and even their politically active neighbors, just too hard to take. All this shouting and name calling, the scandalizing, the fear mongering, the crazy claims and outright lies are enough to put any reasonable person off. The politicians and the more politically active among us have come to look like a bunch of self-absorbed intolerant bores. The most extreme of them can seem downright scary.

And scary is not too strong a word for it. There are lots of Americans out there who are fearful but often extremely angry with governmental policies, and laws, and fellow citizens they disagree with politically. What will come out of the political fear and anger that has been simmering ever hotter, over the past several years? Allow me a bit of a confession. As I have approached the project I have also been goaded along by a growing concern, a concern that all this verbal conflict might very well lead some day to violence between extreme political factions in this country.

To summarize, if you don't get it when it comes to politics, you are part of that solid and persistent other half, who opt out, when it comes to voting in most elections in the United States. My plan, my purpose, my promise here is simple. I want to try to convince at least some of those in that other half, that politics is not that boring or hard to understand, and that it just might be worth a lot more of our attention. In the pages that follow, who knows, you might work out your own reasons to begin to engage in politics on your own terms. At very least you will be able pass unnoticed among the political partisans, and converse with them on your own terms whenever you choose to.

My Approach

So, a book about politics for people who have made up their minds that they are not interested. Try to think of what you are reading as a kind of promotion designed to pull people in. To give you an example of what such an effort might look like, a few years ago promoters of professional football wanted to increase the fan base among women. In the process they went to great lengths to get more women interested in televised football. They brought in female sports commentators. They made other efforts to get women viewers to become a bigger part of the fan base. The efforts paid off and women football enthusiasts can be thankful.[7] But who's doing anything similar for politics, certainly not the loony talking heads that fill up the television screens. Where is that calmer voice out there, explaining the interest and excitement of the political game that is going on? Who is giving us objective commentary along with insights about the customs, and rules, the stats and records; whole bodies of information that can really help us identify with the teams and the individual players, both on and off the field, so that folks like you can make enough sense of it all to get interested in the game and its outcomes"? What about the political parties? Trust me; the parties are not going to do it. You might not realize it at this point, but they support your indifference. The low levels of interest in politics are just the way they like it. More about that later. For now, let me have a try at it.

I think that the women NFL fans example is apt. But how do we apply it to politics? In some ways a sport like football is simpler. Aren't they just after scoring points and winning games? What do you think would have happened if the NFL had printed up millions of football rule books and sent them free to subscribers of popular women's magazines? Letting disinterested women in on all that stuff about four downs and time clocks, and even play diagrams wouldn't bring in many new fans, right? What kinds of knowledge and understandings convert people from ignoring to engaging in a scene, any scene? Knowing more about how elections are conducted and how a bill becomes a law is probably not going to mint many new political junkies. If you happen to be a football fan, I am confident that you see what I am talking about. For starters you'd probably be reminding yourself of how betting on the outcomes generates game day interest. But that isn't going to get us very far with politics because you folks in that other half are already convinced that you don't have any skin in this politics game. So take a deep breath, and continue reading with the assurance that I am not about to lecture you about what is personally at stake for you in Bureau of Land Management policies, or future Supreme Court appointments. And besides, the Bureau of Land Management doesn't even offer a trendy line of casual apparel.

It is my feeling that the knowledge and understandings that might open you up to our politics has to go deeper into how the game is played. We need to get closer to the people involved, their beliefs, their strivings. Politics is first and foremost about ideas. ,Let me elaborate a little. Sticking with the notion of games and moving beyond sports and football, in any game there are goal seeking participants who at times cooperate and at other times confront one another while acknowledging rules which are specific to that situation. And of course there are all kinds of rules of the game, (some clear some fuzzier), rules that say what people there can and can't do to get what they are there for. But the thing that can get us interested is understanding that each of the participants is trying to get some things done, that he or she can't get done alone as individuals. It is this process of finding like-minded people, and then getting them to act together that will benefit our understanding of politics most.

When researchers travel to remote places to observe how the people live, we call it anthropology. They try to understand the group life they observe by finding out what is important to the people there, their positions, their history, the rules of their game, things they consider sacred. I am convinced that the political world can be better appreciated in this way.

A good bit of the research that went into this book used a technique that actually came out of anthropology. It has been called "participant observation." Though some might use the jargon of social science to describe it, participant observation is not a whole lot more than hanging around with people enough so that you start to understand how they see things and what they think is important. It's a fact: we all use participant observation skills in order to grow up and mature. But when it comes to our subject here, politics, people just seem to naturally not want to hang around with people they disagree with; Republicans stick with Republicans, Democrats stick with Democrats and so forth. Not me. For some strange reason, I've liked hanging around with people of all political variations trying to figure out how they see things and what they think is important.

Trying to Make Sense of It

Let these people rant while we take a closer look at what this politics stuff is really about. Just because some among us dismiss, and even demonize people with political beliefs they don't agree with, that doesn't make it either necessary, right, or even helpful, for us to do the same. Good anthropologists seldom take sides in tribal affairs. Oh, that reminds me. Let me also be straight about something else. This is not going to be some disguised attempt to fill page after page with my own personal political beliefs. Books like that come out every day. I have political beliefs, but I'll try to keep them out of the discussion. Publishing harsh polemical tracts is now one of the few growth areas in our otherwise weak economy, and we'd be a lot better off without 99% of those kinds of books. What I have tried to do is give you my best attempt to explain our politics and how they got to be this way. If I am at all successful, ideally, you will be prepared to set this book down and begin digging into this thing, politics, on your own.

So, my aim here is not to convert you into an ideological hot-head. Neither is it to discuss the US Constitution or how a bill becomes a law. Again think of the NFL example. Just like that game, our game of politics needs more fans right now...desperately. I perceive that this is because our politics is careening off track, and I have become convinced that what it needs is a bigger audience; more fans. In addition, there is the irony that the closer that governments get to us the less interested we seem to be. This 50% stuff is really about national elections. In the city or county where you spend your days, where you encounter government directly, voter turn-outs like the 13% in New York after 9/11, are routine. The essence of our representative government has, from the beginning, been majority rule with respect for the rights of the minority. What the country needs is more care and concern from you folks in the other half.

Politicians are prone to say things and make commitments they couldn't possibly be sincere about. This alone is a big part of what keeps a lot of people away, especially young people. So part of what we will try to do will be to look at what people are saying and then try to cut through the crap and find out what they are actually concerned about, and what they are trying to accomplish. I believe that a good understanding of the political divide we call its right/left dimension is key to our understanding. What makes these folks take sides on almost everything and what makes them so consistently sure that they are correct and the other side is not?

As we dig in to this it should begin to make more sense if we see the whole process as resulting in *Minority Rule* government Let me explain As I mentioned before, many of these people, the politicians and their appointees, advisers and consultants, don't have any problem with alienating folks like you. They have their loyal base; a substantial and stable percentage of people sure to vote, and sure to vote for them. Then there is that much smaller percentage, that sliver of folks in the middle, (the people who dependably vote but don't always vote for the candidates from the same party), the swing voters. Politicians focus almost entirely on these two categories: the base and the swing vote. So if you are a nonvoter, just think for a moment. For a politician to get your vote he'd (most of them are still men), first have to expend the effort and resources necessary to get you to show up at the right polling place: a big learning curve right there. Then that same politician would have to be confident that his persuasiveness had assured that you would vote for him. Quite a stretch; too expensive in the first place and beyond that, too risky. Thus it is that today's politicians are probably not at all interested in answering to you, the unlikely voter.

This is perhaps most clear in the primary elections in which candidates compete to get on the ballet. A candidate can easily win with only a tiny percent of the electorate's votes. So it is not at all surprising that the appeals these politicians come up with sound so hollow to you the nonvoter. What gets almost no attention though is the fact that, in most times and in most jurisdictions, we live not under majority rule but under *minority rule*, with highly motivated extreme minorities all too often choosing our leaders and the direction our government takes

You have probably heard it said that generals are forever preparing for the last war. Whether this is true for military planners, the world of politics exhibits this backward thinking quality quite clearly. The positions and perspectives of the partisans often echo struggles long past. I think that this fact is one of the main reasons non-partisans find it all so unintelligible and boring. It is for this reason that we will need to reach back into history to get a hold on some of the major events that animate the contemporary political scene. As I hope to show you, our disagreements about economic issues really make more sense in the context of the events of the 1930s than they do today. With some of the basic moral differences of opinion that emerge in our politics, making sense of it all may take us way back to arguments among the ancient Greeks. While I will try not to get us bogged down in lots of names and dates, here and there I'll try to give some credit where credit is due by citing an important historic person who is usually credited with certain political ideas

As an added feature, we should also prepare for the fact that whenever you might encounter people who are involved in politics, they often tend to be rude, overbearing and down-right intimidating. There is no reason to let them get away with this. Your accumulating knowledge and understanding should give you the ease and confidence to hold your own. But let's address this problem; there will be times when you may need some extra defenses. Nothing major, just a little glossing up to give a term or topic a bit more depth and sophistication. Let's put it this way, if some self-absorbed, true believer, is about to put you down by stating that everybody should know this or that tidbit of information, you don't need to let it pass. The kind of information I am talking about here may be either profound or trivial but there are certain facts that make up that "everybody knows" stuff/BS. This thing I am calling gloss, can be the difference between being taken seriously and being seriously ignored. To address this matter of political sophistication, throughout the text I have inserted a number of "gloss notes" to offer general background information which may be a help. Some of this stuff you might already know. Some not. Here's one:

> **Gloss Note:** Actually, our word "politics" comes out of the ancient Greek word which we know as "polis," their word for the city; the community; the setting and the living arrangements shared by fellow citizens. This entity, the polis, was distinguished from other human groupings such as the family or the military. A lot of what we now know about how the ancient Greeks thought about politics comes from the fact that various

> students of the philosopher and teacher Aristotle put their lecture notes together to make the book called Politics that they attributed to his authorship. This book Politics takes up a consideration of the structure, organization, and administration of the polis; how it is governed, who are its citizens and what is expected of them; in short, the affairs of the city.[8] From Greek to Latin to the French politique and we first see the word politic appearing in English in the year 1420.

Other writers might call these "footnotes" and bury them in the back of the book. No big deal, I just think that would be inconvenient. I have indented these gloss notes to make it more easy for you to skip them, if you like. In fact, there might be whole sections of this book that cover things you already know. Please skip over them. Your time is valuable. As for footnotes, I have cited references when necessary and also sometimes only when I thought you might want more information about something. Perhaps with some overconfidence in the survival of things as they are now on the internet, a footnote will often direct you to an http:// address. But if your searches are coming up short a lot, better check the publication date in the front of this book. After all, this primer isn't intended as a timeless classic.

A Preview

Like our example of getting more women interested in pro football, my aim is to make it so that you can listen to politicians and immediately figure out not only what they mean, but also what team they play for. Part I is a preliminary survey of the landscape. In the first chapter we will begin by reckoning with just what politics is. Then in chapter two we will take the first of three short trips back in time: to France in the late 1700s. Many of the dominating ideas in contemporary politics have their origins in tumultuous political times. The French Revolution is certainly a prime example. Not only did our modern notions of conservative and liberal, (right and left) began to solidify in this chaotic episode, but in reaction to these events in France, politicians in representative governments like ours have since that time sought to avoid extremism and violence as they settle their differences. In chapter three we'll jump right into the fray of politics today and get to understand how the partisans part company on a whole range of issues. This will put us in a position to take a first stab at recognizing some of the more basic differences in points of view that we find on the right and the left side of the ongoing debate. As we will see, some of the political arguments we can hear every day actually go back at least a couple of hundred years. By the end of chapter three we should be able to begin to appreciate the political game going on around us.

Our ultimate aim is to come away with a much deeper understanding of the activists on the left and the right in our politics. Parts II and III take up what are obviously the two subjects that they differ most dramatically about, namely economics, and morality. What we are after in both cases is an understanding of the differences in how the right and the left view these two subjects on the level of the every-day common sense assumptions they carry around with them. Common sense assumptions are important because even if the facts change, assumptions can often remain. And assumptions that cannot ever be proved can have just as much influence on judgment and facts.

Of the two, economics and morality, the economic dimension is the more straight-forward, so we will take it up first, in Part II. A person could spend years listening to politicians go on and on about our economy, and come up with little or no solid understanding of this subject. So in chapter four we will go back to basics and do a quick tour of the intriguing subject of free markets. In the decades after the fall of the Soviet Union, the vote has been virtually unanimous worldwide: free market economy is the only way to go. But outside the fraternity of the economists, there is very little understanding of how free market economics actually works. With some of the economic basics behind us, in chapter five, we will be ready to better understand the way the left and the right seek to put our economic house in order. This chapter will necessitate a second trip back into history, this time to the world economic collapse we refer to as the Great Depression of the

1930s. Just as the French Revolution wrote much of the script for conservative and liberal thought in general, political responses to the Great Depression shaped a whole lot of our modern thinking about how government should relate to the economy.

In Part III we get religion. Well, I really should say morality, which does come from religion, but it also seems to come from other sources as well. Like economics, morality is a major and a critical factor in our politics. Though I have made great efforts to keep all these chapters on a light and easy-going level, this morality stuff is a definite challenge. So as preparation for digging into this subject, in chapter six, we'll need to get a more complicated understanding of the beliefs people have and how these beliefs function in their lives and in their politics. Chapter six takes on the enigma of human beliefs. I use the word enigma because, while we can never be certain about what another person believes, our very existence day-to-day demands that we constantly act on assumptions about the beliefs of others. Don't worry; I think I have been able to keep the theorizing over on the light side.

But when we get to Chapter seven, and take up what an important part morality is playing in our contemporary politics, I think you will agree that some of this psychologizing has been necessary. As the chapter's title, The Moral Divide in Politics, puts it, the partisans on the left tend toward a distinctly different account of right and wrong than those on the right. And if you, dear reader, don't appreciate it at the moment, I trust you will come to see that moral confrontations are not easy work for political institutions dedicated to peaceful resolution of differences.

In Chapter eight I introduce the increasingly popular alternative to the old line righty and lefty political morality battles that are grabbing most of the attention. Through a whole series of developments, we can document a newer way of perceiving our world and its politics which has been emerging. And as you will see, it brings both good and bad news. The good news though, is that this postmodern perspective, as I've labeled it, takes a lot of people away from each others' throats politically.

With all this economics and morality stuff under our belts, Part IV takes us back to where we started, and gets into how the politics game is now being played. Chapter nine ponders the huge and even intimidating wealth of information that is at hand; information about governments, issues, politicians and the world these exist in. An essential task we all face consists of sorting through the mountains of facts and claims to arrive at what is real and true. Chapter takes up how the legions of professional political consultants work in the tired old economics and morality trenches of the left and right, and refine and perfect the old arguments of the left and the right to mobilize dependable voters. Chapter eleven brings politicians and office holders into focus. I mean this literally. If there is a single thing that has transformed contemporary politics, it can be found in the way we come to know the politicians and what they stand for. There we will see the changes that the technology of the movies and TV have brought to our politics.

Fear not, the final chapter is not going to walk you through my own private plan for the future of the United States. Even if I had one, which I don't, that's not what this book is about. Chapter eleven just brings up some things you might reflect upon the next time you rank the things you do, or could do to spend your time. And if my aim has been achieved, the rank of politics will have moved up in your priorities.

Part I: Preliminary Approaches

PRELIMINARY APPROACHES

Chapter 1 What's Political & How do we Know it When we See it?

"The end move in politics is always to pick up a gun"

R. Buckminster Fuller(1895-1983)[1]

"I have come to the conclusion that the making of laws is like the making of sausages—the less you know about the process the more you respect the result."

Often attributed to Otto von Bismarck (1815-1898)

So, we've made it past the introduction. Great! Remember our goal, dear reader, is to get you to be able to think politics and talk politics the way folks do inside the game. But whenever we try to enter any unfamiliar world of goings on, we have to be prepared to come up against a lot of stuff that people just take for granted and seldom talk about. Its stuff that just never comes up, because it is like what you'd call "duh!" stuff. For instance, bikers know a whole lot about the geometry and physics of two wheel vehicles, especially ones that are going over 70 mph. They twist the handle bars slightly to the left when they want a nice right turn. They never trust the rear brake to stop them. And they don't park on a down-hill grade and kick down the stand expecting that the bike won't spill over as they walk away. And they almost never talk about this stuff. Then there is the whole realm of cultural taken-for-granteds; dress, accepted ways of talking. There are most certainly even biker political understandings that don't get discussed; understandings about how to show dominance and deference to one another, and what is at risk if one doesn't act accordingly.

What I mean is that it is hard to imagine political activists sitting around talking about what politics really is. That does not happen. But for us it is a pretty good place to begin. We need to get a grasp on what is and what is not politics and, more important for our project here, what political partisans think it is. I aim to break through this basic definitional barrier now. Consequently, this chapter has two objectives. We need to have an understanding of what is political. And in accomplishing this, we will take a first look at how writers and partisans talk about it when the subject does come up.

When approaching a new topic it can be helpful to consult some of the authorities on the subject. If we go back to Aristotle, (about 340 BC), as was mentioned in the introduction, then politics is simply, and quite literally, the affairs of the community. Besides sounding kind of boring, this won't take us very far. If we are to get it right, we need a definition that will serve us when folks are talking about national politics, state politics, office politics, sexual politics, or whatever kind of politics. We need a much more general definition to work with. How's this one; a kid's dictionary says, politics is: "social relations involving authority or power."[2] This one's better for us. The emphasis is more on how potential conflict gets worked out. Along the same lines Mao Tse-Tung, (1893-1976) is once supposed to have said that "Politics is war without bloodshed."[3] Definitely a little edgier, no? The emphasis is again on conflict, but, conflict short of violence. Consider it for a minute, politics is a way to live with one another so as to avoid the incidence of violence. Then just try to imagine how things would be without politics by this definition. On second thought, you don't have to, because 16th century English political theorist, Thomas Hobbes, (1588-1679) did it for us. His imagery of a world of individuals confronting one another without political restraints is downright haunting. He wrote that without some form of political order we'd find ourselves in a continuous war of "all against all" and life would be "solitary, poor, nasty, brutish and short."[4]

Fortunately, for most people, at least in most places, a lot of the time, life is not like Hobbes describes it. Consequently, we can take this as a point of departure for finding just what kinds of restraints on violence there are. I hope that you can see though, that seeing politics as restraints on violence is consistent with my motive of wanting to appreciate politics as vital, and a part of the essence of our existence. Furthermore, since violence is at least potentially present whenever two or more humans are together, thinking of politics as restraints on violence makes politics something that you might begin to see easily everywhere around you. For this, Hobbes' statement of what politics is not, becomes a pretty good jumping-off place. We have to build our understanding of what politics is by starting from his "solitary, poor, nasty, brutish and short." In other words Hobbes starts us from political zero, so to speak.

There are four very general ways of thinking about politics that we can relate to violence. Taken together they should be enough to get us a good way into our subject:

Politics: *A substitute for violence*

Politics: *Who can do what to whom without committing violence*

Politics: *Agreeing on how to disagree so as to avoid violence*

Politics: *The raw power of potential violence is implied through the use of harmless symbols*

A Substitute for Violence: On the subject of violence, consider the idea of the pecking order. It actually happens to be a great way to see politics as a channeling of the raw power of violence and threats of imminent violence into organized behavior. In chickens and in people, even when we don't see it at first, the pecking order is always there. Here is how it works with chickens. From the time they peck their way out of the egg shells, the chicks begin to work out their pecking order. (You can watch this yourself on YouTube.[5]) The pecking is mostly about the head and neck and certainly meets the definition of baby-chicken-violence. Little by little a pattern emerges with some chicks meeting out more pecks and others either taking more pecks or learning to back off. Once this pattern is established deference among the chicks, (literally, the question of who comes first, who then comes next, and next, and so on), is pretty clear and pretty stable. As the chicks mature to adulthood together, the pecking subsides and they appear to get along together, but the power relations established in that early violence among them, remains pretty constant, even though the group's relations have become relatively peaceful.

The similarity between this chicken behavior and human behavior is of course limited. OK, some of you will have to admit that this kind of thing went on with your brothers and sisters when you were little. However, the pecking order model is a vivid illustration of how, under the surface of peacefully coexisting, there can exist a history of violence and threats that has been worked out over time and accepted by the players. A history of violence casts its shadow over the present in that the power relations remain in effect, without a need for those past conflicts to come to the surface physically. Similarly, as we observe people around us, interacting we are usually watching them disagree with one another, make demands, and appeal to one another based upon pre-established rules and customs. These rules and customs have, over time, become substitutes for actual threats and actual violence. But there is an important difference for us humans. Unlike chicks, as lots of people come to live together in communities, they do not have to fight it out anew with each generation. As time goes by, they can avoid a lot of hassling by teaching their young who is boss and who comes next, etc. Humans can get their affairs organized over generations and generations, so that the occasions when there is a direct threat or actual violence against somebody are minimized. In this way human groups can come to an impressive level of peaceful consensus that is surprisingly stable over time. But underlying any such consensus

PRELIMINARY APPROACHES

there must always be shared understanding, as to who can do what to whom, and under what circumstances they can do it. Politics is all about working out and maintaining this kind of consensus through time so that people can live with one another and, at the same time, minimize the use of actual threats and violence.

Who can do What to Whom without Committing Violence: We actually have a name for these human pecking orders that are worked out over generations. We usually refer to them as "hierarchies". You are probably familiar with this term as it is applied to the Roman Catholic Church, but hierarchies are part of the character of all kinds of human organizations. For example, there is the chain-of-command in the military, or the reporting relationships down from the CEO in a corporation or the cabinet secretary in a governmental bureaucracy. This pecking order or hierarchy is a stable part of the character of whole families, from the patriarch or matriarch on down to the babies. In each case, they involve shared understandings about who can do what to whom and under what circumstances, without having to resort to violence. Our ability to develop all these kinds of cultural hierarchies is what has allowed us humans the unique ability to coordinate the efforts of many people in the pursuit of big accomplishments. But in all instances, these hierarchies harness power relations so that threats and violence within the group are pushed back.

It is important to point something out here. The people who find themselves in a particular hierarchy, may share an understanding of its rules, but they need not share any agreement about justice or fairness of the way that the rights and duties are assigned. They only have to understand that bad things could happen to them if they were to break from adherence to those rights and duties. Back when I was being raised in a family hierarchy, I didn't always think that my parents were fair and just authorities over me, but I did learn early on that they could make threats and make good on those threats.

So to summarize, we started out with the kind of chaotic political vacuum that Thomas Hobbes pictured for us. The world he describes for us is a world of raw power where threats and actual violence are what rule relations among humans. This raw power is gradually replaced by a set of power relationships that, by mutual understanding, push direct threats and violence nearly out of the picture. People get on together and don't often disagree openly about when it is OK: a) to make other people do things, b) to threaten others, c) to take things from others, d) to hurt them, f) or to even kill them. But isn't all this talk about threats, and pecking orders, and hierarchies getting kind of dense? I am beginning to get the distinct impression that we might be slipping off the edge and falling into a trap of abstract theoretical nonsense…

Let's take a break and go to the movies. We can get back to this definition stuff later. Maybe we can use a movie as an illustration of what we are trying to think through here. The movie I picked for us to see is an old one, which is based on a novel. In point of fact, there were two movies, and they both were based on this same novel. The novel is Samuel Golding's Lord of the Flies.[6] The book has been a staple of high school reading for many decades. Both of these movies did pretty well at the box office, and though Golding didn't get an Oscar, he did pick up a Nobel Prize along the way. If you have not seen the movies or read the book, or you just don't remember, the story is about a group of schoolboys stranded on a remote island after a plane crash. In that crash, all the accompanying adults are killed. The plot covers the transformation of these kids. It is about their political transformation. At the onset of their time on the island, they are all civilized middle class school boys. But as events transpire, they regress to become a barbaric and violent bunch of little fellows. Without justification; they threaten one another, they take from one another, they injure one another, they even kill one another. As you may know, the author's title, "Lord of the Flies," by the way, is a translation of the Old Testament word Beelzebub, which is usually thought to be synonymous with Satan. His clear suggestion is that even well behaved children are just a short way away from relying exclusively upon violence and coercion to govern their relationships. If this is at all reasonable to you, readers, then it should make some sense that we started this definitional discussion by viewing politics as the control and channeling of violence and potential violence.

So, on the most basic level, politics makes up the ground rules we have created to live and work together so as to avoid a lot of nasty behavior. Good going. Don't you think we humans can give ourselves a nice pat on the back here? Haven't we obviously made a lot of progress against brutality and barbarism in the last few thousand years. Not so. And this is important to our goal of understanding politics. Peaceful politics might even be thought of as an exception. With the rise of modern representative governments, the just-past, 20th century became the nastiest and bloodiest of all of them. Ineffective political arrangements mean that people can lose the ability to channel the nasty stuff. Working democracies have in a matter of weeks, deteriorated into gangs of violent street thugs, and then to all-out war. We certainly got more of that kind of thing in the century just past than in any preceding century. Estimates put the deaths by just the intentional violence of World War II alone, at over 60 million. At various times and places throughout the 20th century, population bombing, mass imprisonment and genocide became accepted practice. So there is no good reason to think that civilization has put all this behind us.

There are today, many political entities that hold physical threats and violence quite close to the surface of every-day life. Tyrannies and dictatorships are alive and well in the world. Terrorist networks are thriving. For instance, it was reported that within its first six months of rule in the city of Raqqa, ISIS executed over 1,100 civilians. Furthermore, the militants like to make sure that parents bring their children to witness beheadings so that they will grow up being used to them.[7] Sorry to hoist such a curtain of gloom. But I think it is important to be mindful that we might never be very far from having politics fail us.

Thus, it is essential for us to accept that disagreement and conflict are always with us. They never cease. It is within politics that they can sometimes be handled through peaceable channels. But glib terms like "peaceable channels" don't tell us anything. We need to be able to see politics, it's various dimensions, how it operates. Let me try to begin to do this by taking a closer look at some of the ways we push use of raw power away so that we can handle disagreements politically.

Agreeing on How to Disagree so as to Avoid Violence: By following specified rules or conventions on how to resolve our differences peaceably, groups establish ways to handle disagreement and conflict with a minimum of violence. This can be true for nations with a wide variety of forms of government. The peaceful ground rules differ from place to place. Nevertheless, there are always some with the power and/or authority to keep things orderly, and then there are the folks who are kept in order. The arrangements vary a lot as to how much influence the people under the rulers have over those with the power and/or authority at the top of the political hierarchy. This is why it is important that that we do not exaggerate the level of acceptance and agreement by those governed that might exist in a given instance of peaceful politics. An apparent agreement about keeping things peaceful can often conceal one or more of a number of alternative degrees of consensus:

> People who appear to knowingly and willingly agree on rules for settling conflict peacefully and the settlements thus brokered might well be agreeing due to ignorance or trickery.
>
> Seeming peaceful consensus can also be the result of serious threats that are not directly apparent. In totalitarian régimes, many live in constant frustration and terror. Their peaceful conduct is merely a strategy to avoid certain harm.
>
> And then there is always the possibility that some of the peaceable participants are simply not willing to expend the effort. "Can't fight city hall." "It's pointless to argue with him/her, a huge waste of time."

PRELIMINARY APPROACHES

Then again the apparent consensus sometimes is complete and real. All concerned might agree that disagreements are being resolved for good and just ends, or at least that decisions they disagree with might be corrected peacefully at a later date. In other words, we need to be mindful of what a rare and even fragile thing real consensus may be when we are considering what that kids' dictionary refers to as "social relations involving authority or power." When people knowingly, and willingly agree on how to settle their differences, we use the term legitimacy. So when people knowingly, and willingly agree on the methods of peaceable dispute resolution we can call the government legitimate.

The Raw Power of Potential Violence is Implied through the Use of Harmless Symbols: There is one additional aspect of this invisibility of violence in politics. The exercise of power is camouflaged by the use of symbols to represent it. These symbols are themselves essentially harmless. Clothing is for instance, very often a way that the facts of unequal powers are harmlessly expressed in group settings. Sure, we all know that power relationships are overtly displayed for all to see in the way that people dress in the military. They literally wear their power status on their sleeves. So it is with dress in a court room. The judge, who is likely to be wearing long black robes and wielding a gavel. That gavel is practically speaking useless, but it is clearly there as a crude symbol of a weapon. The sound of the gavel insists on silence, and, if that doesn't do it, there are marshals, uniformed and armed, to back it up.

In less formal settings dress connotes power in more subtle ways. As conflicting ideas about power relationships between men and women, racial, educational, and economic categories are being challenged, this subtlety has given way to a certain amount of confusion. Back at the turn of the last century, author, Thorstein Veblen (1857-1929) could easily point out that the high heels, constraining undergarments, gloves, veils and such that women were wearing, were symbolic of their assigned roles as weak, dependent, objects in a world where men had the power.[8] There was a time when the expression "who wears the pants in the family," made sense both literally and symbolically. Though these customs of dress for women are no longer to be found in many informal settings, they still hold sway for many more formal settings like the "red carpet" and some contemporary weddings.

Recent decades have brought down a lot of the old power suggestions of clothing in the workplace as well. The symbolic inequality that existed when all the bosses wore suits, can only be recalled in the sentimentality of TV shows like Suits and Mad Men. These days, only attorneys and politicians (male or female) typically work in suits.

As the suit and dress symbols became less popular, retailers and manufacturers, stepped in to provide us with a new symbolic language of power. Clothes have taken on an additional symbolic character. They have retained their use in suggesting power distinctions, but in addition, each of us is now expected to dress so as to express a type. It is as if you and I were cast in a movie with a quirky provision in the employment contract that assigns all wardrobe responsibilities to the individual actors. As a result, we must figure out the type we are playing and dress to that type. Marketers have even made it easy for people by offering complete lines of clothing. Are you playing the Nike guy? The DKNY girl? I'm not about to check, but I'd bet that a lot of you Harley dudes and chicks can even have your underwear marked with the HD logo.

But don't think for a minute that dress is no longer a camo-proxy for power either at work or in more informal situations. When you pick and choose how you dress, you pick the costume of the character you want to present and all these dress-up characters project their own power aspect. They suggest how we should be treated in the pecking order as we move through our days. And it should be no big surprise that the magnitude of our clothing budgets is central to this symbolism. This metric has become objective because most folks can distinguish Burberry coats, or Lucchese boots, or Valentino dresses, or Gucci jeans, from the substitutes Walmart offers. After all, people with a lot

PRELIMINARY APPROACHES

of money to spend on clothes, surely are more likely to have more resources (friends, allies, lawyers, maybe even paid thugs, etc.) to bring to bear when it is time to settle differences. And the symbolism of clothes doesn't stop with things you put on your body. Arguably, your transportation vehicle choices and the street address you occupy are just additional aspects of the way you dress yourself up to confront the world.

Besides clothes, the power relationships that we face daily are reflected in the very words we use. Many children and all basic trainees in the military are taught to use the terms "sir" and "ma'am" when conversing with certain people. This practice in both contexts is explained as a way that proper respect can be expressed. However, when viewed from the perspective of hierarchical power relations, it is easy to see this practice as a means of voluntarily differing to those who have power to do you harm. But terms like sir and ma'am just scratch the surface. We all take great care whenever we address somebody who can lift us or knock us down. It is part of the script we are continuously creating on the spot. (A student from Nigeria I once knew claimed he got a traffic ticket dismissed by going to court and addressing the judge as "your highness.") This is why it can be so calamitous when we can't see clear symbols of the power structure. I once went to work at a company where, I swear, I was just about the only person who wasn't somehow related to the, pain-in-the-butt, CFO. Need I say, it didn't go well for me until I could identify all of the last names that made up the clan?

> **Gloss Note:** Here is an example of how power relationships lurk in the very language we use every day without thinking about it. In our past, a women always took the last name of their husband at the time of their marriage. This replaced the last name of her father, which we referred to as her maiden name. In recent decades this practice has been resisted by many women. While the old fashioned word, maiden, did mean first, as in the ship's maiden voyage, it more commonly referred to a virgin. The resistance to taking the husband's last name can thus be seen, in effect, as a political act of rejecting the

implied power relationships between men and women, i.e. that females belong to their father, until they are permitted to have sex, and, thereafter, they belong to their husband.

Maybe I should have stopped all this definitional stuff back at the kids' dictionary, "social relations involving authority or power." But my aim has been to get us to a complex definition of politics; one that can be applied to a range of settings; one that works for an argument between eight-year-olds on a playground just as well as it works in the halls of the Versailles Palace at the end of the First World War. I think that we have enough to move on now. We are going to be talking about:

Politics as power exercised without violence. This is accomplished either through persuasion, or through various kinds of threats short of violence. When participants accept the politics they live in, we can say that they consider the allocation of power relations as " legitimate."

Consequently, rather than something remote that only goes on in Washington D. C. and the Statehouse, politics is all around us. Either we agree with others or we don't agree. But when we don't agree, we try to resolve the disagreement without using the raw power of violence. So when the playground eight-year-olds try to settle disagreements, they sometimes make it and other times somebody gets hurt. When diplomats and heads of state try, sometimes they make it and other times they forge a path to the intentional, destruction and death of war. With this in mind, let's get back to that irritating shouting match we began with. At least now we can recognize that these people are mostly just trying to get their way without having to hurt anybody. These partisans are using politics to harness some legitimate power for themselves.

In the chapters that follow, we will try to dig into the ideas and beliefs that underlie this endless arguing about what should be accepted as legitimate in the power relations that we live within. Our politics is thus not just a particular arena we call government. In a broader sense it

PRELIMINARY APPROACHES

includes activities that are going on everywhere that people are. Taken together it can be thought of as a kind of national pecking order that justifies and enforces: --who can do what--who gets to use what--who gets to do what to whom.

UNDERSTANDING U S POLITICS

PRELIMINARY APPROACHES

Chapter 2 The Story Behind the Left and the Right

"Today the claims of the masses are becoming more and more sharply defined, and amount to nothing less than a determination to utterly destroy society as it now exists..."

Gustave Le Bon (1841-1931)[1]

"Conservatism has its vice, and that vice is selfishness...radicalism, too has its vice, and that vice is envy."

Russell Kirk (1918-1994)[2]

"The representatives of the French people...believing that the ignorance, neglect, or contempt of the rights of man are the sole cause of public calamities and of the corruption of governments, have determined to set forth in a solemn declaration the natural, unalienable, and sacred rights of man..."

Approved by the National Assembly of France, August 26, 1789[3]

Yes, this chapter might seem to some to be quite a way off our track. It's not about our subject: contemporary American politics. It's not even about the United States. So I guess I have a bit of explaining to do. The quickest explanation I can come up with is this. We are trying to understand this political game we are forced to watch every day. A good way to get a start at doing this is to become more familiar with the thinking that orients and motivates the players. So, let's go back to the earliest days of the game; the place and time that the play began. If you are resistant to a little history, I just ask that you cut me a little slack on this. After all, I might have insisted that we start with the direct democracy they tried out for a while in BC Athens. Those ancient Greeks did certainly have plenty of political lessons for us today. But, I need to keep you awake while at the same time keeping my pledge. My pledge that is, to get you just enough primer-level politics so that you will be able to pass unnoticed among all the opinionated political partisans. For this I think we at least need to go back to that great train-wreck that was the French Revolution. This is because it is the point in Western history where much of the lore and lessons of politics emerged for the folks now on the right and the left.

Having said this I should follow up with a WARNING! Beware of historical arguments in politics. Things that happened in the past are often misrepresented and abused to make them fit with a point somebody is trying to make. This should put you on guard, my reader. History seldom, if ever, proves anything beyond question. Arguments like, "We must do so-and-so because look what happened way back then, when those other people faced the exact same problem, and did such-and-such…" But I am not about to do this. All I am claiming is that there is an event, the French Revolution, that represents a unique turning point in the way partisans think about their politics in the West, and a good part of the rest of the world as well. All kinds of political activists on both sides of the political divide have used this great upheaval over 200 years ago as "proof" that is support for their opinions. And besides that fact, it is a fascinating, even shocking, series of events which are quite well documented.

We will review the events that took place and then see what writers had to say about them as the main lines of modern political thought was coming into being. This is far from a complete account of the events of the French Revolution. I'll try to be brief about what happened, and then I'll just mention a few of the principal writers who took inspiration from it; just enough to anchor us in how these happenings brought out the beginnings of modern political thinking. I'll focus in particular on a few Brits who had a lot to say. Starting here, you can always read more elsewhere if you care to.

The main point we take from the French Revolution is that in a period of just a few years, 1789 to 1804---the political conversation among a group of well-meaning, peaceful, rational, very well educated men---things went horribly wrong. This was a shocking, unprecedented development. As late as 1788, Thomas Jefferson wrote to James Madison from France saying. "I think it probable that this country will in two or three years be in the enjoyment of a tolerably free constitution and that without its having cost them a drop of blood."[4]

As we will see, ever since the Revolution in France, political life everywhere distinguishes between two kinds of activists. There are those who insist on working through democracy and representative institutions to settle disputes without violence or oppression and those committed to getting their way by any means.

With this as context, I hope you will be able to appreciate how the French Revolution was such an astonishing event for contemporaries that it became the historical record; the case study; or what we might think of as the primary data set from which many of the central ideas of modern political thought are fashioned.

France 1789, the Cradle of Modern Politics

The Revolution in France which began in 1789 was only one among several political events that together brought an end to the absolute monarchies and the feudal societies they ruled. Royal families and their nobles owned everything, including the common people who did their work and fought their wars. The French were certainly not the first to challenge their monarchy. The British, for example, had executed their king 140 years before, but after a brief experiment in kinglessness, they went back to a monarchy with a parliament. Also, just prior to the revolutionary events in France, thirteen North American colonies, severed their connection with the parliament and king an ocean away from them in Britain. In fact, the French monarchy lent decisive assistance to the colonists in their victory over the British. But the turmoil over the monarchy in France in the years that followed was an epoch-marking break with the past, launching a veritable explosion of political writing theorizing and speculation. Afterword, France and politics everywhere, were never the same. What is perhaps most unsettling about what happened is that it all took place at the height of the intellectual movement we refer to as the Enlightenment, a flouring of scientific and rational thinking like the world had never before seen.

Here, in briefest summary, and with apologies to the French, are just some of the major events that took place in the 10+ years starting in 1789.

1789:

In May, amid hard times and war debts, the French king, Louis XVI calls church officials, (the First Estate), the nobility, (the Second Estate), and other notables from the various cities and rural localities (the Third Estate) to Paris to meet as État-général, (the Estates General).

In June, that faction of the attendees, the Third Estate, (those associated with what we'd think of as the business, professional, and trade interests) finds that they are locked out the proceedings and so they convene a meeting at a near-by indoor tennis court. At this meeting, by a 576 to 577 vote the group resolves to continue working together until a new national constitution is established.

In July this group along with representatives of the clergy and the nobility come to be called National Assembly, and take on the task of formulating a constitution for France.

PRELIMINARY APPROACHES

Later that month, citizens lightly armed yet numerous, take control of a prison (the Bastille) in Paris. They free the few prisoners being held there and take possession of its armaments. July 14th is still celebrated among the French as Bastille Day.

In August the National Assembly decrees an end to feudalism and adopts Declaration of the Rights of Man and the Citizen. (A quotation from this declaration appears at the beginning of this chapter.)

In October a group of Parisian women invades the palace of French King Louis XVI, at Versailles. In the following days the King and Queen are relocated to their Paris residence, the Tuileries.

1790:

In June, nobility and titles are abolished. In July a Civil Constitution is established, which also subordinates the Catholic Church to the civil government.

1791:

In June, the King and Queen attempt to flee Paris, but are recognized and forcibly returned.

In August in the French colony Saint-Domingue, African slaves revolt.

In October the newly established Legislative Assembly takes control and becomes the government of France.

1792:

In August, members of a political club known as the Jacobins (named after a former convent on Rue St. Jacques where they held their meetings) storms the palace and imprisons the King.

In September over 1,000 supporters of the monarchy being held in Parisian prisons are killed.

1793:

In January, after his trial, the king, Louis XVI executed. In April the Legislative Assembly's Committee of Public Safety is established to defend against those who threaten the Revolution.

In June the Jacobin faction's proposed Constitution is implemented.

In September the "Law of Suspects" takes effect, and a period of mass executions begins. This bloody period of just under a year is referred to as "the Reign of Terror," or simply "the Terror."

In October the Queen of France, Marie-Antoinette is tried and executed. A new French calendar starting time at year two is decreed.

1794:

In February, the French National Assembly abolishes slavery. (Back in the French colony of Saint-Domingue the eventual success of the revolt of former slaves, brings the Republic of Haiti into existence and its diplomats are later welcomed in Paris.)

In March Jacobin leader Maximilien Robespierre, of the Committee of Public Safety, becomes virtual dictator of the country.

In May Robespierre decrees the new state religion of the Supreme Being.

In June new procedures for mass trials and executions are implemented. Victims will go to the guillotine now in batches of 50 or more.

In July, Robespierre arrested and executed and "theTerror" ends. It is said that, in Paris alone, over 16,000 had been executed during the Terror.

PRELIMINARY APPROACHES

1795:

In October, a new government, the Directorate takes power.

1799:

In November, having returned from his campaign in Egypt, Napoleon Bonaparte comes to Paris, in what we now call a Coup d'état and the general takes power with the title, "First Consul."

1804:

In December, Napoleon, having consolidated his power, and considering no one on earth worthy of the task, he holds a splendid ceremony during which he crowns himself Emperor.

That's it. In a mere 15 years, France goes from a long stable monarchy to mass executions. Along the way, slavery is abolished, the French national motto "liberty, equality and fraternity" came into being, a successful slave revolt took place in Haiti, while more than 18,000 citizens met their end at the guillotine. The tumultuous times also saw wave upon wave of powerful crowds, parties, factions and dictators who successively struck down ancient codes and customs, started a brand new calendar and a new reason-based religion all of which seems to have come to nothing. After a military dictator had installed himself as Emperor in 1804 there followed over a decade of wars throughout Europe.

While the revolutionary period is our focus, it doesn't end there. By 1814 the various European powers had had enough and they restored France's monarchy under Bourbon king Louis XVIII. But this only lasted until the next upheaval in 1830 when the Bourbons once again lost power. This series of events beginning in 1789 shook not only France but all of the European world. How could a centuries old country and its governance and customs, so completely fall apart, repeatedly gather back together only to fall apart again. Political actors who bonded tightly together into factions at one juncture, fragmented at the next, condemning one another to death. Based upon these events it was obvious that the cement that holds society together was nowhere near as dependable as had been thought. From royalty to violence and from chaos to military rule. And all of this among some of the most enlightened, civilized people on earth.

> **Gloss Note:** the terms "right" and "left" as applied to politics actually originated in the early phases of the French Revolution, (1789) when supporters of the king sat to the right of the chair of the National Assembly's leader and the opposition to the king's government sat on the left. Thus conservatives, or the "right" are generally thought to support present or past arrangements and liberals, or the "left" are generally thought to want things to be changed.

Lessons Learned

Our contemporary sophistication, acknowledges that all enlightened and civilized people are fully capable of civil wars, totalitarianism, and even genocide. But these are things that Europeans of that time couldn't know. It is important for us to step back and imagine the shock of how incomprehensible all this was to Europeans living at that time. All these events took place at the height of the optimism and faith in the powers of science and human reason. All that was taken for granted about how politics works was brought into question. Even to this day the events of the French Revolution are the mirror that political thinking is reflected from. Since that time, modern political analysis has remained tethered to the wild events of this 15 year period in French history.

I want to point out three things our political heritage starts to recognize after the events of the revolution in France:

1. First, there was **the issue of the violence itself.** A debate developed over whether, and if so, under what circumstances it was even possible

PRELIMINARY APPROACHES

to introduce significant changes in the political arrangements within a society without committing serious violence. In the center were reformers who held to the possibility that change for the better could come more gradually yet peacefully. These reformers faced two varieties of opponents: there were advocates of violence on either side; those who saw violence as necessary and preferable either as counter-revolutionaries bent on bringing the clergy and the nobility back to the power they previously wielded and on the other side the radicals committed to violence as their means for completely replacing the existing political arrangements with a system more beneficial to the masses. To be more complete here, a third category of radicals should be mentioned. These were folks who viewed it unlikely that either legislative reform or violence could change existing societies to their liking, and instead sought to isolate themselves and design and establish their ideal society from scratch.

2. In addition, critics and commentators began to address and argued over the consequences of the fact that **political participation of lots of ordinary people, the masses as some called them, was here to stay**. The genie of citizen participation in government was out of the bottle, so to speak, and few believed that this genie could ever be put back in. Henceforth, the task of governing would need to involve far more care and concern with what common folks were thinking and how they were likely to react to political events. A debate arose as to whether this mass participation was a good thing or whether it was a disaster.

3. At the same time, many observers began to call attention to the fact that the bold thinking of Enlightenment had forcefully rejected the sacred religious traditions that had prevailed in Europe for centuries. After the events in France, it became clear that **messing around with what is considered sacred can be dangerous business**. Without these unifying beliefs that bind people and whole societies together, things can fall apart. Back in the decades following the revolution in France it was becoming clear that's simple substitution of unquestioned human reason for the doctrines of the prevailing Christian faith had failed.

> **Gloss Note:** This is not to say that the Enlightenment inspired French revolutionaries didn't acknowledge the importance of sacred beliefs at all. In their own strange way, they sought immediately to reinvent the sacred. For instance, in 1793, after over 120 Catholic priests had been barbarically executed. The "dechristianization" revolutionaries in Paris proclaimed a public cult of liberty and equality, and converted iconic Notre Dame Cathedral into what they called a "Temple of Reason." Then, just two months before he met his end, Robespierre declared a new state religion. What could possibly go wrong?[5]

To see how these three lessons (the reality of political violence, participation of the masses, and challenges to traditional religion) were acknowledged by political partisans and thinkers in the decades that followed the French Revolution we could begin wading into a whole catalog of authors and activists. However, I think we can come away with enough of the historical background we will need later on if we focus on just a few of the more influential contributors. In the headings that follow, we will divide the field into four categories. First, to be complete we'll touch on the activists who are of less importance to us: the escapist utopians who advocated walking away and starting over, and the radicals who were convinced that no real political improvement would never come without a fight. After that we can focus in on a couple of fellows, one on the left and one on the right, who devoted their efforts to doing politics peacefully within the institutions of existing representative government. These two, one an example of the reformers on the left, the other an example of the conservatives on the right, are widely acknowledged as representing the foundations of kind of peaceful representative politics I am trying to get us to better appreciate.

The Utopians

One category of writers and activists who emerged, in effect, retreated from the extremity and violence of the national politics of the

PRELIMINARY APPROACHES

Revolution and fixed their attention on designing what they believed to be optimal human political and social arrangements. Rather than being confrontational, many of these writers were more apt to advocate withdrawing from existing communities so that they could implement completely new ways of living together. Think of these utopians as continuing with the unlimited faith in reason of the Enlightenment. These were the radicals of best planning and practice. Among the utopians the Frenchmen Henri de Saint-Simon, (1760 –1825), Charles Fourier, (1772-1837), had actually lived through the events of the Revolution. Saint Simon was released from a Paris prison when the Reign of Terror ended. The utopians sought out isolated areas in Northern Europe and the United States to establish experimental communities where participants could be free to pursue communal ownership of property, and other fundamentally different social, religious, and political practices designed to bring about more perfect political entities than those already in existence. Though he didn't actually found a commune, from the standpoint of influence on his 19th century contemporaries, Auguste Comte (1798-1857) stands out. He pioneered the scientific study of society that later became the discipline of sociology. The plans he laid out for his scientifically correct society left nothing to chance. He was especially concerned with our third lesson from the French Revolution and stressed the necessity for a replacement for traditional religion. Accordingly, he devised a new "religion of humanity" that he insisted was essential to its success of his plan.[6]

While these utopians and their experiments no doubt had profound effects on participants, little from their work gained any traction in our national politics. Though the post-Revolutionary period saw a blossoming of utopian thinking, the prospect of withdrawing from ongoing societies was not unique to this period. The Mayflower pilgrims and the Massachusetts Bay Colony are earlier instances. The kibbutzim in Israel and the numerous communes that were established in the US several decades back suggest that the attractiveness of withdrawal to more perfect ways, has been, and will continue to be with us.

The Radicals

As we trace our three issues through the decades that followed the French Revolution, the first thing that becomes apparent is that the advocates of political violence were on the ready to jump in at the least opportunity, either to create empire, restore monarchy, or even to establish communist governments. Of all the possibilities, it wasn't that easy to be a writer on the radical left side of politics after the French Revolution deteriorated into chaos. This shouldn't be surprising. After all, what we call the French Revolution was, in large part, a series of miserable attempts at radical reforms. But political radicals were far from quieted. Paris and other places in Europe erupted in political violence a number of times during the 1800s. Of the radical writers on the left, Karl Marx (1818-1883) and Fredrick Engels, (1820-1895) are of course the most famous. Together and separately they endlessly ridiculed the utopians as they formulated what they considered their own scientific theory not of society but of history and change; a theory that saw future revolutions as inevitable. For them history itself was an unstoppable series of revolutions and in each instance the ruling economic classes go down to defeat and the underclass takes power. In the last of these revolutions, the working class would defeat the owners of economically productive entities, and this history of economic conflict would come to an end. Enormous efforts to promote this supposed communist inevitability are of course among the main historic and political currents that show up in the 20th century.

If only so you'll know what it is about when partisans get into name-calling, the communists aren't the only leftist radicals who deserve mention. The anarchists represent another line of radical left thinking that you should be able to identify. The difficulty in part follows from the fact that the term is applied to so many variants of anti-government thinking. Generally anarchists would seemed to identify the very existence of government as the source of all political ills. But the simplicity of a plan to end all political problems by abolishing all governments sounds comical, and it should. Actually, the anarchists were opposed to the great harm they attributed to uncontrolled concentrations of power that governments and other hierarchical organizations can come to wield over people. They held that in such circumstances, some people treat other people, not as human equals, but as mere disposable means to whatever ends they might seek. While not all anarchists are bomb throwers committed to political violence, their radicalism came from the contention that such power concentrations would never give ground without a fight. Theirs is not a politics without government, but one where purely voluntary non-hierarchal groups could relate to one another peacefully.

> **Gloss Note:** In a sense the anarchists are the original anti-big-government folks. Brit, William Godwin (1756-1836), (father of Frankenstein's author, Mary Shelly), contributed to anarchist thought of this period. This might seem strange but according to author and volunteer soldier, George Orwell and others, anarchist troops actually took control and "governed" briefly during the Spanish Civil War, in the 1930s before Stalinist forces destroyed their initiative.[7] On the contemporary scene, MIT linguistics Professor, Noam Chomsky, is typically considered to be in the anarchist tradition on the left. In his popular video "Manufactured Consent" he argues that the enormous concentrations power in our society have warped our perceptions.[8] Contemporary anarchist folks on the right are easier to find. They would certainly include a number of government shut-down advocates in Congress and the self-identified splinter group called "libertarian anarchists."

The Beginnings of Modern Liberal Thinking

We have mentioned the utopians and the radicals to simply be more thorough. Our main concerns are with the partisans right and left who rejected violence. Returning to the three lessons partisans took from the French Revolution, it is helpful to begin the discussion of those on the left as placing a lot of their emphasis on the importance of our second issue: they fully acknowledged that political participation by the common people was here to stay, and for the most part they saw the common sense of ordinary people as a very good thing.

These partisans had their own celebrity, Jon Stuart, the British politician, writer, and reformer, John Stuart Mill (1806-1873). I want to single this fellow out for a moment only because, in his parliamentary career and his many writings, Mill set a standard for the modern reformer. He presents us with a vision of a representative government which would work to continuously improve the lot of the people. Through education and expanding knowledge, problems could be addressed on a massive scale, bringing improved living to most of the people. So long as politics could be conducted in peaceful mutual respect, incremental changes could be legislated, implemented, tried, and kept in place or further corrected with additional lawmaking. The resulting overall pattern would be improvement for most and maximum freedom and equality for all. Mill and these progressives envisioned a democratic society where free speech and toleration reigned supreme.

I want to point out three aspects of Mill's writing that were firming up in the politics of the left during this period: liberty, utilitarianism, and humanity. Of the three, Mill, himself is probably most closely identified with the first. In his famous essay, *On Liberty,* Mill describes the circumstances under which everybody might live in maximum personal freedom.[9] Do whatever you like, say whatever you like, and so long as we maintain mutual respect and keep from hurting one another, things remain great and probably continue to improve. In such liberty a nation could be in the best situation to confront any problem that comes up. These were the times in the US and Europe of increasing literacy and an explosion of all manner of readily available books, pamphlets, magazines, and newspapers. Think of a kind of free market place of thought, where the best of the fresh ideas rose to the top. Popular government could be relied upon at every turn to overcome adversities, as the people freely argued about their options and brought in rational policy solutions with their votes. We now label the society thus envisioned as "pluralist," because in such a society people with many different deeply held beliefs could coexist and work out their differences in mutual respect and peace. Talk about optimism!

> **Gloss Note:** Since his time, Mill has kind of had it both ways. Partisans on both the right and the left have tried to make exclusive claim to his brilliant characterization of liberty. On the right Mill fans emphasize the unrestricted liberty he advocated for the workings of the marketplace. The doctrine that the government which governs best is the one which governs (business and the economy) least, is labeled with the French term "laissez faire", (loose translation, let everybody do as they choose.) On the left Mill's words about liberty are the used for justification of some of the most far-reaching defenses of free speech, free press and civil liberties.

Utilitarianism is the name we give to a way of thinking about ethics. In particular it has been used to offer a logical way of making decisions about the appropriateness of laws and policies. There are many variations, but, in the main, utilitarianism goes like this: It is a universal truth that when we decide what to do, at the most fundamental level, we consider whether the consequences of an action will avoid pain and/or bring happiness. Recognizing this fact, government laws and policy decisions become pretty straight-forwardly simple. The right thing to do is always the thing that will bring the greatest happiness to the greatest number of people. Mill's mentor and teacher, Jeremy Bentham dubbed this "the happiness principle," and he even developed mathematical formulas for use in determining the precise degree of pain/happiness that would follow any proposed action. Imagine this, we have a government agency, The General Accounting Office, that determines the cost, over time, of laws and proposed laws. If there is anything to this utilitarianism, maybe we should have a General Happiness Accounting Office too.

Gloss Note: To know of Mill it is almost expected that you know at least something about this quirky fellow Bentham. A fiction writer couldn't possibly have made him up. He famously referred to the French National Assembly's 1789 appeal to "sacred rights of man" as "Nonsense Upon Stilts." But as a radical reformer he was opposed to slavery, the death penalty, all physical punishment, and the laws against homosexuals. His connection with John Stuart Mill came when he hired Mill's father, James Mill, and the poor child, John, became the guinea pig for their radical ideas about education, learning Greek by age three and Latin by eight. One of Bentham's most quirky gestures was the gift of his body. In accordance with his will, he was dissected before audience at a public lecture, and later, per his instructions, he was placed in a wooden box with padding for his skeleton and dressed in his clothes and hat. In that box Bentham remains on display, today accepting visitors there at University College, London.[10]

Mill's version of utilitarianism steered away from Bentham's math and complicated things by pointing out the fact that all pleasures were not equal nor were they ranked the same by different people. Even so, critics then and now, attack this whole line of thinking as being simplistic in principle yet impossibly complicated in its application. For example, are we after maximizing total happiness or the average level of happiness? Can happiness really be the same thing as justice? Nonetheless difficult, simple, or whatever, an active and persuasive school of utilitarian writers continues to this day. Just as one example, we now even see a form of the happiness principle in the arguments of animal rights advocates. The point, for our purposes, is that Mill and other early reformers had brought up an easily understood notion of ethics that, when applied to politics, put the masses of common people at center stage of policy determination. The same logic also helped to make Mill one of the earliest champions of rights and suffrage for women.

The final feature of Mill's reformist views I want to consider is his concern for our third lesson from the French Revolution, his belief in the need for religion. True to the heritage of the enlightenment, Mill dismissed existing faiths as hopelessly inadequate for the task of bringing the participants together as the new political democracies developed. Besides, many religious beliefs made people focus on themselves when what was needed was a system of beliefs that expanded the sympathy and concern of average people so that they could identify with larger and larger groups and leave the past of feuding families, warring tribes and national identities behind them. As was his optimistic way of approaching many other subjects, Mill conceived of this religion of humanity as a natural process taking place almost without efforts and leadership. The main impetus was to come from the society's commitment to mass literacy and education. With the cultural emphasis on the general happiness that his liberal utilitarian society promised, the age-old myths and superstitions of existing religions would lose their hold. The same cosmopolitan and worldly perspectives would introduce people to an ever widening expanse in their respect and compassion for others, who they would recognize as sisters and brothers sharing in their humanity. All that was really needed in the belief department, to hold this society together, was a mutual open-mindedness and respect for one another. A broad-based faith in humanity would grow as time went on.[11]

Once again, we see in Mill and his fellow reformers a confidence and optimism that harks back to the Enlightenment almost as though the events of the terror and the military dictatorship had never come to France.

The Beginnings of Modern Conservative Thinking

The unbridled optimism of the reformers seems naïve to us today. Didn't they get the message from the Revolution in France? Those who rose in opposition to the reformers clearly did get a message. For them, the Enlightenment's rejection of Christian morality had brought crisis. Western civilization set adrift from the stability that 15 centuries of

Christian dominance was a central issue. In addition to that, the political participation of the masses really forced things to unravel. The violence was clearly the product of the entry on all those ordinary people into politics. These ignorant commoners were the recruits for the mobs. Separated from their Christian constraints, such people were a clear and present danger. I quoted Gustave Lebon (1841-1931), at the beginning of this chapter as a way of capturing how completely conservative views of events of the Revolution in France could differ from the jubilant optimism of reformers like Mill. The quote comes from what Lebon called his scientific study of the psychology of crowds. In it he asserted that unconstrained, the masses always revert to the mentality of beasts. He leaves us with the images of herding animals swept from one direction to another by ideas that register with the lowest common denominator of their intelligences. Scary stuff!

But Lebon's analysis leads only to fear and probably repression. His is not a perspective that contemplates a conservative plan that might take us forward in a politics of peaceful representative government. However, for that kind of conservative perspective, we are indeed fortunate that the events of the French Revolution had such an articulate and practical conservative analyst. The fellow I have in mind is ideal match on the right for John Stuart Mill on the left. His name is Edmund Burke (1729-1797). At the time things began to fall apart in France he was following the developments from just across the English Channel. Burke managed to use the facts of the matter as they were taking place to develop some of the basic elements of the modern conservative way of approaching politics.

Originally from Ireland, Burke was, like Mill, a writer and member of Parliament. Earlier, when the American colonists resisted British taxes and eventually declared their independence, Burke consistently supported their claims that taxes to the British Crown were not just or reasonable. But in the first months of the French Revolution, he quickly wrote a book-length essay in opposition. There is nothing much better for selling political books than to make a good prediction about the outcome of controversial events and Burke's book, *Reflections on the Revolution in France*, has got to be one of history's best examples of good predictions with really good timing. In it, he managed to heap criticism on the revolutionaries and predict that their plans were destined for dismal failure. While his arguments are often elegant his characterizations of the French radicals throughout his 407 blistering paragraphs shows them to be a crew of self-possessed, disrespectful, usurpers.[12] Like-wise, he attacks their supporters on his side of the Channel with varieties of nasty name-calling that include suggestions what might be his anti-Semitism. While Burke was obviously worked up, what was important at the time was that he was able to predict the failure of the plans and actions of the French revolutionaries long before the reign of terror, and all the bloodshed, which eventually provided Napoleon the opportunity to take over. What makes this analysis so prescient is that Burke never saw many of his predictions come to pass. He died in 1797.

However, Burke's book along with his other writings is far more important than a commentary on current events of his time. It is the rationale of his argument that we need to take in. It is in the way that he supports his certainty that the French Revolution will fail, that Edmund Burke is often thought of as father of modern conservatism. Burke's conservatism is elegant, yet at the same time, it is really quite simple and straight-forward. He is such a master of words that it is tempting to explain him by giving you some quotations. Though I recommend him to you, it wouldn't be fair to compare his prose to Mill's whose awkward paragraphs can go on for pages. So I'll resist. Keep in mind that Burke is not presenting some kind of action plan to bring about the ideal society. His subject is change itself, and the prospects of great change then only being considered in France. His promptings are aimed at how careful we all must be about such things. Let me try to describe his approach.

Burke explains how change and conservatism relate to one another by taking up the history of property inheritance. The rights/rules of property inheritance come to us from past generations. Not just the past two or three generations, but from time-out-of-mind. While these rules have been with us for eons, it is not true that they have never changed at all. Over the centuries the rules of inheritance have certainly changed but they have changed gradually to account for contemporary circumstances. Using property as an easily understood example, Burke points out that people owe to their ancestors those things they inherent. And likewise, during their lifetimes, they owe to their future generations the care and preservation of those inheritances that they will pass on. As it is with property, this passing of value from the deep past---into our hands--- and then from our hands to future generations, is no different when it comes to our liberties. These too are inherited from our predecessors. They come to us from the gradual development of the past, we make use of them, and then pass them on to the next generation. In the course of his essay we can pick out five basic underpinnings of what is recognized as modern conservatism:

1. That it views social/political arrangements as extending through time. We are merely the contemporary custodians of what we receive from past generations. And it is our duty as custodians to conserve what exists in the present so that it will be passed on to future generations.

2. Democracy has severe limitations so far as this generational handing-off process is concerned. Minorities are unprotected from majority rule. Viewing things at any one single place and time, the living participants are bound to exaggerate their importance, their understanding, and their wisdom. To put it in other words, since our past and future partners in this historical process cannot cast votes, they cannot be properly represented by the majority rule of democracy.

3. From time to time, adjustments can be made to these inherited arrangements. But the only changes we ought to permit are those that seek to recognize current needs while preserving as much of the critical past/present/future continuity as possible. Thus the orientation to change and the scope of potential changes must remain small scale and

pragmatic. This should rule out transformative reforms, social engineering and revolution.

4. In all of this we are acknowledging that any living individual (or even a living group or faction) has ideas and perspectives that are severely limited to the here-and-now, whereas the political community has a much broader existence through time and space. For Burke, the fascination of the enlightenment with human rationality is one such limited perspective, and as such it is a dangerous trend. This is because, in actual practice, what we take to be purely rational is actually colored by passions and emotions we often do not admit to. We humans and our customs are far too complex to figure out. So rational plans to redesign human societies are always bound to fail.

5. There is an additional feature of what went into modern conservatism that Burke's formulations are less explicit about. That feature is the idea of natural law. We will have occasion to take natural law up in later chapters. But it might be helpful to simply mention it at this point. The concept of Natural Law gets at the idea that all us humans, regardless of place or time, as part of our very natures, have, and will always have, the very same inclinations, or predispositions that incline us toward good things, things like life, love, truth, and perhaps even toward God, and also selfish passions that pull us in opposite directions. Think of this common morality inborn and unchanging in human minds as resulting in the way that people have always, and will always live amongst their fellow humans. Some see this kind of thing at least implied by Burke while others have claimed that they cannot actually detect the notion of natural law in his work.

To Summarize:

We have taken this look back into history to understand where some of the central characteristics of modern politics came from. I maintain that the French Revolution is a critical historic event for that reason. We looked into the reformist left by example, visiting the work of John Stuart Mill, and the conservative right through the example of Edmund Burke. In terms of our three lessons of the events in France, both writers were committed to the peaceful ways of representative government. Both fully recognized that the political participation of ordinary people was not going away any time soon. And both were of the opinion that the French revolutionaries had misunderstood the role of religious institutions in binding the people together as a nation. Though both were British, both are widely recognized for their contributions to ongoing political conversations on the left and right that continue to this day in the United States. Whereas Mill's perspective is a program of reform and change, Burke is a cautionary advisory that argues for doubt and emphasizes the importance of traditions over what might seem more reasonable today. Mill's reformist perspective is alive and well among modern progressives. Burke's conservativism is still commanding respect on the right. In particular, his disapprovals of the actions of the French of his day are echoed among today's conservatives when they charge that we must back-track from government actions in recent decades which have changed our way of life too much and taken us on a destructive course.

As important as these historical anchoring points might be for our understanding of contemporary politics, I want to bring this chapter to a close by returning to what I suggested was the main point that people took from the events in those few short years in France: the point about how---the political conversation among a group of well-meaning, peaceful, rational, very well educated men--- had gone so horribly wrong. This point, I'd suggest, informs everything that goes on in every truly representative government. The basic principle that must lie beneath it all is that differences are to be settled peacefully. The events in France remain a constant reminder of how fragile this principle can be.

I don't want to exaggerate the point. Granted this lesson for non-violent and non-coercive customs in politics is of central importance. (It forms

PRELIMINARY APPROACHES

the very definition of politics that we came up with in the last chapter.) But please don't miss the fact of its limitations. Even in the United States, where we hold the democratic way of settling differences in high esteem, critics will remind us that our peaceful American political customs governed over decades of slavery and its aftermath, a race war which our predecessors conducted against Native American peoples, a military deployment in which we took half of their country away from the Mexicans, and a breakdown that resulted in a bloody war between the states, to mention only a few more prominent examples. Such examples should only serve as reminders to us of just how rare such peaceful politics can be. And once in play, how fragile such peaceful politics always remain.

As a result, our republic, what we think of as the representative government, is something we can be proud of. Lucky we are that it has characterized most of our politics in most times and places. This is how our partisans do it. And not only that, these peaceful partisans seem to get it right a lot of the time.

One further thought about the political lessons from history. In politics, everybody seems to take lessons from history. The problems come from the fact that different folks take different lessons from the same history. Leo Tolstoy, for example used his enormous novel, War and Peace, to teach his lesson that so-called great leaders, and Napoleon Bonaparte in particular, are not much more than blind instruments of history. Whether it is the Napoleonic Wars or the War on Drugs, whatever the topic, the records are there to pick and choose from and in doing picking and choosing political writers are forever identifying historical causes and placing blames.

In doing political history, writers often give us arguments about how things could have been different; "what if, or "if only." "If only Louie XVI hadn't gotten so in to debt," "if only John Wilkes Booth had missed," or "if only Hitler hadn't been a vegetarian." Whenever historical matters are approached in such "if only" terms the writer is engaging in what's sometimes called counterfactual history. It might be interesting and even fun to do this, but doing it should come with a warning: significant historical events are complicated. Most often they involve numerous forces and the thoughts and actions of countless numbers of individuals. Nevertheless, with the French Revolution, and, as we will see later, with the crises that came between the First and Second World Wars, our politics thrives on placing historical blames and "what if" historical speculations that partisans embrace as unquestionable truth. As with issues in the present, our interest here is not to take sides in the arguments. What we want instead is to better understand how partisans are using history to back up their way of looking at what we face in contemporary politics.

We will have an opportunity to get back to history as it figures into the basic differences that orient the right and the left, but before that, I suggest a change of time and place. In the chapter that follows we will jump forward to the present and instead of looking for underlying anchors and currents we will stick to the surface and check in on how the current political argument between the left and right has been busy defining the issues and their positions on those issues.

PRELIMINARY APPROACHES

Chapter 3 What's the Difference?

"Conservative, [a noun], A statesman who is enamored of existing evils, as distinguished from a liberal who wants to replace them with others."

Ambrose Bierce(1842-1914)[1]

One way to get a better understanding of our politics is to merely listen. If we listen to what the partisans identify as the problems we face in our politics and listen to what are being proposed as solutions, how can we not better appreciate what our politics is about? At least it is a start. Accordingly, our goal in this chapter is to take a look at some of the issues that get the attention of political activists. Our purpose is not to get into the ongoing arguments and take sides. What we want to accomplish is to see what issues have been in play and where those on the left and the right come down on them. We just want to get a handle on how the sides share some of the very same concerns, while, at the same time, their specific approaches to these concerns may diverge dramatically.

To use this issues approach, we'll want to steer clear of a whole lot of the political debate. I refer here to all the name calling and character demolition we hear so much of. Politicians can be scoundrels and most Presidents, at least since the 1970s, have been in legal hot water from time to time. But name-calling, whether justified or not, will not contribute to our political understanding at this point. The tactic of name-calling is a completely different order of political argument. It boils down to "Trust me and don't listen to him/her because he/she is loony/a criminal/a liar/an evil human being/a Nazi/a communist/or whatever." Almost all of this stuff takes place completely outside of legal proceedings and hard evidence. It is the stuff that comes packaged under titles like: *Why Liberals Hate America* or *Lies: And the Lying Liars Who Tell Them*. The practice of demonizing the political opposition is a staple in our political life. This is unfortunate both because it turns many people away from politics, and even if it does not turn them away, and they remain engaged, it can take their eye off the ball, so to speak. In later chapters, I intend to explain how and why specific political issues like the ones we take up here are coming to take a lesser role as the polarization in our politics has become more intense. But even so, we need to look at the issues themselves as an important part of the political conversation.

Issues come in all sizes; local, state, federal and international. (In fact, it is not uncommon for a discussion of which of the levels of government should handle the issue, to become a central part of the political debate.) A local zoning question or a bill revising rules and procedures for elections can get partisans deeply divided but here we will intentionally stick to issues that divide the right and left nationally so as to stay on a fairly general level in this discussion. To actually gain any insight, the political issues we need to look into are the ones that have real content and consequences. And the positions advocated on the right and left, take things in very different directions.

Though people have very strong opinions about some of these issues, I want us to withhold judgment as much as possible. Correct or not, people tend to think of their political beliefs as being correct. Generally, we think of correct beliefs as those that can be factually demonstrated to almost anybody. Nonetheless, there are a lot of political beliefs out there that do not meet this requirement. Sometimes people think a belief is true because they possess only part of the facts that have a bearing, when these same beliefs would be obviously untrue were the believer to have all of the facts. In other instances, people cling to beliefs in the absence of any factual support. But let's just try to get the gist of the positions. After all, in many instances the heat generated by an issue merely involves opinions about what will happen in the future if something is or is not done by government; to back off, or intervene or reverse some trend. What is more, government actions desired by just one side or the another are very seldom adopted in pure form with no compromises. Thus, the ideas and theories that underlie these positions are not likely to ever be tested and proved entirely right or wrong.

I will try to be as objective and straight-forward as I can in describing these various positions on issues. I'll probably miss the mark a time or two. Disappointing both sides equally will be the best a guy like me can do. We will have occasion for a more thorough look at political beliefs later on. But as we proceed in this chapter, let's just remind ourselves we cannot look directly inside people's heads. We have to rely on what they say they believe; and these expressed beliefs are all we can get at. This is, of course, better than listening to how the political opponents on the other side of the issues would have us understand them. If we depended on the opposition to understand right and left beliefs, we would quickly come to the conclusion that the vast majority of people interested in politics are just plain stupid. However, with a discerning eye, we can identify some reasonable examples of the political beliefs of the partisans on the left and right, as people apply these two labels in everyday political life. If I do a half way decent job, I will soon have you, my readers, using these labels yourselves with some comfort and satisfaction. So much for preliminaries; again, it is our purpose here to look at political beliefs as elements in the political process. With the above considerations in mind, we can proceed.

Under each of the headings below, there is an issue followed by a comparison of typical political reactions to it. In each case, the positions of folks on the left are summarized, followed by summaries of the positions people on the right typically take on these same issues. This is neither an exhaustive list nor a full expression of the views that these issues bring out. Some of the issues obviously overlap with one another a bit. There is no attempt to put the issues in any kind of rank order. There is a lot of detail here so it won't hurt my feelings if it bogs you down and you just skip it and go on to the generalizations that start after these "Issue:" headings:

Issue: **The government is too big and too expensive**

Typical Left Attitudes and Concerns:

Agree, but: Government is too big, but government is where we must go when the private business economy and other institutions do not effectively address real problems. For example poverty, recession unemployment, hiring undocumented workers, pollution, species extinction, civil rights. On the other hand, the Cold War ended over 25 years ago. With no nation to nation armed force confrontations threatening the US during this period and with no other nation coming near us in the size and capability of our current conventional military capability, it is time to bring down our military to reasonable size and expense levels.

Typical Right Attitudes and Concerns:

Agree: Government is too big and very inefficient. As the largest employer, government drives up wages. It intrudes into people's lives and into their businesses with senseless regulations. It siphons off economic productivity with high taxes. Besides crime control, national defense and court enforcement of contracts, it contributes little of value. On the other hand, it was with a robust commitment to national defense that the Cold War was won, and this same commitment to a large, up-to-date, and capable armed force is essential to making

PRELIMINARY APPROACHES

military confrontation with the US unthinkable to enemies, both actual and potential.

Issue: **Poverty is a serious problem**

Typical Left Attitudes and Concerns:

Agree: Poverty is for the vast majority born into it, an insurmountable handicap. While there are those million-to-one exceptional people who beat the odds (most often in the fields of sports and entertainment) for the vast majority of the poor, our free market economy just doesn't work to improve their lot. When they can get jobs, their inferior education, place of residence, and access to transportation entitles them only to jobs with no benefits, which don't pay enough to live on. It is for this reason only that we must rely on the government to meet some of the most basic needs of the poor, (and especially poor children whose plight is obviously no fault of their own). But, in addition, these people need substantial government intervention to develop the skills and resources necessary to be able to pull themselves up out of poverty. Only by bringing people out of poverty, can we make them productive members of society. As such people enter the middle class, the entire economy expands and is strengthened.

Typical Right Attitudes and Concerns:

Agree, but: Poverty is a fate that stalks every one of us. However, most modern poverty should be unnecessary in this land of plenty. The problem results from well intentioned government programs designed to help people escape from poverty. Instead of helping to end poverty, these programs have created an intergenerational culture of people completely dependent on government. Rather than striving to better themselves, all but a few among the poor seek only immediate pleasure, as rates of drug use and teen pregnancies among them indicate. They can do this with the assurance the government will sustain them. Government should not be in the business of redistributing wealth or leveling incomes. Doing this results in reducing the effort, initiative and personal responsibility that should be expected of each one of us. The needy should be helped, but that's what charities are for. A free and growing market economy is the best way to pull people out of poverty. Economic prosperity has brought countless more lives out of poverty than government programs.

Issue: **Crime is a problem that needs much more government attention**

Typical Left Attitudes and Concerns:

Agree: The justice system is unfortunately a blunt instrument. Threat of punishment will not deter crime among the hopeless or the very poor. We need extensive reform to: 1. Assure that we are convicting the right people, 2. assigning fitting punishment, 3. Preparing properly punished individuals for their return to productive places in society. The overall objective of government is not only to protect the law abiding but also to keep at a minimum, that portion of the population that must be isolated from the rest for their crimes. There is no reasonable justification for the fact that the US houses a larger percentage of its population behind bars than any other advanced nation. Also, no government should have a right to execute its people.

Typical Right Attitudes and Concerns:

Agree: Strict law enforcement and stiff punishments including the death penalty, are effective ways of turning people away from crime. Actions must have consequences, and this is nowhere more critical than in the case of criminal behavior. In the current situation, this clear relationship between crime and punishment is hamstrung with red tape and delays. Only with knowledge of clear and swift negative consequences can criminal law have significant deterrent effect. Criminals can sometimes become rehabilitated through deep personal effort and commitment. Government rehabilitation programs designed

PRELIMINARY APPROACHES

take this out of the criminal's hands, and do it for them, dependably result in subsequent conviction and imprisonment.

Issue: **Personal Responsibility is a vanishing trait in this country.**

Typical Left Attitudes and Concerns:

Agree: People aren't born with a sense of personal responsibility. It must be instilled and cultivated within families, and in our educational system. Furthermore, it must be fostered by a supportive community that rewards the trait. For decades now, discrimination and government supported residential segregation have provided inferior schooling and a hostile climate of law enforcement to communities of poor whites and those of racial and ethnic groups commonly judged by prejudice to be less likely to succeed. In such circumstances, attitudes of personal responsibility, no matter how strong they might be, cannot save the overwhelming majority from predictable failure. And the results of this fact are reflected in the size and make-up of our prison population. If every child could grow up with a good education, a confidence that he/she had at least a fair shot at success, and respect from the society he/she lives in, this apparent problem of personal responsibility would disappear.

Typical Right Attitudes and Concerns:

Agree: Irresponsibility, laziness, and lack of proper self-control should not be permitted. However, if these traits are not discouraged, life-long patterns of irresponsibility result. This problem has two main causes, the welfare state created by the New Deal in the 1930s, and the counter-cultural movement of the 1960s. In the process, we have replaced our reliance on personal responsibility with wholesale dependence on the government. From birth to death people rely, not on themselves and their families, but on the government to satisfy many of their needs. The new health care law is just the latest step in our retreat from personal responsibility. What is worse, the bill for all this government dependence has now far exceeded our ability to pay. We now live in a society with dominant values that cannot sustain it into the future. Harsh medicine in the form of cut backs on government entitlement programs are not only necessary, but, realistically speaking, such cut backs are all we can afford at this point.

Issue: **We've made progress in Civil Rights**

Typical Left Attitudes and Concerns:

Agree, but: Since the 1960s there has been marked improvement. However, intergenerational poverty and remaining discrimination continue to segregate members of certain minorities out of the mainstream and de-motivate them with inferior schools, high unemployment, and oppressive policing.

Typical Right Attitudes and Concerns:

Agree, but: The civil rights laws, while well intentioned, have had the actual effect of making minorities feel entitled and dependent upon government to satisfy their desires. Well organized minorities have leveraged the political system in directions that the majority of Americans do not support.

Issue: **Our immigration laws and their lax enforcement have created enormous and complicated problems for Americans**

Typical Left Attitudes and Concerns:

Disagree: Over the past several decades, weak immigration law enforcement was understood as a benefit to businesses, because it brought in millions of low-wage workers who were never likely to complain or unionize. As a result of this practice and other laws which favored immigration of relatives of US residents, we have become a far more diverse population. We must now reckon with the fact that among the millions of these newcomers who have lived productive lives and enriched our culture, many still live in fear that they can be separated from loved ones and deported. They are just the latest additions to our tradition as a nation of immigrants seeking a better life, and should be welcomed into citizenship. As the portion of our population of European ancestry ages, these newcomers are poised to become the backbone of our economy

Typical Right Attitudes and Concerns:

Agree: Our immigration laws are the laws of our land, and they must be enforced. People who have entered this country illegally are law breakers and must be treated as such. This problem of illegals is the main problem but there are other related problems as well. Rather than joining us, these immigrants often don't even take the trouble to speak English. They are a drain on our economy and on our government services. While this is true enough for great numbers of the Latinos among us, the immigrants from Muslim countries are even more problematic, since there have been a number of dangerous radical Jihadists among them. America is not, and never was, a nation of immigrants. We are a nation and culture established by European settlers, and these newcomers, both legal and illegal, are a threat to America and our way of life.

Issue: **Economic Classes are the basis of politics**

Typical Left Attitudes and Concerns:

Agree: Group political action based upon economic self interest has brought real gains to lower class groups. This is the way the politics which characterized the union movement and the civil rights movements brought the comforts and securities of middle class life to millions of Americans. However, during the past 40 years, the poor and middle classes have lost their sense of common political identity which has allowed an ever smaller ever richer proportion of the population to capture political dominance.

Typical Right Attitudes and Concerns:

Disagree: Economic classes are simply income categories economists talk about. Class-based politics misses the point that people can, and do, become rich all the time. Political class can do nothing but harm to economic stability and growth. The class-based politics of the 1930s and 40s only brought us the virtual explosion of the welfare state and the government regulation has made it more difficult to get rich in recent times. Those who have become rich should be valued and respected because they are the only people who have the resources to invest and create jobs.

Issue: **Religion should have a greater influence in our laws and government**

Typical Left Attitudes and Concerns:

Disagree: The founding fathers specifically put a barrier between government and the tenets of religions. Accordingly, people cannot be forced by the government to abide by the dictates of any religion. Besides, on a whole, the moral behavior among those professing Christianity (or any other religion) has not been particularly impressive. The history of most major religions has included violence and hatred that has no place in our politics.

Typical Right Attitudes and Concerns:

Agree: Without religion people are turning away from the moral and ethical ties that bind us together as a people. We can acknowledge the religious beliefs of other good citizens but, Christianity is the main religion of the United States, and as such, should be embraced by government for the moral/ethical impact it can have. Without exception, our greatest leaders have openly (and rightly) appealed to America's religious traditions and beliefs.

Issue: **Effective Diplomacy has an enormous role to play in our current national security**

Typical Left Attitudes and Concerns:

Agree: The potential for security gains through diplomacy should never be underestimated, but they are even more critical now as we face this new century. The immediate threats from the international terrorist criminal gangs that call themselves Jihadists, demands close cooperation and information sharing among legitimate governments world-wide, as do issues such as trade and global warming. Our experiences since WWII, first in Viet Nam, then in Iraq and Afghanistan, remind us that military campaigns seldom bring about their desired ends or any lasting results. In this era of world economy and modern instantaneous communications, we should build upon the United Nations and other international organizations to foster international peaceful coexistence. National leaders committed to attacking other nations militarily will not cease to exist, but they can be effectively confronted by a unified international community devoted to peaceful dispute resolution and actively promoting health education and improved standards of living globally.

Typical Right Attitudes and Concerns:

Disagree: There will always be war, so long as truly evil people can take control of whole countries and develop resources of military might. Our national interests will naturally precipitate conflicts from time to time, and we must recognize this and be prepared to defend those interests militarily. Furthermore, the United States is not, and will never be, just another nation. Our leadership role in the world is nothing less than the flip side of the freedom and prosperity we enjoy here at home. Consequently, we will probably always be the object of hate and envy for some world leaders. Diplomacy is not an end in itself. It is little more than the front we present to other nations; a necessary front to be sure but no less a front. As such, diplomacy is useless whenever it is not backed up by clear and decisive military threat. Consequently, our world leadership is assured by projecting our military dominance in both potential and actual conflicts. We must recognize the fundamental fact that international politics is little more than pure anarchy and that all attempts at international law violate our essential national sovereignty.

Issue: **Human Equality is a basic principle of the United States**

Typical Left Attitudes and Concerns:

Agree: Equality, as envisioned by our founders has two aspects. People should have equal legal rights under the laws and, partly as a consequence of this, people should have equal opportunity to better themselves through their own efforts. Neither of these aspects of equality have ever been fully realized, so while we must celebrate the way we have progressively realized an expanded sense of equality over time, we must continually commit ourselves and our democracy to this important, but unfinished task.

Typical Right Attitudes and Concerns:

Disagree: All people are not equal, especially in terms of the effort they put forward, but also in skill and ability. Equality under the law is desirable because it maximizes our individual freedom. On the other hand, efforts to use the laws and government to ensure equality of opportunity have often morphed into schemes that endeavor to bring about equality of outcomes, or worse, advantages to particular groups. Inequality of outcomes has to be understood for what it is, the result of good, fair efforts and competition between naturally unequal individuals.

PRELIMINARY APPROACHES

Issue: **Competition in commerce must be supported and encouraged by our laws and Regulations**

Typical Left Attitudes and Concerns:

Agree, but: Small business start-ups are the fertile ground from which our economy innovates and improves. Laws and regulations need to acknowledge this continually by maintaining a level playing field for the competition. But giant corporations are quite another thing. In sector after sector of our economy, a few behemoth international corporations prevent any real competition, depress average incomes, and stifle real innovation. Both the Republicans and Democrats (and their lobbyists and various think tanks) now serve the needs of the huge corporations and not small businesses or average citizens. Consumers must be protected from abuses from unethical businesses and businesses must be held accountable for the costs they create for our environment.

Typical Right Attitudes and Concerns:

Agree: Businesses come in all sizes, but what is true of all of them is that they create both investment opportunities and the jobs that we all depend upon to live. They provide us with a standard of living never before dreamed of in history and not known in most of the rest of the world. Government must recognize this and support the activities of businesses. While there may be a need to tax and even regulate business, we must be mindful that taxes and regulations subtract from business' bottom lines, and thus put limits on a company's ability to expand, hire and pay employees. In recent times our government has created numerous business taxes and regulations that are far too burdensome on business and on the entire economy.

Issue: **Abortions should be eliminated**

Typical Left Attitudes and Concerns:

Agree: Women should avoid abortions if at all possible. But because of the simple fact that only women experience pregnancies, it must remain a woman's decision whether to carry a pregnancy through. Furthermore, the lion's share of all the efforts of child rearing also still fall to women in our society. With single and divorced women, this responsibility is often total. This special standing of women has been recognized by the US government as the law of the land for over 40 years. Our goal in eliminating abortions should recognize that, in a society that assured nurture, good health, education, and opportunity to all newborns, abortions could be virtually eliminated.

Typical Right Attitudes and Concerns:

Agree: The issue of abortion is an extremely simple one. Abortions end the life of a human being. In the years that followed legalizing abortion in the Supreme Court decision, Roe v Wade, millions of women have used abortion to simply evade their moral responsibilities to their unborn babies and to their inherent place, their very nature, and to society. This is a terrible part of a much larger problem. Without consequences, sex roles and sexual behavior have been significantly degraded from what has always been the natural order of things. If abortion were to be seen for what it is, a form of murder, it could be virtually eliminated.

Issue: **Since the collapse of the Soviet Union, the United States still remains under threat from socialism**

Typical Left Attitudes and Concerns:

Disagree: The United States was once in a huge decades-long military confrontation with a threatening block of nations that was identified as socialist. But socialism is a name applied to many forms of government, some good some bad. At their worst, socialistic governments have been militarist, totalitarian dictatorships; at their best socialistic governments have created a good place to live for most of their citizens. We can learn from the worst and the best of these instances of socialism.

Typical Right Attitudes and Concerns:

Agree: Socialism is at best a fool's utopian dream. Whenever it is attempted, it first swallows up personal liberty and then goes on to rule by violence and terror. Under socialism the state controls the individual. Socialism's fatal flaw is that in all of its manifestations, it ceases to recognize that effective laws allowing for acquiring and using private property are essential to human freedom. Governments that play the role of Robin Hood will always be taking that freedom away from all their citizens.

Issue: **World-wide Islamic terrorism now threatens the US and all Western Civilization**

Typical Left Attitudes and Concerns:

Disagree: Worldwide there are over a billion peaceful and religiously tolerant Muslims. By comparison, Muslim terrorists number in the tens of thousands. The terrorist attacks that came on 09/11/2001 were indeed tragic events, but it was a mistake to declare this the beginning of a world-wide war with Islamic terrorists that threatens our civilization. Rather, it is a major instance of a kind of provocation by alienated extremist individuals and groups. They want their horrific violence, and the media coverage it causes, to set all non-Muslims against all Muslims. This strategy is neither new nor very clever. In fact, it is the same approach taken by the Manson Family in the 1960s in their attempt to precipitate race war between whites and blacks, or in the 1995 bombing of the Federal building in Oklahoma City in which militia movement fanatics were bent upon motivating an armed uprising against the Federal government. This time, however, the perpetrators are high-tech, very well financed and aimed at precipitating a world-wide confrontation. All such provocateurs are nothing more than violent criminals and should be sought out and apprehended as such.

Typical Right Attitudes and Concerns:

Agree: We have given Islam the benefit of the doubt too long. History tells us that it is a religion that leads believers to warfare and violence. Consequently, it cannot be accommodated in the concept of religious freedom that our founding fathers envisioned. Though it rises and wanes, conflict between Muslims and Christians dates back to the Crusades, and amounts to nothing less than a clash of civilizations which in the end will leave one side in triumph and the other in subjugation. The longer we take to fully recognize the reality of this fact, the more imposing our Islamic Jihadist enemies become. Furthermore, allowing non-Christian refugees from civil war devastated Middle East countries to settle in the US is almost sure to plant these violent Islamic terrorists among us. More generally, though, its shape and form change from time to time, evil is an ever-present danger in this world. In the last century such evil took shape in the communists and fascists who threatened us both internationally and from within our country. Though we must remain vigilant about Iran, China and North Korea, these radical Muslims are the emergent face of that evil in our time.

Issue: **Torture is sometimes necessary.**

Typical Left Attitudes and Concerns:

Disagree: Torture is illegal under treaties that the US has signed and ratified. It is a practice that the West has condemned for several hundred years. We are looked up to in the world as an example of a nation that respects human rights and torture is simply beneath human

PRELIMINARY APPROACHES

dignity. Torture is beneath us and should never take place under any circumstances. Besides, the overwhelming evidence indicates that it is not effective.

Typical Right Attitudes and Concerns:

Agree, but: While not something to be undertaken lightly, recent use of "enhanced interrogation" had three justifications. 1. Because the techniques were designed not to cause permanent tissue damage, they were not torture, 2. They were required to get captured terrorists to tell us things that ultimately saved lives. 3. The evils that these terrorists have done should disqualify them from any rights as humans.

Issue: **The National Debt must be permanently eliminated.**

Typical Left Attitudes and Concerns:

Disagree: The US Constitution does not seem to anticipate long term Federal Government debt. It says that the "public debt of the United States...shall not be questioned." Unfortunately it does not say that such debts must be paid. Over time, conservatives have used this fact to underfund and defund the laws that they don't like. Much of the expense for our recent wars in Afghanistan and Iraq have not even been put into the annual Federal budgets. Consequently, these costs were added directly to the National Debt. The result is a growing National Debt, currently at around $18.5 trillion. A responsible Congress would pay for our Federal Government by passing only laws we can afford and paying for those laws with whatever taxes they require. Instead, virtually all of the Republicans in the House of Representatives have now even signed a pledge against voting for tax increases. Even so, it is important to realize that the Federal budget is not like a household budget. Its real limit is the level of faith people have in the US dollar and US Treasury Bonds. Both are valued very high, world-wide. The realistic solution is careful concern with the costs of our laws and seriousness about collecting sufficient taxes to cover them.

Typical Right Attitudes and Concerns:

Agree: The deficit grows and grows without stopping. It represents needs for mind-boggling taxes for future generations as this borrowing comes due. It is the shameful result of spending money we do not have. Think of it as a credit card that we use today and just hand the bills over to our children and grandchildren to pay. The main cause of all this debt is the expansion of the size of the Federal government in the past 80 years, or so, and the "entitlements," programs that pay out money to almost everybody. The democrats have since the 1930s been introducing costly programs that pay income and medical expenses to hundreds of millions of people without so much as a thought about whether we could afford them. Since our population is now aging and Social Security and Medicare go primarily to older Americans, the tax burden on younger people is becoming terrific. It will take discipline to cut back on spending and bring our national finances into balance. Since we know that all taxes are a drain on our economy, going forward, we should work toward taxing only for absolute essentials like, for example, national defense, law enforcement.

Issue: **The Second Amendment is essential to our form of government**

Typical Left Attitudes and Concerns:

Agree, but: It authorized the State governments to maintain the National Guard System, and allows for personal gun ownership for self-defense and hunting. But the Amendment does not prevent laws and regulations for firearms that increase public safety. The power and sophistication of modern firearms is far beyond what the authors of the Constitution could have imagined In their world guns were loaded through the barrel shot, by time consuming shot. For example military assault weapons should not be available to civilians, and all arms purchasers should be subject to background checks.

PRELIMINARY APPROACHES

Typical Right Attitudes and Concerns:

Agree: This Amendment to the Constitution confers the right of individuals to own guns. Beyond the language of the 2nd Amendment itself, any attempt at restricting gun sales or ownership through law or regulation should be opposed because wide-scale private gun ownership helps ensure that the government will not risk confrontation with a free and well armed citizenry. The dangers of oppressive government are one of the purposes for which the 2nd Amendment was adopted.

Issue: **Over the years the Federal Government has usurped many matters which should properly be left to the states and local government to address**

Typical Left Attitudes and Concerns:

Disagree: It is true that the Federal Government has taken on issues that previously were governed at State and local levels, but in each instance this was because the lower levels of government neglected basic Constitutional principles. Two main areas of such expansion came from the Federal Government's constitutional role in "free trade" in interstate commerce and "equal protection" of all citizens under the laws. A third instance is in the expansion of national defense into "Homeland Security" that cannot reasonably be coordinated by the states.

Typical Right Attitudes and Concerns:

Agree: During the years after the Great Depression, Democratic controlled Congresses and liberal Federal judges repeatedly invented new ways for the lives and interests of citizens to be brought under Federal jurisdiction. The constitutional justifications have been dubious at best. The cumulative results of this process have been a stifling of economic freedom for both businesses and individuals, and the rise of identity politics where groups like African Americans, Latinos, women, LBGTs and such have become forces in our national politics that never could have been imagined by our founding fathers.

Issue: **America can become energy independent**

Typical Left Attitudes and Concerns:

Maybe: There are some major obstacles to achieving energy independence with fossil fuels: 1. multi-national oil companies would object to being forced to refine and sell American crude only in the US rather than getting the best price for their product anywhere in the world. 2. Producers would have to be assured that they would never face the economic consequences of high risk to the environmental activities like fracking and mountain top coal removal. 3. It would put off addressing the threats climate change (which the scientific community has definitively demonstrated). However, with proper start-up support from government, the alternatives of wind solar and even tides could together make substantial advances in that direction.

Typical Right Attitudes and Concerns:

Agreed: With known petroleum and natural gas reserves, and with the participation of other North American nations, we could easily produce all the fuel we need and cease to be dependent on oil cartel sources in the volatile Middle East. The arguments against this policy, which come from the global warming opposition, are either fabrications or exaggerations put forward by interests who seek government subsidies for the nuclear, wind and solar industries. Besides, globally, climate has always been in change, and if warming, from any cause should actually be taking place, any negative effects would reliably be confronted by innovation and investment. That is the strength of our market economy.

PRELIMINARY APPROACHES

Issue: **All Americans should have government backed health care coverage**

Typical Left Attitudes and Concerns:

Agree: Until 2010 the US was the only advanced country that had no national health care plan. Access to the world's finest health care system should be a right for all Americans. The reason is simple. Freed from the economic catastrophes that health care costs can bring, and the competitive edge that good health can give children as they grow up and enter the workforce as adults, future generations with universal health care will live better and far more productive lives. Obamacare was a start, but we are not finished with health care reform. When we finally bring health care to all Americans the way we do it for older people with Medicare, we bring costs down by eliminating the legions of useless middle-men in the insurance industry. Nothing will stand between Americans and their health care.

Typical Right Attitudes and Concerns:

Disagree: Just what we don't need, nor can we afford: another hugely expensive Federal benefit program. They called it "affordable" because the government pays. Prior to 2010 no Americans were denied medical care. Uninsured people could go to any hospital emergency room and get the kind of excellent care that this country is known for all over the world. There are two main problems with the new health care law: First, the fact that adults of working age were responsible for paying for health care for themselves and their children, was a good thing, because financial responsibilities are the key to what motivates people in a correctly functioning free market economy. Second, Federal health care legislation means a Federally regulated health care industry with Federally mandated standards of care. With regulation and standardization, innovation in this critical industry suffers.

This is only a sampling of issues that have been in play in recent years, (though some of them have been around for much longer). It is not an exhaustive list. We will get into some other issues in later chapters. But I offer this list as being representative of some of what is out there. By the way don't, seriously, please, don't anybody take this list and use it as a check list to determine if you are conservative or liberal. I was just trying to be accurate; not persuasive. We must leave it to the partisans to sell their stuff to you. In fact, I am quite sure that some liberal and conservative partisans would even take exception to the very terms I have used here to represent their positions on these issues. This list is placed here for two purposes: 1. to begin to consider some of what all the arguing is about, which I hope you have been able to do, and, 2. to prepare us to start to see, some of the ways of thinking that separate conservatives from liberals, on a more general level.

In the headings which follow, I'll try to point out just four of these more general ways in which conservatives and liberals seem to see things differently.

Historical Optimism VS Realism

This first difference came out in the last chapter. The left has had a tradition of an open-ended optimism about change and the future that simply does not register well on the right. The typical way that they used to explain this was with a quotation that was claimed by many and attributed to still more. "If at 20 you are not a communist, you have no heart, but if by 40 you are not a capitalist, you have no brain." The idea being that the total agenda for change that people on the left embraced was only a reflection of youthful sentimentality. With demise of the communist world and the popularity of libertarian ideas among many of our younger folks, this presumably fake quote may have lost its relevance. But the idea that the left carries an optimistic view that the right scoffs at as being naïve, is no casualty of history.

PRELIMINARY APPROACHES

The only additional clarification that we need at this point is to try to give each side of this difference its due. The left sees human progress not as wishful thinking but as the reality of history. Their focus of attention is on the ordinary people that have always made up the vast majority of those living. Horrible things have happened to these kinds of people, but over the long haul, things are better for them now than ever before. This history has been punctuated by a series of events, each one of which has tipped the scales a little bit in the direction of justice for these people. Each event has its story and its heroes. In the US there were the brave men and women who created unions to bring home a better life for their families, the fearless marchers and protesters who attacked and vanquished much of the overt racism that was Jim Crow, the young activists who wore down the resolve of the most powerful political military force in the world and help end the long, punishing conflict in Viet Nam. Sometimes the gains are made strictly within the legislative arena, like Social Security, Federal Deposit Insurance, Medicare, Americans with Disabilities, Family Leave, Affordable Health Care, but gains for the ordinary people never just happen. They take effort and planning. People have to be made aware. The constant pressure for change has to be applied to politicians, at the polls and elsewhere.

People on the right see this list of instances where pressure and protest brought change as a mixed bag at best. When masses of people pressure for and bring about changes, their cure can sometimes be worse than the original problem. When masses of people are mobilized to pressure for change, are they led by like-minded people or are they actually being manipulated by leaders who do not have their best interests in mind.

Underlying this skepticism is a view which runs counter to the way that the left sees history. It is not quite pessimism. I've called it "realism," not because the thinking on the right is necessarily more correct. The folks on the right just tamp down on the optimism and consider their expectations for the future more neutral. On a whole, history can bring us really great changes, but sometimes things don't turn out well. The uniting together to accomplish big things is possible but really pretty limited. So we are better off if we stick with the notion that the best we can count on is cooperation with other people for limited purposes. Whether people are in elite positions or common folks in the masses, there will always be those trying to take advantage of us and of the power our government can exert. And beyond these advantage-takers, there are lots of people out there both at home and abroad who either think that they can only succeed at our expense, or are just plain evil. Realistically speaking, to deny this reality is, yes, naïve.

Liberty VS Equality

As should be apparent from the issues about equality and socialism, each of the two sides takes different positions on which of these values to favor. The right is definitely on the liberty side. The left hangs out on the equality side. But it's not quite that simple. This left/right alignment focuses on economic matters. When it comes to other issues they switch sides in the liberty/equality debate. Since this difference of opinion about liberty and equality goes back at least 300 years, I will stick in one of those gloss notes right here.

> **Gloss Note**: The British Philosopher John Locke (1632-1704) is generally identified as the source used by the Founding Fathers for a critical passage in the Declaration of Independence. In his Second Treatise of Government, John Locke wrote that men, "being all equal and independent, no one ought to harm another in his life, health, liberty or possessions." This of course became the phrase, "all men are created equal, that they are endowed by their Creator with certain unalienable Rights, that among these are Life, Liberty and the pursuit of Happiness." Locke also had a lot to say about when it was justifiable to dissolve tyrannical government and start a new one.[2]

PRELIMINARY APPROACHES

I think it is noteworthy that this critical liberal/conservative difference was written right into the script from the beginning. It says right there in the Declaration of Independence that we are pursuing two core values that are in conflict with each other a lot of the time. The Declaration rests on an assumption that we are all created equal with the right to be free from harm from others and from government. The two; liberty and equality, seem inseparable. But, just because we see these two words together a lot does not mean that they fit together logically or complement each other in real life. In fact, when a community of people pursue liberty and equality simultaneously, the two principles can very quickly come into conflict with one another. To the extent that we have equality some people end up with less liberty (that power to act however he or she pleases). To the extent that we have liberty some people end up with more of what they want, and some end up with less, i.e., there will be less equality.

I can hear some readers saying "nonsense!" Right from the beginning it was clear to everybody that both liberty and equality were to be limited so they would not come into conflict with one another. Nobody had the liberty to hurt other people. And as for equality, it only covered certain rights. People were to have equal rights, not equal possessions. So, the way it is supposed to work, the requirements for equality leave off where the entire range of liberties exist. And likewise people do not have the liberty to interfere with the equal rights of others. But let me persist here. The seemingly neat co-existence of liberty and equality in this country is actually more apparent than real. For starters, when we have the liberty to pursue our happiness unchecked, some people end up quite influential and wealthy while some others end up poor and powerless.

Granted, it is easy to disagree with this equality goal. Just because somebody wrote that all men (and just because we are told that "men" now includes women, legal immigrants, and sons and daughters of former slaves) are created equal doesn't mean they should all end up with an MA in Business, a college chum in the US Senate, two kids attending Yale, and a BMW in the driveway. We'd be foolish not to acknowledge that people have different capabilities and different motivational levels. Nobody ever said that everybody has equal potential, or luck for that matter.

But let me persist just a bit more. Let's peal away I.Q., good looks, luck, and resources of personal charm, for a moment and just look at the economic aspect; the money available as a resource. Consider how much money you might have access to at the start of your career. Money, a liquid asset, is as close to a perfectly plastic resource we probably can come up with. Arguably, money can make up for some missing I.Q. points, for lack of luck certainly, and for big charm deficiencies. Heck, now-a-days money can even do a lot for good looks. As they say in Mexico, "No hay mujeres fea, sólo mujeres pobres," (There are no ugly women, only poor women). In fact, liberals are always saying in one way or another that money trumps almost everything. Most certainly, money can make up for almost any disadvantage a person can face at the beginning of their career or their life's journey, or whatever we want to call it. And it is this equality of opportunity, the opportunity to reach one's potential that liberals really get excited about. Beyond that, equality about some minimum standards for food clothing and shelter concern liberals as well. To liberals, people born into poverty are simply not created equal to people born into wealth. So when we hear politicians and others are using words and phrases like "we are all in this together," or "black white and brown, we're all a part of the American melting pot," or "Christian, Jew, Muslim, we are all Americans", or even when someone refers to our representative government as a "democracy" you can usually interpret it as a kind of language as liberal code language that sets a priority on equality as a core value of the United States. For liberals, equality is the national core value that must be emphasized, protected and expanded.

By the same token conservatives get excited about any and just about all attempts to increase economic equality, because these attempts always seem to be hacking away at liberty. Taxes take away my freedom to decide how I want to spend my money. Who could possibly disagree with the argument that at least some of their tax dollars are being spent on things that they personally really disapprove of. Anti-discrimination laws force people to associate with people they might not otherwise choose to spend time with. And now the government tells us they tell us that we might have to pay a fine unless we buy health insurance. For conservatives, personal freedom is the national core value that must be emphasized, protected and expanded. Substantial personal liberty is nothing less than the engine that has propelled our country to greatness. Each new government initiative aimed at making life chances more equal gets them to feeling like a little push down the slippery slope to un-freedom; that place where individual choices are all gone.

As I mentioned, this right/liberty—left/equality alignment seems limited to the sphere of economics. When we look at questions of religion, culture, and life-style, liberals are all for liberty. Their extreme tolerance, and even advocacy for gays, exotic peoples and their cultures, even atheists can sometimes be upsetting to conservatives who are often less comfortable and sometimes even hostile to such diversity. Issues involving religion are argued consistent with this left/right reversal of the usual positions.

Society or Individuals

This one might be a little harder to grasp, so I'll appeal to an expert. Former British Prime Minister Margaret Thatcher was one of the leading conservatives of her time. She once famously said, "there is no such thing as society." This statement was apparently so astounding that it was given to Meryl Streep's character in the Hollywood movie about Thatcher. But, from a conservative point of view, that statement can make perfect sense. In fairness to "The Iron Lady," as Thatcher was sometimes called, let's put her no society quote into some context. What she said was,

"I think we've been through a period where too many people have been given to understand that if they have a problem, it's the government's job to cope with it. 'I have a problem, I'll get a grant.' 'I'm homeless, the government must house me.' They're casting their problem on society. And, you know, there is no such thing as society. There are individual men and women, and there are families. And no government can do anything except through people, and people must look to themselves first. It's our duty to look after ourselves and then, also to look after our neighbor. People have got the entitlements too much in mind, without the obligations. There's no such thing as entitlement, unless someone has first met an obligation."[3]

With this additional context Thatcher starts sounding more like the responses on the right side for issues like poverty and personal responsibility. If she were to have eased up a little, we might have gotten her to go so far as to admit that societies consist of groups of people who actually know one another. The point being that beyond personal relationships, the concept of society is not *real* in our direct experiences. It is merely an abstraction that we have come up with to put some kind of label on the entirety of personal relationships out there. We can see and have direct experiences with a lover, our family a boss. a cop, even strangers we meet. But as hard as you might try, you cannot actually see society. If we look at it this way, it becomes clear that our knowledge from personal relations is direct and concrete, while our knowledge of that totality we call society is nothing more than bunch of abstractions and assumptions. If you admit this, it follows that any efforts to characterize this "society," and launch programs to cure its perceived ills, are far more open to error and mistaken assumptions, than what we might do in the context of real face–to-face relationships.

We have Ms. Thatcher to thank, not only for this insight, but for the implication she draws from it as a conservative thinker. You say that you suspect that you are a liberal and this distinction seems phony to

PRELIMINARY APPROACHES

you, like just a convenient way of dodging obvious social responsibilities? Well let me go at it another way. When is the last time you went to see a music star, somebody like, Beyonce or Tim McGraw or even somebody on the second or third tier of music stars? Chances are excellent that the sounds you heard were way worse than the recording you bought or even YouTube. Chances are even better that you were far enough away that your eyes kept on going to that big screen blow-up over the stage. So why did you, and the 45 hundred other people there, bother? Fact is that even in this high tech age, even liberals are still placing a personal value on the difference it makes to be with one of these people, face-to-face with nothing in between the two of you. You were actually living there with her or him in real time. And if that is important, maybe you can appreciate the significance conservatives can place on how abstract and fraught with error our ideas about society are.

While this distinction does not come up directly in partisan arguments, it is almost always apparent from the way arguments are made. Liberal arguments are typically peppered with statistics and claims about categories of people. They lament the plight of undocumented US residents, minorities, working women or people serving time for non-violent conviction for drug possession. They condemn giant corporations, climate change deniers, or misogynists. Notice that in each of these examples, they are taking large numbers of actual people, people who relate directly to many others in complicated real lives and literally abstracting a single aspect of these people and using it to label them as a member of an undifferentiated mass in society. For many conservatives this just doesn't feel right. They may make generalizations about people but theirs is a definite preference for generalizations on a much lower level. I'll mention two. Just as we see in the Thatcher quote, in general we all must look after ourselves, and this means developing and maintaining our livelihood, as we compete for our needs in the economy. Not so much the whole big abstract economy of the economists, but the web of personal relationships that together make up schooling, career, marriage and such. This is of course a conservatism on the liberty side of the liberty/equality difference we just got into.

The second lower level generalization relates to the equality side. Folks on the right are likely to focus on the idea that we all live our direct face-to-face lives with others in the same a moral dimension, a dimension that is universal for all us humans. Nobody is exempt. We are thus continuously faced with choices about good and evil, and further that we should judge our own actions and those of others in terms of these categories. Where this second generalization surfaces most clearly is in the way liberals are criticized as moral relativists who try to escape from this universal moral dimension with a stance of situational morality. Folks on the left might have strong and enduring moral beliefs as individuals, but they are less likely to hold that their sense of morality holds uniformly for all people and all situations. The two sides have this difference in their whole level of analysis. We will spend more of our efforts on these matters later on.

For now, a quick illustration might be helpful: according to surveys of income, women in our country are consistently found to be paid 75% or less than men, for the same work. For the left, this is a problem that needs fixing with laws to insist on equal pay. This might be true. This might be unfortunate. But following the logic of the conservative argument that we are considering here, if the solution to this problem requires that the government step in to interfere with the lives, the liberties, or the properties of individual citizens, it is a violation of the very principals of our constitution. What is more, the task that this intervention would set in motion would require that the government intervene into every one of the millions of relationships between a woman and her employer to determine if a wage disparity exists, the amount of that disparity, and once so determined, government action would be necessary to enforce an ongoing correction. Think about it. The task is so enormous and complex. What are the chances that the government would get it right without entirely disrupting the economy? It would be almost certain to guarantee problems for people, both men

PRELIMINARY APPROACHES

and women, as they participate in commerce. At the very least, somebody from government would become a player in every relationship between a woman and her employer. And nobody is saying that women should be paid less than men for the same work. This is only one example of the problem this difference in perspective has for the left. Call it a difference in toleration for abstractions or the "no such thing as society factor", but I think you will be able to recognize it in the political rhetoric you confront each day.

The United States: Republic or Democracy?

Like so many questions about our politics, the answer depends on who you ask. The last of the differences we will take up doesn't reveal itself to us from the list of issues. As basic as this difference is, it hardly ever comes up as a matter of issues and arguments. Many might not realize that this difference really even exists. Not unlike religion, when it comes to politics, people often head into adult life carrying the faith that they grew up with, the beliefs of their parents. Based on this fact, I can speculate that if you grew up in a liberal household you are quite likely to have learned that this country's government is a democracy. If yours was a conservative household the government of our country is much more likely to have been called a republic when you were growing up.

So what? Everybody knows that we don't all meet in one humungous stadium somewhere and raise our hands to vote on every law passed. Left or right, everybody knows that our democratic activities are limited to electing representatives, and in turn, having them and people who work for them, govern us. What is less clear is that, what everybody knows, ends about there. The left and the right have fundamental differences about this subject. To start with, the US Constitution refers to itself as a "Republican Form of Government" and not a democracy. The fact is that the word "democracy" does not appear in the Constitution.

The idea of a republic goes back at least to the ancient Greeks. The republic that Plato wrote about was a community ruled not by kings but by philosophers. His student, Aristotle, argued in favor of a republic that he thought would more adequately meet the requirements for a good life for all citizens, (with the stipulation that citizenship might well exclude slaves, women, and the working classes). Aristotle's concept of a republic is actually a good starting point to understand much of what conservatives are about when they apply the distinction between republic and democracy to the United States.

New ideas about republics and representative democracies emerged among European thinkers in the 1600s and 1700s, as part of the intellectual movement known as the Enlightenment. In essence, a republic is a political system that maintains justice for its citizens by adherence to a constitution rather than the capricious dictates of whoever might be king or tyrant, and how that person might be feeling on a particular day. While it is not necessary that this constitution be written down, it is essential that consistent rules for governing guide the activities of the political entity. The way this is accomplished in fact is that the citizens administer this system of rules, (their constitution), by governing themselves. In practical terms citizens might vote on issues or elect representatives to govern and adjudicate disputes. The rules that the republic operates under set limits on what those who govern, at any particular time, may do. These limits protect against a danger that many saw in the idea of pure democracy, namely that the majority might take actions to harm the minority. (e.g. What would prevent the 51% from passing a death sentence on the 49% or casting them all into slavery?)

That the United States came to have a written constitution which recognizes essential human rights, and operates under the governance of elected officials, is clearly consistent with the definition of a republic. Within this republican framework folks on the left often take quite an expansive view when it comes to who elects and who the elected representatives represent. As a result they are more likely to

PRELIMINARY APPROACHES

think and talk about our government as a democracy, a "representative democracy". By contrast people on the right often tend to fear what might happen if the government were elected by and worked for the interests of the great masses of people. Theirs is a more limiting view as to the "who" that is to vote and be represented. Nonetheless, both sides can accurately claim to remain well within the principles of the US Constitution.

Who should be the citizens of our republic if we are to live long and prosper? Should people who don't own property vote and be represented? How about people who don't pay taxes? Can we trust the votes of people who lack an education? Or folks who cannot understand English? What about children ? Convicted criminals? It is simply a matter of where one draws the line on this question of voting and representation. Just because people on the left envision a much larger pool of people who they think should vote, it doesn't mean that theirs is the only correct way to understand the Constitution. From the point of view of many on the right, maybe we are just too damn democratic these days. There is no reason that future Supreme Court decisions or even Constitutional Amendments couldn't shrink or expand the principles that define our self-government.

This right/left difference goes further when we consider how (to what end) we should govern ourselves. Generally the left seeks a representation of the rights of most all of the population and the assurance that government will prevent the privileges held by one segment of that population from doing harm to other segments of the population. Theirs is a government that should represent the rights of all. The right seeks a representation that maximizes freedom for individuals so that they can do as they wish and thereby achieve their own ends without government interference. In this sense the republic/democracy distinction is a reflection of the equality/liberty difference.

Gloss Note: As a child, you probably recall reciting The Pledge of Allegiance, with it's clear identification of the United States as a "republic." The Pledge was written in 1891, by Francis Bellamy, a socialist who had to leave his position as Baptist minister because of reactions to his left wing sermons. His Pledge became adopted nationally in a campaign addressed to state superintendents of education. Bellamy had initially considered including the word "equality" in the Pledge but given current levels of opposition to equal rights for women and African Americans, he apparently thought it unlikely these state officials would find this wording acceptable. The Pledge remained the same until the words "under God" were added, June 14, 1954, just 23 days after US Supreme Court announced Brown v Board of Education, mandating public school desegregation, a decision that was one of the most significant government recognitions of equality in this country's history.[4]

Historically the democratic aspects of our republic were fairly limited at the beginning. This has changed through the years through constitutional amendments, laws passed by Congress and court decisions, which expanded voting and legal recognition, first to freed slaves, then to women and also expanded the recognized rights of proper treatment of all citizens. In recent years there has been some correspondence between the concepts of republic and democracy that match up with the Republican and Democratic political parties, with the latter putting more emphasis on voting rights and civil rights. This was not always so. After all, first Republican President, Lincoln, probably gave our representative government the most expansive definition ever when he referred to it as "Government of the people, by the people, for the people."

Even so, we never got completely carried away with this "by the people" notion. Let's not forget that Presidents still are not elected by popular vote, and the nine unelected justices of the Supreme Court often rule against the majority of voters and the majority of lawmakers without any serious repercussions. In fact in 2000, without any substantial blowback, they took over a national election before all the votes were counted and picked our President.

PRELIMINARY APPROACHES

Besides, the representation thing turns out to be a bit messy upon closer examination. For example, in terms of the number of people represented, according to US Census figures an Alaska Senator represents a bit over 500,000 voting age people living in that state but, given the low turnouts, he or she will need only about 150,000 votes to get in or remain in office. In California on the other hand, a Senator represents 27,500,000 voting age people and needs about 7,000,000 of their votes to get elected. This same kind of state disparity exists in the way we divvy up the electoral votes when it is time to elect presidents.

The point for us is that because of this republic VS democracy stuff people on the left can see the very scope and purpose of our government in a different way than people on the right. Who is the government supposed to represent? How are they to be represented?

Some people take the facts and the history and call it a republic, while other people take the same facts and the same history and use them to support the idea that ours is a democracy.

> **Gloss Note:** You might have noticed that we've pretty much neglected the courts in all this left/right, conservative/liberal discussion. That is because these terms are thrown at judges and their decisions in very confusing ways. In theory a "conservative judge" should generally seek to stay close to past precedents, and avoid expanding the meaning or the application of laws beyond the intent of their authors. Furthermore, in criminal cases such a judge would support the rule of law by leaning toward the side of the government. In an even more extreme variety of judicial conservatism the judge must always avoid going outside the "original intent" of the authors of the US Constitution. In contrast, an "activist judge" might seek to increase justice by issuing rulings which expand the meaning or the application of a law. In practice, these legal theories often fail us. Not only do judges often bring their partisan biases into their judgments, but the term "activist judge" is now freely used by both the left and the right to criticize any judge they disagree with. Critics of the "original

intent" approach point out that the US Constitution would, among other things, not permit the US to maintain a standing army. The judges, might wear robes, but all too often they are just a part of the same partisan battle.

Chapter Conclusions

With a look at some of the contested issues, we should have enough of an understanding to follow where the politicians and the talking heads on either side are coming from. Hopefully, with our discussion of these four more general level differences, we should be able to start to figure out just how far apart their points of view really are.

Contemporary politics really emphasizes two clusters or ideas and issues. To enter our political world and follow the play, we need to become more familiar with how both of these disputed areas align our partisans. One cluster of ideas and issues focuses on how the government should relate to the economy. The other cluster of ideas and issues takes up nothing less than the subject of morality. We will take up the economy in Part II, first by laying out the components that make up a free market economy, and then by reviewing the historical background that brought the right and the left to their respective views on our actual economy. In Part III we will get into how important morality is for our politics. But morality, being such a ponderous subject, in Part III we will first need to backtrack a little and consider the subject of belief itself; what people say they believe, what they believe deeply and how such beliefs bring humans together and unite them politically. This will enable us to take a good look at the core beliefs which differentiate folks on the left from those on the right, as well as those who seem to be gravitating to a third moral territory.

Part II: Economy and Politics

Chapter 4 Some Basics of Free Market Economics

"It is not from the benevolence of the butcher, the brewer, or the baker, that we expect our dinner, but from their regard to their own interest. We address ourselves, not to their humanity but to their self-love, and never talk to them of our necessities but of their advantages."

Adam Smith(1723-1790)[1]

"From each according to his ability, to each according to his needs!"

Karl Marx(1818-1883)[2]

"For what is a man profited, if he shall gain the whole world, and lose his own soul?"

Jesus [3]

In any considerations of politics, the subject of economics is sure to come up repeatedly. With this in mind, the time has come for us to get under the surface and look more directly at that subject. As we began to see in the preceding chapter, while liberals might think of freedom in connection with life styles, philosophic or religious beliefs, or artistic license, conservatives typically use the words like "freedom" and especially "liberty" as references to free markets where investing, buying, and selling goes on with a minimum of government involvement. This market freedom is for these conservatives most important: it is the defining characteristic of liberty. Limitations on free markets are, as a result, always to be suspected of being misguided and ultimately futile.

Liberals, on the other hand, never seem to tire of pointing out how free markets fall short when problems confront us. They tend to downplay the dramatic increases in living standards associated with free markets and instead they dwell on the instances of waste and misery that an unregulated market economy leaves in its wake. Could both sides possibly be talking about the same thing? In one sense they are. The two sides are talking politics, or more specifically, they are concerned with what government should do for and to the economy. One path that might take us outside this perpetual argument would be to step aside of the praise and blame being heaped on the subject and try to get a better idea of what is and what is not meant by the term "free market." Accordingly, in this chapter we will be examining the concept of free markets, by covering three of the components that make them up: *market pricing, limited liability investing, and international free trade.* This will lay the groundwork for the chapter that follows where we can look at some of the formative historical events that brought free market economics front and center in our politics and gave it its distinctive twists to the right and to the left that are found in the contemporary political debate.

> **Gloss Note:** The practice of using the term "liberty" to refer to free market economics goes back at least to the late 1700s. The intellectual father of this view of economics, Adam Smith, uses the term "liberty" this way. The term "capitalism," that refers to free market economics was not invented until the 1800s. (Since liberty is now used to refer to a number of very different kinds of freedoms and capitalism is sometimes used in harsh criticisms of this kind of economy, I will try to stick with the terms free market economics and private enterprise in these pages.)

ECONOMY AND POLITICS

Components of Market Economy

Market Pricing

There is almost universal agreement that a free market has been the best way to effectively connect buyers and sellers economically. Not only that, unless buyers and sellers are forcefully prevented from getting together, markets seem to emerge naturally everywhere as a way of distributing things needed or wanted. This occurs naturally, regardless of place and time. Think of EBay, or better yet, let's put all of the essential ingredients together in one place. Think of a small isolated town where the butcher, the brewer, and the baker mentioned in the quotation above each runs a small business. These three and others in the community each specialize to satisfy common needs.

This example of a small isolated town gets us almost to the heart of the matter, but not quite. As any introductory economics text will tell us, the central dynamic of a free market is found in the way it operates to set prices that are optimal for all concerned. To understand this pricing dynamic, let's imagine ourselves in that small isolated town. It is a Saturday morning in August, and let's say that we are going to a farmers' market to buy tomatoes.

When we get there, we take in all the sights and smells. We see that lots of farmers have brought in tomatoes and all kinds of other things, and there are lots of people who have come to buy. Let's say, for example, 20 farmers have brought their tomatoes to sell (our market's supply) and 300 people have come to the market wanting to buy some tomatoes (our market's demand). We could use other numbers but if we assume that we see 20 tomato sellers and 300 tomato buyers, (and also maybe that they are all pretty tasty beefsteak tomatoes), it will keep things easy for us to imagine. With these numbers there can be enough tomatoes for the buyers and enough buyers to get the tomatoes all sold. As the trading takes place, the sellers hawk their wares and reveal their asking prices. This is an important ingredient because even before the first sale, we are observing a scene where relevant information is free to all. At first we will probably see some big differences in sale prices. But after a short while the tomato sales settle into a small range of prices. Just think of it. Given the number of farmers, the quantity of tomatoes there this morning, and the number of people who want them, it is difficult to conceive of a more efficient way to come to the most reasonable price for tomatoes there, that day. I picked these numbers to describe a situation where, at least hopefully, everybody leaves happy, happy at least about tomatoes.

With different numbers everybody is not as happy. Either we have surplus tomatoes and the price settles at a lower point, (unhappy farmers not reasonably compensated for their efforts) or alternatively we get a tomatoes shortage and the price settles at a higher point, (unhappy shoppers). But happy or not, nobody said this has to turn out fair for everybody. What we can say though is that the transactions settle on the best price for that market that day. And with this knowledge most of the participants can go away satisfied that they got the best price they could.

At this point it should be mentioned that this desirable buyer/seller chaos was not always recognized as the way prices could or should work. Early on, fair pricing was thought to require items involving equal consideration for both labor and expense. Even after various kinds of money came into use, this labor plus expense idea of pricing continued to hold sway. The realization that price was simply a matter of whatever sellers and buyers could agree upon is a cultural belief of fairly recent origin.[4]

Nonetheless, market pricing has become a foundational feature of commerce almost everywhere. To emphasize this point, try to imagine some alternative method: maybe all the buyers call a "Tomato Bureau," and tell them how many tomatoes they will want that day, sight unseen--then the bureau calls the farmers to see what they will have—and then what? I defy you to come up with a better way of getting everybody satisfied about the price, that is to say, setting the best price. This is the essence of market pricing. It's simple, it's natural… come on, you have to admit, it's down-right elegant. And nobody has to be telling anybody else what to do.

But of course to be more thorough with this descriptive illustration we should acknowledge a few additional things about how the buyers and the sellers are behaving. We have to assume that:

1. None of the sellers brings a big enough proportion of the tomatoes that day so that she or he can withhold them to insist on a higher price,

2. The farmers don't get together ahead of time and agree to fix a single price, and likewise that the customers don't get together and agree to the same kind of concerted action. (When sellers do this illegally it is called price fixing. When they can do it legally, it can sometimes be called a co-op and other times a cartel and other times a syndicate. When buyers act together it can be a co-op or it can be a boycott.) These names for organized sellers and buyers are important for us here, merely as a way of emphasizing that market pricing can only work when all the participants act as individuals. Concerted actions among participants tend to distort that best price that market pricing gives us.

3. No buyer (or seller) has enough money to buy up all the tomatoes and thereby become the only seller and then offer them for sale only to those willing to pay a higher price (known as cornering the market).

So long as there are a lot of participants selling and buying and that all the participants are roughly equal in the power that they can assert over the market, there exists competition over the price. And this competition works to set a price that is optimal: the lowest reasonable price that sellers can accept and the highest reasonable price that buyers are willing to pay. The more participants and the more independent they are, the better.

This reliance on having lots of roughly equal participants buying and selling illustrates what some statisticians might call a low mean deviation. Let's say we can view this process from some ideal vantage point where we see each exchange of tomatoes for money as it occurs, and record the transaction on a spreadsheet. We could see that the use of that optimum price tends to grow as the number of trades goes up, so long as none of the participants buy or sells with an advantage over his or her fellows, in resources or knowledge of the market. Overall, the sale prices form a normal curve with a few high-price sales and a few low-price sales and most of the sales prices lumped in the middle of the curve, the optimum price thus being about the average and the most frequent one. As it turns out, this market pricing is a dependable, effective, sturdy, reliable and universal social/economic phenomenon.

Economists are fascinated by this. Those of you who have already had occasion to delve into the subject of economics will know that rather than the bell shaped curve of sale price frequencies, economists show us a point where the graph line representing the buyer's desired prices, (called demand) crosses the graph line for the seller's desired prices (called supply). This point they call *equilibrium*. But for our purposes, an abstract theoretical concept like equilibrium is not particularly helpful, because it gives the impression of a market almost as though it were a single event thus hiding the countless decisions and actions which are the very essence of free markets. In economics the market place can seem to become a kind of separate reality. We even get people talking about markets as if they were living things.[5] Go to CNBC or one of the business channels and you'll hear statements like, "There is good reason to believe that the markets are saying we are about to see shortages in this or that". When commentators talk about markets as though they are living breathing persons, they are grossly oversimplifying what is going on. This alone is a reason for us to continuously maintain some reservations about what people say about economics.

Let's get ourselves back to the sights, the sounds and smells of the tomato buyers and sellers. This should remind us that there is no overall rationality among the participants as the market price settles in. What we are talking about is not a democratic consensus. It is not even necessarily the best price for the over-all economy of our isolated little

ECONOMY AND POLITICS

town. After all, what gets spent on tomatoes might better benefit people in the community some other way. It is simply the end result of a large number of individual desires, decisions, and actions that take place in that farmers' market that Saturday. And it is the same with other free markets everywhere. The price is best because it satisfies the requirements of a great number of participants. When we achieve the conditions for this optimum pricing, we have come to call this process a "free" market. As we've pointed out, nobody is ordering people to do anything. The only control each participant has, is their personal choice; they are free to sell or not to sell; to buy or not to buy.

To get a more thorough feel for this subject we need to call attention to some features that are important to market pricing but not as easy to pick out as we stroll among the stalls in the farmers' market. We can think of these as necessary background features. Here are four such features:

• The first of these features might actually be pretty obvious. To get through the buying and selling, we have to have some degree of peaceful order. We cannot have a gang of thugs busting into the market and taking tomatoes. For that matter, we better be sure that the market isn't overrun and sacked by foreign invaders. Freedom to sell or buy at any price people choose cannot exist without orderly public spaces; that is to say civil order. We might take this point for granted but there are lots of places where this feature presents serious problems. For example in the extreme, there are political entities we refer to as failed states where internal and external threats abound. If we were to find ourselves in one of these places, we'd recall what old Thomas Hobbes told us about life without politics. Effective governments are what give us assurances against such threats both internal and external. The government's efforts to maintain an entities' external boundaries and to assure who's OK to be inside, that's the job of a military. Within the political entity, government can assure that activity is conducted in peace by enforcing the laws or rules of the game. Here within the farmers' market we cannot see most of this peace-keeping apparatus.

The military, CBP (border patrol), the national, state governments, and the county council are nowhere to be seen this morning at our farmers' market. At most, if we look around the place carefully, we will probably see some police officers and perhaps a weight scale with a certificate attached to assure its accuracy.

• For our second background feature we need only consider how the tomatoes get paid for. The Adam Smith quote at the beginning of this chapter might well be describing a moneyless barter economy. The baker can trade some of his bread for beer, and some more for meat etc. But these days almost all free market transactions use some kind of money. Even back in the days of seashells and gold coins, good, trusted, money with generally agreed upon value, was a vital feature of the marketplace whenever trade expanded beyond subsistence level economics. And reliable money is only possible where there is a stable political jurisdiction. Whether the money is issued by a government or is privately created, it takes a stable power structure to give market participants the assurance they need to trust the values being exchanged. These days, besides the Euro used in many European countries, most currency is created and managed by banking systems within individual countries.

> **Gloss Note:** In the US we have a system of 12 Federal Reserve Banks that are chartered by the government. Among the officials who manage the Fed, as it is called, some are appointed by the Federal government and others are selected by the banks themselves. The Fed is responsible for more than just maintaining a ready supply of money. It is also supposed to maintain enough currency out there to foster growth, while minimizing both unemployment and inflation. Many observers suggest that these objectives are, at most, impossible, but at least contradictory. For example, if we get anywhere near full employment, market pricing of wages and salaries will go up, and these higher prices for workers will probably stimulate inflation.

ECONOMY AND POLITICS

- The third background feature arises from the fact that human interaction is always going to produce arguments and misunderstandings from time to time. And it is far more efficient if, when people get to those "He said---She said" situations, they don't have to resort to knives and guns. They have the confidence that their actions are backed up by a good system of dispute resolution: a court system of some kind. Our courts can fine and/or confine people who break laws by taking from others. The court system also enables people, and other economic entities, to seek what they think is due them by civil suit.

- Finally, are you old enough, to ever have seem Monty Python's dead parrot skit?[6] It is about a man who discovers that he's just bought a dead parrot and tries to return it to a shopkeeper who seems incapable of saying anything that might be true. This video, and many of their others bring us to the last of our four background assumptions. Our market of individual free choices is not going to work if many, or all, of the participants are not acting and communicating somewhat rationally. I say "somewhat rationally" to point out the unfortunate fact that until recently, most academic research and writing about economics follows from the obviously incorrect assumption that people always act rationally in their economic self interest, when they make buy and sell decisions. Nonsense! Anybody who has just had to have that--- toy, or sweater, or car, or house, or that yacht---that would surely make you forever happy, or content, or attractive, or popular-- knows that there are limits on the rationality requirement in free markets. If that doesn't convince you, how about the well named "impulse racks" of sugar candy and magazine candy we have to negotiate at the food store check-out, or the relentless advertising of that recreational drug they call Viagra? Calculating rationality no: what free market pricing does need though is for the participants to be able to communicate and to trust each other's statements, sufficiently to get a lot of transactions accomplished.

Ok, so even in this simple farmers' market example, we can see that a free market is an effective and desirable way to set the prices for things. But at the same time we can see that a free market is not an easy or even the most natural thing for us humans to pull off. There are a lot of must-have ingredients. We need public order, rules and laws, money, a good way to settle arguments, and of course somewhat reasonable participants. And as the transactions take place we are not going to get that best price if some of the participants can assert control over the proceedings. It also should be clear from this example that there is no guarantee that on any given market day, the price determined in the trading will be satisfactory to a majority of the participants.

This brings us to one last point to think about: time. Not time per se, but uncertainties about what prices will be in the future. The tomatoes in our example are not as durable as many things that are bought and sold. But whatever the item, if buyers and sellers begin to imagine that prices are going to change at some point in the future, their imaginings can begin to drive serious price changes. Here are some examples:

- When sellers get worried that in the future the price will go down, they will begin to settle for less in anticipation of these imagined future lower prices. The actions of a few fearful sellers thus lowers the average price. When others notice this, the same fear of future lower prices can convince more sellers that they must accept less. Fear and lower prices can reinforce each other and feed into a vicious cycle. When this happens to a whole economy and not just tomatoes at a farmers' market, it is called a panic. When the prices of things trend downward over a longer period, it is called deflation. Panic and deflation are among the most serious problems that can confront a free market economy because they are situations where sellers want to sell but buyers believe that there is a serious advantage in delaying all the purchases that they can. Economic activity can all but come to a halt.

- Now think about what happens when buyers get worried that prices are about to go up. Sellers are more hesitant and buyers are naturally more likely to consider paying a little bit more now before prices go up a lot. Again upward anticipation can affect not just tomatoes but whole economies, and the opposite kind of vicious cycle can begin to feed on itself. When prices trend upward generally, it is called inflation. When prices on a particular item or group of related items take an upward surge based on anticipates future prices that is prolonged, we call it a bubble. In the extreme, economy-wide inflation can bring down the money system that underwrites all exchanges.

- These distortions in market pricing come from both hopes and fears about the future. As such, these are beliefs which cannot be demonstrated by facts. And since these kinds of unsubstantiated ideas can have real power to influence prices, it should not be surprising that the exaggeration, false information and other varieties of outright lying are a common feature of the dynamics of market pricing. Unless we are presented with guarantees in writing, with a dispute resolution system to assure compliance, there is scarcely a limit on what buyers might imagine and sellers can claim.

> **Gloss Note:** Over the centuries of free market activity, definite customs have emerged about how far one can go in exaggerating, whether it is boasting and bragging about the value of ones goods and services, or instilling false hopes or fears about future prices. ***Caveat Emptor***, a term that the Romans coined for us, serves as a proper warning: *let the buyer beware*. As it has come down to us, this means that it is up to the buyer to sort out the claims and the hype that the seller sends our way.

Back in the days of the street bizarre, the game was probably simpler. In the bargaining back and forth we generally understand that both the buyer and the seller are pulling each other's legs much of the time. We have all become accustomed to a lot more of this leg pulling on the sellers' side these days, but let's not forget that it is the objective of every trader to get the advantage wherever possible. We have old sayings like, "buy cheap-sell dear," and "there's a sucker born every minute," to remind us of this. For our purposes, it is enough to note that the expectations created by various kinds of false representations are part of what participants have come to expect and take for granted in the operation of market pricing.

Glancing back at the last several paragraphs I fear that I might be leaving the wrong impression; an impression that free markets are so fragile that they seldom exist and then only for brief periods would be misleading. Once the components come together market pricing emerges easily and naturally all over the place. All these requirements and background factors are important for our consideration though, because they are what enable free markets to actually come to that best price for both buyers and sellers. The market pricing system depends on how well these requirements and background factors are satisfied.

Though perfect market pricing seldom, if ever, exists, we get workable approximations all the time. And on the other hand we often get flawed and biased pricing systems that are erroneously presented to us as though they were the result of ideal free market dynamics. Please keep in mind that our purpose for digging into this economics stuff in the first place has been to get ourselves into a position to understand and evaluate political claims and counter-claims about free markets and market pricing. This is why our subject is an essential part of any reasonable working knowledge of our politics.

We now should be able to go forward with a practical notion of the idea of market pricing, and with that we are on our way to a workable understanding of what people are referring to when they talk about market economies. There are just a couple more components to add to it, limited liability investment, and free trade, and then we will be there.

ECONOMY AND POLITICS

Limited Liability Investment

Though market pricing is an essential feature of market economies, there is a feature which is perhaps an even more critical. What is called limited liability investment starts with market pricing and then uses it to give market economies their enormous potential and scale. Not only that, but if you think that people are talking about supply and demand market pricing, when they use words like "free economy" and "free markets," I am here to tell you that you are way off the mark. Lots of folks out there would tell you that liability investment is front and center when they define the word "freedom" for themselves. After all, limited liability investment is the feature of private enterprise economics that undoubtedly has launched a scale of economic activity previously undreamed of, and had the power to transform the standard of living of billions of people in countries all over the world. Maybe, to do it right, we should have a trumpet fanfare here. It's that impressive!

Instead of trumpets perhaps some numbers will help us get an idea of the potential and scale we are looking at. In 1800 the US population was 5.3 million. Using 2005 dollar values to take out the effects of inflation, we can say that this population was annually producing $7.4 billion worth of goods and services (in equivalent 2005 dollars) within the country's borders. To consider just how productive the economy was then we can just divide the total dollars by the population and see that they were up to producing the equivalent of $1,400 per person. Not so bad when we realize there are a whole lot of babies in our divisor. But by comparison, in 2000 the US population of 282 million produced goods and services valued at 11.2 trillion in 2005 dollars. Dividing the total by the population the same way we can see that per person the US was producing about $40,000 per year, just short of 30 times more productive.

So how does limited liability investment operate? And how did it become such a powerful economic force? The answer to the first of these questions is that a separate market place devoted to investment emerged and that marketplace took on all the characteristics of the farmers' market I've been talking about. But instead of tomatoes, this market deals in "stock" shares. Each of these stock shares represents a fractional portion of the total investment in various business ventures. The stock market thus trades shares in many different ventures. Investors buy and sell shares in various ventures hoping that they get back more than they paid in as the business venture conducts its business. If the business venture does well the investors who own shares can benefit in one or both of two ways. 1) The investor can go back to the shares market at a later date and get somebody to buy his/her shares at a higher price. Or, 2) The venture can reward its investors by paying them a portion of the profits as "dividends."

In this marketplace where business ventures obtain the money they need to invest and operate profitably, stock shares are the most typical item bought and sold. However, there are many other variations. With bonds, for instance, the business enterprise promises to pay back a specified additional amount at a later date. Nor is the trading limited to individual investors. Various groups bundle their money together and put the resulting fund in the hands of professional investment managers. But let's not get off track. We are out to grasp the significance of free market economics for our politics. For this, it will be enough if we understand the notion of a market for investment shares that values these shares by market pricing. That is pretty much what we need to keep in mind for the "investment" part, of limited liability investment.

We just covered what happens when the venture goes well; the venture prospers and the investors can get dividends and they can also profit from selling their shares at higher prices. What happens when things really go south? As the business fails to make profits, there are no dividends to expect and the share price falls in the stock market. If things go very bad, the business venture eventually shuts down because, even if it was to sell off everything it has, or has taken in, there is not enough to pay off its suppliers, employees, consultants, investors and everybody else. We are now talking bankruptcy here. In the extreme case the managers of the business essentially hand everything over to a court and the court decides which claims against the venture get paid and how much of what's left, they each get. But as the remains of the venture are divided up, the claims of stock investors rank among the lowest. They don't expect to get any of their investment back.

Why should they though? First of all, those stock shares they own are probably market priced at zero. But let's step back a bit. Aren't the investors, the owners of a business that owes a lot of people a lot of money? Consider what is going on. The business they own fails not just to make a profit. It fails to pay for the materials and supplies it purchased. Isn't that sort of like stealing? The business they own probably owes wages and salaries to employees, and maybe pensions and other benefits. Aren't their employees being cheated? Everybodys got the blues, except maybe the attorneys. (In this court supervised pecking order of bankruptcy supervised by former attorneys who are now judges, you should not be surprised that the attorneys often do pretty well.) Granted, I have cooked up an extreme case of a failure of investments in a business venture. At the same time I think that we have conjured up a scenario that gets to the very heart of the "limited" part of limited liability.

As all these claims are being worked through, nobody has the right to reach back into the pockets of the shareholders and get more money from them. It is the genius of limited liability investment that we don't let the stock share owners lose any more than the price they originally paid for their shares. In other words, their liability, (what all those owed money by the venture can get legally from them) is limited to the amount they put in for their shares in the first place. This is a very big deal because even though you might hear people talk about "losing their shirt," people can invest and never lose their shirt or their car, or their house, or their bank account or even their Louis Vuitton handbags. Their risk of loss is limited to whatever they decided to put up in the first place.

This combination of limiting the risk and pricing investments in a market situation unleashed economic potentials that are powerful indeed. Market priced shares that individuals and companies buy and sell with the understanding that when things do not work out, their losses will never exceed their investment creates a kind of economic leverage. This is because it spreads the risk of business ventures out so that if they fail the losses are tolerable losses spread over large numbers of individuals, and even more important it limits the degree to which business failures discourage future investment. So even on the downside there is this added plus. It makes failure of even enormous business ventures bearable. But on the upside there is also an enormous plus. Business ventures are able to gather up huge amounts of money from many investors and accomplish things that most, or all, of the participants could not ever hope to do individually. Huge business undertakings can thrive, even on a global scale.

So while market pricing involves freedom to buy or sell at will, limited liability investment involves a very different kind of freedom. You can call it the freedom not to lose your shirt, but whatever you call it, it has had profound implications. It is a freedom that is in fact far more central than market pricing to what people think and talk about as free economies.

But stop for a moment to consider the unique character of these markets. Investment markets that deal in a kind of economic activity that is completely separate from things that directly satisfy human needs and wants (that is to say separate from gathering things, growing things and creating things directly useful to us). There is certainly a lot of selling and buying, but it is at least, once removed from the more direct dealings of our farmers' market. In a way the trading here is more akin to loaning and repaying loans. If anything at all, it can be thought of as being sold and bought, it would be "pieces of the action" that together represent various business ventures. And it is this buying and selling of pieces of the action that really makes up the central feature of what people mean when they talk about free enterprise and

ECONOMY AND POLITICS

free markets: the freedom to possibly gain from the venture, but in no event to lose more than your share.

Historians differ on the origins of limited liability investing. This is because these entities show some important similarities with certain economic activities going back to ancient Rome, the Medieval Catholic Church and other places. The idea of shares in a business venture has a long standing application in maritime activities with investors in trade voyages contributing a portion of the total expense and even crew members anticipating a commensurate portion of the profits of a successful voyage.[7] By the 15th century there were in Europe, joint stock companies with limited liability for investors, in a number of lines of business, including banking, mining, exploration and many other areas of the economy. As you may know, the premier share trading market, The New York Stock Exchange, might have actually appeared to be very much like our farmers' market. In the 1790s before they went indoors a lot of buying and selling was done on a city street, Wall Street.[8] New York State enacted a law recognizing limited-liability stock companies in 1811.

The terms of risk that this arrangement offered to investors spread to other states and other countries. In the UK such companies often used the word Limited or end with the abbreviation, LTD at the end of their company name. By the end of the century limited liability investment was enabling never before seen levels of capital investment in ventures the world over.[9] To get an idea of the magnitudes that can be bundled together in a business venture when we share the risk and insist that investors can never "lose their shirts," some examples: as of early 2014, Apple Inc. was said to be worth $468.52 billion, Exxon Mobile Corp. $415.14 billion and General Electric Co. $315.26 billion.[10] Big funding can get big things done. And what is more, if you can afford it, you can buy in to a piece of the action, in these and thousands of other business ventures.

Gloss Note: Much is made over a legal theory called "personhood" in connection with stock-share-financed ventures.

It thus might come in handy for you to know some of the historical background. The 14th Amendment to the U.S Constitution was adopted in 1869 to assure equal protection of the law to all citizens. Presumably it was to protect former slaves in the wake of the Civil War. However, it has typically been applied in the courts in defense of the notion that private ventures financed by stock and similar investment: a) have the legally protected rights of human citizens, and more important for us here, b) have no obligations that reach back to share owners beyond the amount of their investments in the venture. In Santa Clara County v. Southern Pacific Railroad (1886), the US Supreme Court preceding is supposed to have commenced with an announcement by the Chief Justice that the 14th amendment clearly applies to corporations as persons. Actual Supreme Court's rulings beginning with Trustees of Dartmouth College v. Woodward (1819), have explicitly recognized corporations as having the same rights as human persons, rights for instance to contract and to enforce contracts.

In summary, just like market pricing, limited liability investment can be thought of as having several must-have background characteristics. However, it is easier to flesh these out because they are the defining characteristics of the early joint stock companies and the legal entities that succeeded them, namely the modern corporation (INC. and CORP.) and the limited liability companies (LLCs). These are the very same characteristics that make them so attractive to investors:

- They are created by a written contract (e.g., a charter, or articles of incorporation) which is typically established and enforced under the laws of an existing government.

- Under the terms of the laws that enable them to exist and support them, the business venture is supposed to be managed solely for the financial benefit of the shareholders.

- The shareholders are responsible for the debts of the entity only up to the extent of the value or the shares they own.

- Shareholders are free to sell their shares at any time, thereby transferring a portion of their ownership, or all of it, to others

- Sales of such shares can be transferred privately but they are often traded in a shares market.

- Shareholders are entitled to any increase in the value of their shares that may have occurred by the time of sale. The business venture may also pay investors a portion of any profits during the period of their investment.

- And finally, in no event is the investor expected to perform any work as a result of their investment. In fact, investors often do not know much more about the venture than its stock exchange symbol and its price.

We've done this quick tour of market pricing and limited liability investment and the two kinds of freedom they bring with them. This brief discussion certainly won't get anybody a bachelors degree in economics, but it will be sufficient to get you in on what is behind what politicians and partisans think they are talking about when they mention free markets, free enterprise, freedom, and liberty and many related terms. We now have only the last of our three bases to cover, international free trade.

International Free Trade

Our third and last feature of free market economies differs from the first two because it is far less precise and settled in the policies of free market economies. Let me try to put it in better words. With very few exceptions, we are now entering one of those subject areas with way more bold assertions than accepted facts. International free trade might be thought of as an umbrella term used to cover whatever seems necessary to bring market pricing and limited liability investment into the international arena. Nonetheless, this international feature is no small detail. By definition, individual countries are sovereign political entities, that is, they are characterized by an independent authority over a geographic area. This sovereignty means that a country's boundaries mark the area within which government enforceable rules and laws can operate.

Thus, sovereignty ends at the boarders. Buying, selling, investing, and in fact all international business activities are quite different, in that there are no internationally recognized rules and laws, and no overall enforcement authority that extends over all countries. Remember those must-have ingredients for free markets? Take two, an enduring civil order and a trusted way of resolving disputes peaceably; these are characteristics of established political entities, within national boundaries. They don't cross borders very well. Then there are language differences which make the necessary communication of traders much more complicated. For many among us, if the truth be told, simple trust of ones fellow humans takes a huge dip when those humans happen to be "foreigners." I am not piling it on with all this. Take another example, we know that both market pricing and limited liability investment also depend on a trusted currency. We could go on but you get the idea.

Now it's not that international trade takes place in a Hobbesian chaos. International treaties do sometimes attempt to extend supports to businesses beyond national borders. Some of these treaties work, and others, do not. Some work for some times and some places and not for others. Consequently, we are left to look at whatever governments may be called upon to do when the free market activities of their economies spill over their boarders.

In what follows we will examine the role of governments in international free trade. To accomplish this we will take a closer look at how governments get involved in some of those must-haves that we previously identified, and see how things get worked out when business ventures "venture" outside national borders. To what extent do governments interfere with market pricing? What happens when only

ECONOMY AND POLITICS

the military is there to keep the trading peaceable? How do the buyers and sellers cope when there is no single trusted kind of money? Along with these topics we will be taking up another question: To what extent should the government act not just to assure that the market is free, but to directly support and advance the country's international business ventures? And finally there is the question, "What the hell, why not take care of all these problems by establishing an international government to protect international trade?

How do Governments Interfere with Market Pricing:

If somebody were to try to interfere with market pricing at our farmers' market, the folks there would not like it. Similarly, American colonists got upset when Parliament passed laws that added shipping restrictions and taxes to their early American marketplace. Just as we would expect, it was in large part political unrest about import and export restrictions that precipitated even the first thoughts of independence for the British colonies in North America. Every school girl and boy learns about the Boston Tea Party and the resistance of the colonists to taxes and restrictions that interfered with market pricing for items coming to or going from our seaports. We learn about the issue with the slogan "No taxation without representation."

But as soon as the colonies had secured their independence, the issue of import taxes arose as a problem between the colonies themselves. The question was about the extent to which the new overall government of the former colonies should go in promoting domestic business interests. From 1781-1787 the former colonies set about to function almost as independent countries. Think of 13 separate countries with a simple mutual defense treaty. The freed colonies had become a group of independent states under Articles of Confederation. Central government authority was extremely weak.

And behaving as independent countries, the 13 states did what was typical at the time. They passed tariff tax laws, on goods imported from other states. A tariff is, of course, a tax on imports that raises the effective price of an item and thereby makes the price of the same thing produced within more attractive. If for instance, brooms from New York were cheaper than the brooms made in Connecticut, the threatened Connecticut broom makers would push for a tariff tax on brooms imported into Connecticut. In reaction, New York might retaliate with their own tariffs on other items. As time went by a lot of people were paying a lot more for a lot of things. It might seem short-sighted to us. As colonists, they had revolted against British taxes on imports, now they were passing similar taxes on each other.

These interstate tariffs were soon recognized as a real problem. This issue and other problems of overall coordination (including the Revolutionary War debts presumably shared by all of the 13 former colonies) led, in 1787, to a convention in Philadelphia that drafted the current US Constitution. Once adopted, the new Constitution created a "free trade zone" within the United States. And this example of states without tariffs or other trade restrictions was so uniformly positive and enduring that it became a model for similar arrangements later applied at various times, all over the world.

> **Gloss Note:** Back to economist, Adam Smith; it is no accident that his *Wealth of Nations* came out just a decade before the ex-colonists were grappling with their inter-state tariff mess. Before Smith's advocacy of "[tariff] free trade" was well known, the dominant theory of international trade, mercantilism, held that, given the fact that international trades were settled in gold, nations should export more than they import, to accumulate more gold, which represented any nation's true wealth. Smith argued to the contrary, that international tariff-free markets were, in reality, no different from domestic free markets, because both fostered the most trade at the best prices for all concerned.

Examples of modern attempts at free trade zones are the North American Free Trade Agreement (NAFTA, 1992) between Canada the US and Mexico, Latin American Free Trade Association, (LAFTA) with 12 member countries, and the European Union, a series of

ECONOMY AND POLITICS

European free trade treaties beginning in 1951 which by 2012 involve 27 nations. More recently we have efforts toward an agreement that includes many countries which happen to have Pacific Ocean Coastlines, the Trans-Pacific Partnership, (TPP).

Even though our brooms example shows clearly that, taxes on imports and exports are ultimately wasteful and foolish, this is hardly the end of the story. All business ventures always seek competitive advantage. This is a given. So as a result, particular businesses and industries, as well as labor unions, are seldom shy when it comes to proposing taxes and other regulations that will give them a competitive edge. Typically such proposals might argue that domestic production is of strategic value to national defense, or that a foreign government is holding prices of their goods down by subsidizing their industries or manipulating the relative value of their currency, or that foreign imports are stifling the early stages of what will later be a thriving domestic industry. Some observers charge that campaign contributions can help bring politicians around to supporting restrictions on imports. It is reasonably easy to gain traction with such arguments against free trade, given that they can be presented as "us against them" patriotic causes.

What is more, ocean, rail, and highway transportation have become so inexpensive, relative to labor costs in this country, that production facilities can now be set up virtually anywhere. This has lead to lower prices of goods but also a large scale export of whole industries from the US with the loss huge numbers of high paying jobs. In the worst cases imports might now come from places where workers include children and captives.

> **Gloss Note:** Since NAFTA took effect in 1994 the US / Mexican border became dotted with masquiladoras, assembly plants where materials are shipped from the US tax free, assembled and packaged for sale and then shipped back, tax free. The workers, mostly women are paid well by Mexican standards, yet at a fraction of what the same jobs would pay here in the US. A depiction of the violent deaths of hundreds of

women near the masquiladoras at Juárez are a stark feature in the background of Roberto Bolaño's novel 2666.

Does the Government Back Up Business Ventures Militarily?

How far should governments go in defending business interests militarily? This question came up immediately for the US. Even before the North American colonies were separated from Britain, trade from the colonies faced a major naval challenge. Ships involved in trade on the Mediterranean had long been targeted by Barbary pirates out of the ports in North Africa, (in what is now Morocco, Algeria and Libya.) Ransom payments, confiscation of cargoes and enslavement of crews and passengers, though not completely eliminated, had been giving way to a system of tribute payments to local rulers. In the first years after independence under the Articles of Confederation, without the power to tax, the US was not only unable to pay the tributes but was also having it's trading ships attacked by France because the war debts to the French were being ignored. That these threats to international trade were recognized as government concerns for all the former colonies is quite clear from the 1789 US Constitution. In spite of the finicky approach the framers had to a standing army (the constitution as adopted, called for land armed forces to be funded for war time in two year increments) that same document clearly called for Congress to establish a permanent navy. Article I Section 8 says Congress is to: "To define and punish Piracies and Felonies committed on the high Seas, [and] To provide and maintain a Navy"

In 1801 as attacks continued and the tribute payments approached 10% of the entire Federal budget the Jefferson administration took action and sent several ships along with US Marines, "to the shores of Tripoli," (as the song goes), to stop this bullying behavior once and for all.[11] On the issue of the war debts Treasury Secretary Alexander Hamilton earned his picture on the ten dollar bill by successfully arguing that protecting the US's financial reputation and trade relations (lately we refer to it as the "full faith and credit of the United States") required that the war debt be paid. Thus, from the early years, it was understood that one of the functions of the new Federal government was to protect US international trade, financially, and even by force if necessary.

What Happens When there isn't a Trusted Currency:

Quite apart from pirates, historically, whenever international trading reached a point that involved large settlements, there was real potential for trouble. Not only did safety and security become a concern, but there was also the matter of what could be accepted as the correct value for the settlement. Originally this potential led to networks of internationally connected individuals who made their living by cultivating sufficient reputation to deserve the trust of the parties trading across borders. They did this by issuing letters of credit that their foreign counterparts could accept and then later by assisting in actual settlement of debts. Even though some of these kinds of networks still exist today, by now most such transactions have been taken over by international banks and other private international financial institutions. The security of international transactions is quite routine these days. The same cannot be said of agreements upon values to exchange. Think for a moment about how important a good and trusted form of money is to effective market pricing and limited liability investment. It is easy to see the difficulties that can come to international trade from the fact that most countries use different forms of money. The rate at which one country's currency values translate into that of another country creates its own instance of market pricing. Currency markets are in one way quite different from the market pricing of our farmers' market. This is because there is no overall trust and very little basis for agreement on the value of the various national currencies. As the stability of national governments and national economies ebbs and flows, so does faith and trust in a country's currency. Guessing or speculating about currency values creates a financial trading market all its own. There are fortunes made and lost daily as speculators buy and sell currencies.

> **Gloss Note:** In one of the most famous currency exchange deals, currency speculator, George Soros sold over $10 billion US dollars worth of British pounds short (think of short sales as not selling, but buying, IOUs for a particular currency or other investment). So when the British devalued the pound soon thereafter, Soros covered his short sales (think of him paying off his IOUs with the cheaper British pounds), netting over a billion dollars. The press called Soros the man "who broke the Bank of England." He has since become famous as an advocate of and contributor to progressive economic causes.

Besides speculation, there is an additional problem that involves international currency exchanges. It might at first seem to contradict the notion of free trade. The problem involves what is called the balance of payments. As individuals and businesses do their cross border trading, they generally, make their purchases in their country's currency. That is to say, they export portions of their own country's money supply. When all the trade between two countries is totaled up, the trade balance can be determined, and having a lot more imports than exports is referred to as an unfavorable balance of trade. This is because more money is going out of the country than is coming in. You might recall Adam Smith on this point, and say "so what?" But economic competition between countries is far from dead. This is because a country can make its products cheaper and its investment opportunities more attractive to foreigners by intentionally maintaining lower values for its money in the exchange rates it supports. But there is no one there to order governments around and tell them how much their currency should be worth.

Why no International Government:

It is incorrect to say that international trade is completely without overall governance. Nevertheless, attempts creating a robust and authoritative world-wide governance of international free trade have not yielded very much of consequence. The world war ending treaties of the 20th Century included attempts at establishing international governing authorities. The first of these, The League of Nations treaty was rejected by the Senate and never really took hold. The United Nations was established in 1945. Several international business and financial authorities came into existence at the same time. Some of them are in operation today. The International Monetary Fund (IMF) operates to stabilize currency relationships and assist developing countries with their market economies. The General Agreement on Tariffs and Trade (GATT) that later became the World Trade Organization (WTO) is devoted to minimizing tariff and other trade restrictions. And the World Bank was set up to lend both advice and funds to developing countries with market economies. In addition, parties to a contract that has international provisions often include provisions in that contract that call for any disputes to be decided by courts of international arbitration.

Though these and other organizations do influence the way that international trade is conducted, by comparison, they represent a weak approximation of the authority and power that actual laws, police, courts represent to the domestic marketplace.

> **Gloss Note**: For our politics there is an important argument that comes from the right which needs mentioning. Any power we give up to an international authority is a sacrifice of national sovereignty, from which our freedom comes. In other words, if other people in other countries could tell us what to do, we would be to that degree, less free. Critics of this argument on the left point out that this argument includes the underlying assumption is that sovereignty, that power that provides us with freedom, has a limited quantity, that is to say it has a "zero-sum" character. By this they mean that by giving up some national authority, freedom for all people in all nations, might actually increase. Once they settle this argument they will be able to go on to the question of how many angels can dance on the head of a pin.

To summarize, our term "international free trade" begins with an understanding that governments have a role in seeing to it that domestic businesses get treated as close to the same way in their international trading activities as they expected to be treated in the market places at home. At times partisans even go so far as to advocate the use of the military to assert the nation's business interests.

For most of us this all seems like common sense. What makes things a bit more complicated is that recent times have seen the emergence of the multi-national corporation. Corporations like Dow, Coca Cola, and American Express earn over half their operating profits in international business, that is to say in other countries under other laws and other governments. Leading companies like Exxon/Mobil, BP, GM, Sony and Microsoft do business in more than 100 countries around the world.[12] It is obvious that these kinds of business ventures cannot call any nation their home country. But as major economic players in the economies of many nations, they can exert significant political clout with many governments. Consequently, some observers see that the new global economy is beginning to overshadow the political significance of national economies. In any case, we are entering a new era for a significant portion of free markets.

Putting it All Together: Free Market Economics

Now that we have the basic mechanics down, we should push enough further to get some idea of how contemporary business ventures can play out. To do this, we might want to focus on what these Corporations or Limited Liability Companies hold as their central objective. There are still old style enterprises mom and pops and little businesses starting up with savings and bank loans. There are still ventures that concentrate on the product or service that they create, and through that, the profits they obtain from the market place. There are still tomato farmers who go to Saturday markets. But in our times the dominance has clearly passed to ventures that can exploit the gigantic funding that the investment markets. For these big players, whatever maintains or increases share price is the chief concern of those involved. We live in a world where the price of shares and not the prices of goods and services has become the laser focus of vast business ventures. A couple examples might help to illustrate:

-While it is fresh in our minds something on international currency will work. A prime example is that since the mid 1980s it has been the Republic of China's policy to maintain a Yuan/ dollar exchange rate that kept their Yuan's value low, (in 2009, the Yuan exchanged for U.S dollars at 6.8339 dollars to one Yuan). Many US economists and politicians see this as a serious threat to the US economy because the cheaper Yuan stimulates US purchases of Chinese products and Chinese investment opportunities. And of course during this time we witnessed an explosion of China's economy. Is it nothing more than a coincidence that China booms and Wal-Mart brings us all manner of things that used to be made here, but now come from there? Unlike the drain of gold that Adam Smith scoffed at, this is a drain of industry. But whatever the case, there is really no international dispute resolution system with sufficient power to force China or, any other country, to change its economic ways.

- Health care, a second example, operates in a market place that confounds and confuses the best of them. This has been going on for 50 years or so. Take the receivers of health care, call them the sick, the injured and the scared of being sick and injured. They are not really the consumers. Back just after World War II there was a temporary labor shortage. Many companies started offering health care coverage as a way of keeping their employees. Since it wasn't very sophisticated back then, health care was a good, inexpensive benefit. So, as a result, employers, and later with the passage of Medicare and other legislation, government, became the "customers" for medical care. But it is a little more complicated than that. Employers and the government don't actually buy the health care, they buy insurance and claims administrator's services and the insurance companies and the claims administrators actually write the checks to the doctors and the hospitals and the drug companies and thus do the buying for them. Over time, as the sophistication and technology of health care virtually exploded, costs went up. And since the check writers, (the insurance companies and claims administrators) typically set their rates as a percentage of the total of the checks they were writing, health insurance prices went up by a double digit percentage year after year. Though they try not to admit it in public, for the actual consumers, in this particular market place, the check writers, the rule of thumb they work by, is that the more it costs the better for them.

Oh yeah, something else about the receivers of health care, the sick, the injured and the scared of being sick and injured. It is not like lots of them are going to look around the market place, asking about prices, and deciding that tomatoes are just too pricy this week. These receivers are actually as close to total ignorance about prices as we can imagine.

As prices in this messed up market place prices for health care have been rising at double digits for decades, for most of this same period most other stuff showed either flat prices or low inflation. As a result health care has been taking a bigger and bigger bite out of the total economy each year. In the process, health care simply became unaffordable for people without employer or government insurance, (and by the early 2000s about 40 or 50 million Americans had none). As the money pours in to this sector of the economy just look in any city in the country, whether large or small. Typically, almost all the new buildings and the biggest construction projects are expansions in the hospital-medical sector.

- Or, for a third example, what about the large multinational oil companies? Of course they are among the most profitable enterprises, anywhere, ever. But profit has become a decreasingly important influence in their share prices. As they produce and sell refined oil and gas, they should logically shrink in value as their available reserves are taken to market. A company with shrinking inventory is almost by definition a company with declining share prices. Having less crude to obtain, refine and sell can only hurt share prices. So what can be done? Only by laying claim to larger and larger untapped reserves can this shrinking be addressed. They must have more and more reserves to protect share prices. In recent years this has meant campaigns to get leases in Alaska and offshore along the US coastline. It has brought them into close association with dictators in troubled and failing countries in Africa and Asia. And perhaps their most creative, they have taken to redefine previously worthless tar sand as a newly recognized kind of oil reserve. The huge emotion charged debate about global warming becomes a no-brainer then for those who embrace the objective of protecting share prices. The very future of these corporate entities demands that they take on all share price threats and expand their asset base. Take care of the asset base and profits take care of themselves. So the intense focus of these corporations has shifted from the gas pumps to governments. Governments have the power to expand inventory by leasing new drilling sites. Government regulations have the power to redefine tar solids as oil and further expand inventories. Governments can grant access to property for pipeline construction.[13] By comparison the gas pump requires little attention. Refined petroleum is refined petroleum. There is no real product competition at the pump. Overall demand isn't much of an attention-getter either. Consumers absorbed huge price increases in recent years, mainly because the bulk of their vehicle operation is not really discretionary.

There we have it: market pricing, limited liability investment, and international free trade make up the underpinnings of what we refer to as market economy, or private enterprise. There is of course much more to it, but hopefully this little illustration and commentary will give us enough of a feel for the subject to allow us to better separate what private enterprise actually is from the political claims and counter claims that come to us wrapped in the guise of economic wisdom. As we will see, though different people mean different things when they bring up market economy in the political context, there is just about universal acknowledgment that the economic arrangements we've just discussed are the most effective and the most productive ever yet put in use. The critical characteristic is the fact that the overall direction things take is not designed or planned by anybody. Direction is the result of millions and millions of separate detailed judgments and transactions.

Earlier, I mentioned that charge about military brass suffering from their tendency to always be preparing and planning for the last war. Whether this is a valid criticism of the military it sure rings true of politicians as they talk about economic issues. This might be the reason that in spite of all their shouting and chest beating, neither the economists nor the politicians have had a particularly good record at fixing problems when economies go sour. In any case, we are now prepped enough to turn to that prior war of words and policies, so to speak: namely our political inheritance from the economic arguments and events of the critical period of economic collapse that took place between the two World Wars. The theories and proposals of that period have shaped the terms of debate as we have inherited it today.

Chapter 5 The Politics of Economics

"The long run is a misleading guide to current affairs. In the long run we are all dead. Economists set themselves too easy, too useless a task if in tempestuous seasons they can only tell us that when the storm is past the ocean is flat again."

John Maynard Keynes (1883-1946)[1]

"Industrial mutation—if I may use that biological term—that incessantly revolutionizes the economic structure from within, incessantly destroying the old one, incessantly creating the new one. This Creative Destruction is the essential fact of capitalism."

Joseph A. Schumpeter (1883-1950)[2]

"Politics is economics by other means."

Michael Ruppert (1951-2014)[3]

Though there is no single authoritative source to add it up for us, various estimates of annual Federal Government spending put it at $3.6 trillion in recent years. Estimates for State and Local government spending come in at somewhere closer to $3 trillion. Let's round it off and try to get our mind around the idea of a consumer that spends $6 trillion a year. This figure represents about a third of the value of all that the economy puts out in a year these days.[4] Nowadays if you can stand to listen to people talking about politics, occasionally, you will more than likely hear them talking about taxes, deficits, government spending, political contributions, and government regulations. One might think that it is all about money, especially at the level of the Federal government. While the talk may all be about money, the real concerns run deeper. The more central issues being debated are seldom discussed fully with any detail.

Most politicians and almost all politically active citizens are not economists. But taken together, the laws and regulations that define the government's participation in the economy, make up a gigantic and extremely complicated relationship. These laws and regulations were drafted, (debated, redrafted, passed and sometimes amended again over time) by highly specialized experts and attorneys. And for the most part, I am not talking about elected officials and their staffers. These people are not on government payrolls. They work at those ominous shadowy entities we know as "special interests." The interests they represent are many and varied. After all, almost everybody wants something from government. Even a person who might say of government, "I simply want to reduce it to the size where I can drag it into the bathroom and drown it in the bathtub," is a person who wants something. [5] The thing that is special about all these special interests is that they have the resources to employ people to pursue what they want. They might seem to be conservative. They might seem to be progressive. It matters little. What is special about them is that they are paying out good money and they expect a return on their investment. They want to access the resources of government to get something made legal or illegal, or paid for by the government or for the government to stop paying for. They all want things in the economy to tip in their favor financially. How did these folks get a seat at the table? How did our politics come to embrace the minute details of our economic activities?

ECONOMY AND POLITICS

With this question we arrive at the heart of the subject of this chapter. The role of our government in the economy has, evolved to become one of the central features of our politics. This chapter will try to outline that evolution and help us appreciate its significance, on a more sophisticated level than we find in the talk of politicians and other partisans.

To get this better understanding of the politics of economics and the concerns underlying it, we have to take another short trip back into history. This time we go back to the period between the First and Second World Wars. The period between the wars began at the conclusion of what has been called the first modern war; modern, because in WWI the technologies of the modern industrial economies (steel, gas engines, automatic firearms, dynamite, poison gas, airplanes, etc.) were put to effective use for mass killing. It is estimated that over 10 million combatants perished. War has never been violence restricted to armies, but dynamite and bombs never target very well. These weapons tended to blur the line between combatants and civilians. An estimated 7 million civilians also died. The shock of such war destruction was followed in 1918 by a world-wide influenza epidemic that took more than 50 million lives worldwide. These terrifying events lingered in the memories of the living throughout this period between the wars, and certainly influenced political attitudes.

This period between the wars is what we will focus on because, if we are looking for a short series of events that had just about as great an impact on contemporary political thinking as the French Revolution, the events from 1918 to 1938 certainly deserve our attention. But unlike the earlier period, the political lessons that our politics took from the history of these years are not so much about rights and freedoms and constitutions. They are about economics.

So let's briefly go over years 1918-1938 so we can better understand the economic issues of those times. Out of the struggles with these issues certain perspectives about the economy came to the forefront of our political thinking. First, a few highlights, year by year that most historians would recognize in the story of these years:

The crisis between the two World Wars

- **1917** in March, in Russia, the Tsar's monarchy falls to a Provisional Government committed to setting up a democratic constitution. By November the Provisional Government has been brought down by more radical factions dominated by the communist Bolsheviks.

- **1918** in March, a peace treaty with Germany ends Russian participation in WWI. A Russian civil war continues for several years before the Bolsheviks consolidate power. In November 1918, European combatants end WWI hostilities. July, in Japan, demonstrations against high rice prices begin. As many as 2 million hit the streets.

- **1919** World War I peace treaties, include one setting up a League of Nations that is designed to preclude future wars. Another treaty sets up heavy penalty payments (Reparations) from the War's losers.

- **1921** in May, the US passes the Emergency Immigration Restriction Act designed to admit new immigrants at the rate of 3% of their ethnic proportions as found of the 1910 US Census.

- **1922** in December, in Russia, the Bolsheviks finally consolidate power ending the Russian civil war and establishing the Union of Soviet Socialistic Republics, (USSR), the world's first national government that claimed Marxist communism as its basis.

- **1923** in September, Germany, is experiencing hyper-inflation (one US dollar became worth 4.2 trillion German marks). In the midst of a declared state of emergency, Munich, political activist and army corporal, Adolph Hitler, and his anti-communist party make a failed attempt to seize government power (the so called Beer Hall Putsch).

ECONOMY AND POLITICS

- **1924** in May, in the US, the Johnson–Reed Act further restricts immigration to 2% of the nation's 1890 ethnic composition and eliminates immigration of Asians altogether.

- **1925** in January in Italy, Benito Mussolini (Il Duce) announces he has become dictator.

- **1926** in May, in Poland, a successful military coup places Jozef Pilsudski, Minister of Defense in power where he remains for the next ten years.

- **1927** in July, in Austria, socialists call a general strike. Amid demonstrations, the Palace of Justice in Vienna is set on fire.

- **1928** in August, Germany, France, and the US sign the Kellogg-Briand Pact pledging not to use war to settle disputes. Fifty additional countries later accept coverage under this treaty.

- **1929** in October in the US, after a decade of sustained economic prosperity the stock market plummeted (the Dow stock index falls from 381.17 in September to 198.60 in November. Stock-holders lose over 52% of the total value of their shares. At it its depth the index dipped below 80). Share prices in other countries behave similarly.

- **1930** The economic collapse known as the Great Depression begins to develop in most of the world's economies, and continues at least to the end of the decade. September, Argentina's, two term president is ousted by General José Félix Uriburu in a military coup supported by conservative elites.

- **1931** in September, Japan invades Manchuria, hostilities between Japan and neighboring countries expand thereafter into WWII.

- **1933** in January, Germany, Hitler appointed Chancellor. In the following year he abolishes the position of president and takes full political control under the title, Leader and Reich Chancellor.

- **1934** in February in Austria, civil war breaks out between socialist groups and forces loyal to the existing government.

- **1935** in August, in the US, the Social Security Act becomes law. October Italy invades Ethiopia and hopes for the authority of the League of Nations to stave off military conflict, fail.

- **1936** in May, in France, the anti-Fascist Popular front brings the first socialist prime minister to power. In July, in Spain, Civil War breaks out between various groups supporting the left leaning elected government and followers of a group of generals supported by monarchists and fascists.

- **1937** in December, in Romania, elections fail to bring in a majority government, King Carol dissolved Parliament and began rule as dictator. December, Japan captures and destroys much of the Chinese capital of Nanjing killing large numbers of its civilian population.

- **1938** in November, Germany, "Kristallnacht," a government inspired and sanctioned destruction of Jewish businesses, homes and synagogues. Large scale arrests of Jews begins.

- **1939** in September, Germany invades Poland: World War II is on in Europe.

The above is not intended as a some kind of history lesson. It is simply to show that a whole lot of major events were happening, and that a lot of it was bad. Democracies fell to dictators economies collapsed. Ethnic mistrust increased both here and abroad. Nations launched unchallenged attacks on other nations. (Folks like me, who would like to see more people voting these days, shouldn't forget that voter turn-out increased dramatically in Germany in the years before Hitler consolidated Nazi power.)

Good things happened too. We got talking pictures, radio news and entertainment, and the first anti-microbial drug, sulfa. To sum up the historical context, just think of what these people experienced: 1. The horror of WWI is followed by, 2. A successful revolution by avowed communists which consolidates control over, the largest national territory on earth. 3, Then less than a decade later, almost as if the aims and predictions of the communists were coming to pass, an unprecedented break down of free market economies occurred all over the world. Using our terms from the previous chapter we can be more specific, about this last development. Limited liability investing and credit virtually collapsed. At first, stock markets crashed, then banks failed, and ultimately entire market economies defied all expectations and ceased to function. The timing was different in different countries, but by 1933 the crisis of free markets was persistent and world-wide. A great economic depression was bringing huge investment losses to shareholders and other varieties of financial pain to millions of people who depended on income from employment.

Industrial nations everywhere confronted failed economies, acute unemployment, and political unrest. Life as people previously knew it was clearly unraveling. Liberal and conservative partisans in the US and many other industrial democracies argued about how to most quickly and least painfully get back to the prosperity that free market economies had brought in the past. But there were other players on the scene. These tumultuous times were a virtual hay day for all kinds of political extremists, partisans who cared little or nothing about either representative government or free markets. These extremists made the economic situation all the more urgent. Their efforts coalesced into huge political movements that came to play decisive roles in both national and international affairs.

The communists represented a radical, yet totally economic orientation. Other extremists like the Nazis and the Fascists preferred to seek solutions in ethnic and nationalist exclusivity. In the pages that follow, we will first look at each of two anti-democratic extremes. Then we will turn to the main economic debate that took place in the United States and other countries where, throughout these turbulent times, governing conservatives and liberals remained committed to both free markets and representative government. When the economy is collapsing, what, if anything, can governments do? Responses in various countries make this period almost seem like a world-wide laboratory for experimentation in government actions to confront bad economic times. The range of responses to these economic issues that emerged has solidified in the intervening eight decades. These responses from the period between the two world wars form the basis for the economic debate in our contemporary politics. This period is the bed rock of our political debate about economics. But first the extremists.

The Communist's goal: An End to Private Property

The communist movements took an aim at the institution of private property. Private property ownership is obviously essential to free market economics. But to get a good handle on the conflicting forces, we need to remind ourselves what we mean when we talk about private property. Consider, for a moment, what is and what is not normally thought of as private property. To begin with, there are many examples of peoples whose cultures use objects but never have the sense that they really own them. For these peoples, the world is to use and not to possess. Such thinking is really not that strange to us. After all it is not unlike the way many of us view our national parks, or better yet, how most of us see that 2/3s of the earth surface that is the dark blue part, the water. By contrast we all have private property. We all have an appreciation of the stuff that nobody else messes with, very personal property; our toothbrush, our clothes, maybe a cell phone, or glasses. Then there are those bigger things that we might not use exclusively but we have title to in writing; a car, a house, acres of land somewhere. Beyond that the private property we can think of becomes much more abstract. Some examples would be dollars, stock shares, easements, franchises, trademarks, patents, copyrights, and such.

ECONOMY AND POLITICS

The point is a pretty basic one. It is only because property is "owned" in our economy (by individuals, by stock holders or even by clubs and coops of various kinds), that having a lot of it, (i.e. wealth) becomes possible. And, with wealth in private property comes its opposite--not so much, or even no private property at all, (i.e. poverty). In most times and places these two opposite states of affairs, private wealth and poverty, are recognized as the critical motivators for all kinds of human efforts. It is what gets lots and lots of people out of bed each morning. Furthermore, as we have seen, free market economies are widely recognized as the best-ever way to create and distribute private property.

By contrast, the expressed beliefs of the communists were truly extreme because they singled out for blame nothing less than private property and free market economics. What is more, they blamed free market economics for almost everything they disliked. For example, religion was for them not sincere and legitimate. It was merely a deception designed by the wealthy to justify their riches in the midst of poverty and suffering. Likewise, art was merely a reflection of the power and glory of the wealthy. From their perspective this old wealth/poverty way of living was about to change. Accordingly, they identified those who benefited most from free market economics not only as villains but also as historical relics. Let me point out that we don't want to confuse these anti-free market extremists of the 19th and early 20th centuries with the Cold War Soviet dictators or the princely party leaders in Republic of China in more recent days. The founders of communist governments in the last century were very different from those who followed them generations later. They were most simply armed and dangerous people, in power for the first time, and bent on solving all the world's problems by attacking and eliminating supporters of the most fundamental component of all known economics: the institution of private property.

As you may recall from our previous historical flash back, the idea that the institution of private property was also becoming historically obsolete had been kicking around at least as far back as the French revolution. But until the events of 1917, the political impact of these ideas had been comparatively minimal. The Bolshevik party had now taken control in Russia, and from all appearances, they looked serious. They withdrew the Russian army of over 10 million from World War I combat and further displayed their break with other national governments by releasing all kinds of Tsarist diplomatic secrets. They fielded their "Red Army" and overcame internal opposition in a civil war. These communists saw that those having power in this dying private-property-phase of world history, could be expected to resist the march of history and put up a fight. That made violent revolution unavoidable. For them, the events in Russia were merely the first instance in an inevitable series that would spread throughout the world. In the long run, the propertied classes, being so outnumbered, couldn't resist the ending of free market capitalist economies and the emerging communal society that must follow.

Transformative changes were under way. These were heady times. They confiscated private property and replaced the existing economy with one that was planned by the central government. Their economic plans came to be designed in five year increments and took as their main objectives a rapid industrialization, and a transformation of agriculture into a new system that organized production the way it was done by factories. The communists had a political philosophy that put a sacredness to their distain for private property and wealth. That sacred distain was not unlike a religious zeal.

This anti-private property zeal was one thing in Russia with the Bolsheviks in charge. Outside of revolutionary Russia it was something quite different. As minority political beliefs, whenever and wherever these anti-private-property ideas showed up, the believers were recognized as a real threat, not only to free market economics, but to the entire way of life that free market economic customs engender. After all, to possess a fundamental disbelief about how appropriate and natural it is to own private property, is to opt out of the notion that there is a basic reasonableness and fairness about the way goods and services are distributed and used in market economies. In other words, even in instances when these anti-private-property folks have been only fringe minority partisans with absolutely no governing power, as individuals, they are seen as threatening because they do not subscribe to the moral foundations of free market economics. Really, how do the notions of right and wrong for such people differ from the morality of thieves? (Biographers tell us that dictator, Joseph Stalin robbed banks in the early years to raise money for the Bolsheviks).

How can such people ever be trusted if they do not even agree when it comes to matters of who has what and who gets what? We are talking about a basic moral principle. This morality aspect of communism is a critical one. It takes us far beyond Russia, the USSR, and the conflict with communism we called the Cold War. So long as everybody might not fully share in the belief that property and wealth distributed by free market economies was right and justly held, supporters of free markets had to be on guard. Whenever people living together cannot assume that they share fundamental moral beliefs, these people live with enemies in their midst. After all, what did these communists make of those biblical commandments about not stealing or coveting? With the rise of communist partisans, a deep suspicion and fear entered politics in democracies. Thus quite apart from international relations, the politics of domestic anti-communism took on a life of its own.

In the inter-war period internal anti-communist politics played a central role in the partisan struggles in Germany, Italy, Spain, Austria, and many other countries. Communism never flourished in the US as a political movement to the extent that it did in a number of other countries. However, the US is certainly no exception when it came to internal struggles involving opposition to the threat of communists in our midst. To mention two examples:

• Just after the Bolsheviks took power in Russia there were a series of bomb threats and actual bombings directed at prominent Americans. Then US Attorney General, A. Mitchell Palmer, whose house was bombed, responded by launching raids that arrested over 6000 suspected communists. Some people were arrested for illegal acts, but many others for things they'd written or said (...or were suspected of thinking). Some were communists but many were not. The legality and the effectiveness of these so called "red scare" raids remains quite controversial. How do you go about rounding up people who have a particular belief? What about free speech? What would you have done if you were Palmer?

- After World War II a military confrontation with communists in Korea took place. It marked the beginning of the Cold War stand-off between the communists and the non-communists that came to color all our international relations for decades. Committees of the House of Representatives such as the, The House Un-American Activities Committee had been investigating alleged Nazi and communist subversives for some time. In 1949 Wisconsin Senator, Joseph McCarthy became famous by beginning a series of investigations and hearings to identify communists in the US government. With communist political activities increasing in the US during the Great Depression and the fact that the Soviet Union had been an ally during much of the just past World War, McCarthy's efforts were quite popular. He eventually identified some Soviet sympathizers in the US government. However, his repeated attacks on people about whom he had little or no evidence, lead to controversy. Eventually his opposition managed to label his investigations a senseless "witch hunt" and McCarthy was censured by the US Senate.

These are strictly domestic political events. However, each of them illustrate the two edged character of opposition to communists, the opposition to communists in control of the economies of the USSR and other countries, and the distrust and fear of people in our midst who seem not to subscribe to popular beliefs about private property. The modern conservative movement in the United States started to develop its momentum in the wake of Senator McCarthy's decline. It marked a new way of addressing the economy politically. The articulate early spokespersons for this modern conservative movement were folks like William F. Buckley Jr., Ayn Rand, Russell Kirk, Barry Goldwater, Phyllis Schlafly. These writers and later President Ronald Reagan consistently supported strong military capability in opposition to the Soviet block and they also shared a vigilant domestic anti-communism as a central tenant in their writing and speaking.

In sum, of the political responses to the troubles of the period between the wars that we are considering, this one, the communist response, has left no real legacy in our contemporary politics. In the US rather than uniting for revolution, the worker's union movement sought a bigger share of the profits from the free market companies that employed them. As for the Bolsheviks, the Soviet efforts to end private property have left us without so much as a trace. In many other countries, communist party candidates were elected into government, and they actually held office within existing market economies.[6]

Though central planning could prove to aid development, communist predictions of the historical demise of free market economics simply never came about. Ironically the five year economic planning introduced by the Soviets eventually came to be standard fare in the US, only here it was effectively adopted not by the government but by managements at large free market corporations.

By the end of the 20th century, free market capitalism had far surpassed the magnitude and scope that even its most optimistic theorists had dared to predict for it. Ironically, communism's declaration of the end of private property, has become the real relic of history. In 1999 the successors to one of the pioneer communist governments, the Peoples Republic of China, amended its constitution to recognize private ownership as having the same status as state ownership. More recently, in communist Cuba there has been a return to private farming with reports of initial success.[7] These days just about everybody seems to agree that there has never been an effective large scale attempt of any duration, to make life better by completely eliminating private property. Instead, oppressive, highly centralized, anti-democratic, police state conditions have become more closely associated with how communist governments actually operate. In fact the most glaring failure of communist governments has been that rather than eliminating inequality, they have only replaced old economic elites with new ones. There are so many actual examples of the tragic descent from the optimism of communal sharing, to authoritarian suppression, that the sad process was famously caricatured as a barnyard fable by George Orwell in his classic "Animal Farm," where, as he puts it, "all animals are equal, but some are more equal than others."[8]

Ultra-Nationalism: It's Us Against Everybody Else

In contrast with the communists, there were several other significant partisan movements of this period that rejected economics as a cause of their troubles. These partisans viewed the bad economy as merely a side effect of other more fundamental and sinister causes. Fear and suspicion about other racial and ethnic groups grows and declines from place to place and from time to time. But in these years it was on the rise and the US was no exception. As our bullet point history summary notes, severe restrictions on immigration were legislated in the US for the purpose of maintaining the ethnic composition of our population, which had been absorbing great numbers of immigrants from eastern and southern Europe, and Asia. In other countries this mood of ethic exclusivity nurtured enormous political movements. The partisans we are considering here saw the ethnic group they identified with, as victims of massive injustice and deceit. Think of it as group-identification-gone-wild. There is nothing necessarily wrong about identifying with a group. "Be true to your school.""Go Packers." That pride of country we call patriotism is usually good and positive. But let's say that we start with ordinary patriotism and we mix it in with some racism and maybe a good bout with the mental symptoms of irrational fear we call paranoia. This will give you a start at understanding what took the center stage in the politics of a number of countries during this inter-war period. But this kind of victimized-super-patriotism is only a start.

For these people the country they are proud of becomes something more than a land and its people. They turn it into an idealized unified conception, more like a glorious, living, breathing, and significantly, a threatened, thing. I am talking about the Nazis of Germany, the Fascists of Italy, and to some extent, the Falangists of Spain. Since these parties were focused on affairs in a particular culture within a particular nation state, it is not surprising that their names differ from country to country. But in each instance there is intense ethnic nationalism combined with fear and suspicion that outsiders are out to get them. In addition, in each case the movement came to focus on a strong-man leader who personified the strength and courage that those dire times called for. To get any insight into these kinds of political extremists, we need to dwell for a moment on how each of these words, *ethnic*, and *nationalism*, come into play here.

First, what are **ethnic groups** and how did they figure in to the politics of the inter-war years, or any time for that matter? We all have some usable understanding of what ethnicity is. What we need to understand is that these extremists groups seemed to be taking it to a whole other level. Writer, Everett Hughes once provided a definition of ethnicity that is especially helpful for us here. He pointed out that we naturally think of ethnic groups as consisting of people who share certain characteristics; like language, customs, religion and such, and even physical features. But he, kind of, turned this view upside down by pointing out that it wasn't the characteristics of individuals but people's beliefs that define ethnic groups. "An ethnic group is not [an ethnic group] because of the degree of measurable or observable difference from other groups; it is an ethnic group...because the people in and the people out if it know that it is one; both the ins and the outs talk, feel, and act as if it were a separate group."[9]

At some level everybody is aware of race and ethnicity, and there certainly is, and has been, discrimination based on race and ethnicity.

What is critical to follow here is that, for these kinds of extreme ethnic political movements, (both then and now), these "in group", "out group" definitions get emphasized to exaggerated proportions. For these kinds of partisans, there are no grey areas between us and them. This clarity is important because, at the very core of their political beliefs, these extremist folks believe that their own ethnic group, its culture and its history had been oppressed, victimized, and prevented from realizing its true historic potential as a people. And what is more, the fault for their plight lies with another or other ethnic groups they identify. So, part of the task of such movements is to further elaborate the strengths and heroism of their own ethnicity while at the same time justifying fear, suspicion, and hate of the group or groups that they blame for their victimization. It is no surprise if you think of it, that this effort to defend ones ethnic group can quite easily get into the biology and genetics. So what might seem to the observer to be a cultural group or a nationality, gets defined by the insiders as a distinct race. It is easy to see that the resulting politics are extremely oppositional and exclusionary. The qualities and characteristics that cause harm; brutishness, selfishness, and other moral or religious defects, are ascribed to other groups. The *thems* are not as good as us. They are lacking in essential aspects of humanity. The *thems* incessantly conspire against us. They are never to be trusted. It's us against them.

> **Gloss Note:** Try this little game in your head. Genetic researchers now claim that there is evidence that our species, homo sapiens coexisted and sometimes mated with Neanderthals over a period of thousands of years. As a result there are, among us, humans with as much as 4 percent Neanderthal DNA. Now take a moment to imagine among the people you know and you know of, who these 4 presenters might be…See we all have the talent to create in and out groups in our heads!

This severe form of ethnic identity is actually not that strange to us today. A visit to any one of many prisons in this country would give us ample instances of groups with these kinds of extreme racial and ethnic

ECONOMY AND POLITICS

beliefs. What's special about the inter-war period is that, in a number of countries, people in huge numbers with these kinds of beliefs, held sway over whole countries. So much for the term ethnic.

This brings us to the significance of **nationalism** the second term in this us-against- them kind of politics. For these ethnic extremists, the nation was much more than the country they happened to be living in. Nor is it enough to say that they were super patriotic. The nation, for them is more like the homeland for a genetically pure, virtual extended family. For the Nazis it was the fulfillment of their mythical Teutonic ancestry. For the Fascists it was the fulfillment of the potential of the ancient Romans. But it is even more. I fear that we might be missing the forest for the trees. For these extremists, the nation, and not the individual, is at the center in their political beliefs. For them, their particular nation state, could best be understood as a kind of monstrous creature with a life, and an existence, and a destiny all its own. So as not to begin sounding like science fiction, it might be helpful to think of an ant hill. I now live in Texas. We have what they call fire ants. The super nationalism that I am trying to describe puts me in mind of these little critters. For the individual ants, the colony is all important. The individual ants are meaningless apart from the totality of the ant hill. Each of them performs great labor to build the community, provide for it and protect it. They can live heroic lives attacking intruders with their powerful venom, with the ultimate self-sacrifice being death in battle, defending their queen.

If ants or even bees seem a stretch for you, maybe, you can follow the lead of the writers who call these kinds of political movements a form of religion, devoted to worship of the state. Either way, these folks were zealots, committed to taking over their country, bringing it to glory by whatever means necessary, and exalting their great one, their leader. This is the kind of nationalism that goes into the ethnic nationalism we are talking about.

I have mentioned the antipathy of these super nationalists with the communists. But there is one important thing that they shared. What defines both of these kinds of extremists, is that regardless of what they might claim, they have no fundamental interest in constitutional government or democracy.[10] Nor do they strive for settlement of political differences without violence or coercion. If they have to encounter politics in a democracy they are more than likely to see it as a hopelessly rigged game. For them, representative governments exist only to legitimize a status quo that is completely unacceptable. They might use democratic institutions, if they can, but only as a temporary expediency. So during this inter-war period, in country after country, we had two sets of extremist partisans, the communists and their like, and these kinds of ethnic nationalist extremists. All of them were pledged to take over by any means. The two sides fed off each other instilling fear and terror into the more moderate more democratically inclined. As economies faltered, tensions mounted and the extremist factions grew. Imagine popular parties in contemporary politics adopting forms of dress and organizational characteristic of the military. The political conversation degenerates into gangs, fighting in the streets.

> **Gloss Note:** It may seem ironic, but the cause of ethnic nationalism that developed into these extremist movements was given a big boost by Woodrow Wilson, the great peacemaker at the end of WWI. Wilson's Fourteen Points, which became the major foundation of the peace treaties, argued against the history of empires in Europe and called for the "self-determination of nations" a principle that was widely interpreted as advocating self-government and territorial integrity for all ethnic groups.[11]

These ethnic nationalist movements were not primarily concerned with economics. But many shared with the Russian communists an impatience with democratic government in favor of the decisiveness of authoritarian rule with and its preference for central economic planning.[12] However, you should be aware that when political labels are handed out (whereas the communists are placed on the far left), these ethnic nationalists are usually discussed as a part of the far political right. There are at least three reasons for this. First there was their rabid opposition to the internationalism of the communists. In addition, the political-right label is no doubt aided by the fact that Nazi leader Adolf Hitler once referred to himself as the "most conservative revolutionary in the world".[13] Beyond this, the rightist characterization probably rests on the way they dealt with business and industry once they were in control. Far from being economically radical, they strove to harness and guide existing financial and industrial elites to enhance their power, and implement their agenda, (in particular their military objectives). Some might find it confusing that the Nazis described themselves as socialist, "National Socialist." However theirs was not a socialism that concerned economic inequality. Nazi socialism, was a socialism of that bee hive that we were just talking about, a collective commitment to the nation. They were strong supporters of the notion of private property. Fortunes could be kept intact, and other new fortunes could be made in these movements, as a part of bringing out the grandeur and glory of the sacred homeland.

If we could go back in time, we would hear their inspiring leaders. Their political messaging began by convincing us we are clearly the greatest among the nations. However, our great historical potential as a nation is being frustrated. Not only that but this frustration is the work of determined enemies both abroad and in our midst. Our potential will only be realized when these enemies are destroyed and we are thus purified as a people. This, they tell us, is our God given national destiny. This is big. This super-state we are realizing is not only an end in itself, but it unlocks all of our human potential. People can warm up to this kind super-nation-state stuff, even today. Get's the blood surging! These are among the ideas that were heart-warming enough to turn the politics of the 1920s and 30s into confrontations and wars resulting in death tolls and destruction that made World War I seem tiny by comparison.

The easiest way to understand the agenda of such movements is to envision a process in which the ranks of the citizens are closed off from outsiders and thus purified. Freed from evil and disloyal elements and thus purified this ultra-nationalist citizenry then is able to capture its true place in the world. Theirs is a moral, cultural, demographic, and ultimately geographic quest. Proponents of such views during the inter-war period sometimes identified economic problems but framed these as resulting from international enemies and domestic conspiracies. The politics of Germany under Adolf Hitler are perhaps the example most called upon to illustrate this kind of super-state politics. Neither socialism nor capitalism characterized the beliefs of the National Socialists. Blaming the Jews was clearly not an economic issue. In fact the Nazi doctrines gave the Jews a curious duel role; sometimes they were the evil bankers who controlled world capitalism, and other times they were the evil anti-capitalist communists. Hating Jews was perhaps the single clear principle in their beliefs.[14] The Nazi campaign to exterminate the Jews and other accused groups, was just the most enormous and determined "us- against-them" effort to eliminate those blamed as impure weakening elements among the population. In Germany, as in other countries, the fears of communists and other partisans and minorities not aligned with the parties of intense nationalism were used to circumvent democratic institutions. Beyond these domestic developments, the international stance of these countries was aggressive and militarily confrontational. It was "us against everybody else," who were characterized as either the weak or the evil.

With this in the background, we can now better appreciate the course taken here in the United States and in other countries where our politics confronted the same economic catastrophe but insisted that democratic institutions remain in full force.

Fixing a Broken Market Economy, Democratically

In the United States the political and economic events took a different path. While the history and the continental isolation of the United States at first buffered us from the dominating extremisms that took over in other countries, we were certainly not spared from the intensity of the economic crisis. To appreciate what was happening in this country, we need to remember that the United States was no longer a land of independent frontier farmers. The 1920 census is the first to show a majority of Americans living in urban circumstances. Unlike rural dwellers, city folks lack any hopes of sustaining themselves directly from the land. They are thus dependent on a functioning economy for most all of their needs. But by 1930 we were in the depths of a collapsing economy. As noted above, almost half of the value of all stocks evaporated toward the end of 1929. Then economic activity of all kinds began to stagnate, sending millions into unemployment. Using the more inclusive definitions of unemployment then in use, about 1/4 of the US workforce was unemployed by 1933. By that time depositors were frantically withdrawing any money they'd deposited for safe-keeping in banks. Since banks keep only a fraction of deposits on reserve and invest the rest, these runs on the banks lead to a crisis of bank insolvencies. Over 9000 banks went bankrupt. The rural population was not spared either. By 1934, years of record droughts and dust storms had affected 27 states and 75% of the geography of the country. I recite these details to underline the sense of urgency that existed in the electorate.

But for the United Stated and for a number of other countries the political task that emerged was one of restoring a once thriving free market economy while avoiding the radical anti-democratic extremes. The politics of the economy that developed at the time and remains with us today focused on two questions: 1. Can a collapsed free market economy heal itself over time? And, 2. can government interventions help to heal a broken market economy and even enhance its effectiveness? There was, and still is, broad agreement that a collapsed free market economy can rebound over time. Historically, the economy had experienced periodic bad and not so bad flops. As we go back in time, the economic data gets more scarce, but historians have been able to pin-point dozens of places when our economy stopped growing for a while. And "stopped growing" is only a pleasant way of saying loss of many fortunes, wide-spread loss of employment, hunger, and need. But that same history demonstrates that sooner or later things get going and the prosperity of economic growth prevails again.

It was the second question, can government interventions help to heal a broken market economy and even enhance its effectiveness, that nicely sorted people into two opposing political camps. As we examine these two opposing political perspectives that emerged in the 1930s and 40s, it is important that we keep two points in mind. First, the profound disagreement that this question created is not limited to theory or principle. The partisans who battled over this question seldom ever agreed about even the facts of the matter. And even today, as they look back at this tumultuous economic period, partisans have yet to agree about the facts of what actually took place. Second, these partisans have been extremely competitive in their advocacy of economic policies. But unlike the anti democratic extremists we just visited, from the beginning to the present, they agree that the contest *must take place within the arena of our constitutional government.* Now let's get a closer look.

Market Heal Thyself

On one side of the political debate in the US, the conservative partisans advocated the patience necessary to allow the forces of the free market to work, and as in the past, a new era of prosperity would naturally and dependably emerge. This might, at first, seem simply to be the do-nothing approach. When economic catastrophe hits, concerned people turn to their government and want something done. There is an understandable bias in us that insists that doing something, anything would be better than doing nothing. It takes some sophistication and effort to successfully advocate inaction in the face of pressure to act. When things seem to be falling apart, how does one go about convincing others to back away and patiently ride it out?

ECONOMY AND POLITICS

These conservative partisans had faith in the knowledge that sour free markets had always healed themselves over time. They argued that the dysfunctions and the resulting pain from the failed economy were unavoidable, and more important, that any government attempts to interfere were counterproductive. Government interference in the economy could only prolong the economic pain and delay that eventual recovery. The reason that there were no easy fixes was that the unemployment and the business failures were both normal and natural economic phenomena. Let's look at three of the main components of their position on government intervention in the economy; their views on unemployment, those which focused on investment and their views on banking.

Unemployment: For these conservatives, their understanding of unemployment brought them to a central tenant of classical economic theories. If labor was something bought and sold in a free market, and there was a lot of labor not being sold, the price was obviously too high. According to this view high unemployment would remain until workers brought the price of their wages down to a point where that price made economic sense to those who might want to buy it. When the rates of pay that made business ventures profitable were achieved, more people would be hired. According to this view, unemployment is thus a direct result of workers inadvertently pricing their labor too high; inadvertent, either because they just didn't understand the workings of the labor market or because they had been propagandized with erroneous labor union doctrines.

Once we begin to entertain this wage-pricing explanation of unemployment, it is easy to see that even the best intentioned government attempts to give aid to unemployed workers, can do nothing but prolong the problem. Within a system of market pricing, when governments subsidize either buyers or sellers, the best price is not obtained. When the best price is not obtained, economic progress is diminished and resources are wasted. When you apply this insight to the government sponsored unemployment benefits for jobless workers, you are only delaying the day when these same people must face the fact that their labor has lost some of its value in the marketplace.

Paying unemployment benefits is not the only wrong-headed mistake that this wage- pricing view criticizes. There is also the temptation to have the government directly reduce the number of workers without jobs, by expanding government employment and hiring them. For these conservatives, this was worse than unemployment benefits. Not only does it prolong the duration until wages settle at a lower price, but the government hires can bask in the false job security of their temporary government jobs and cease looking for employment in the free market. Thus rather than eliminating the economic pain to workers in a downturned economy, the conservatives believed that government intervention in unemployment was likely to prolong or even increase that downturn.

Investment: On the subject of investment, the prevailing conservative view of economic downturns saw such periods as times when free market economies sorted out wasteful unproductive investments from the good productive ones. Free market economies grow as new ventures are put together and take off. These ventures literally represent economic activity that is added to the total. However, as economies progress and innovate, there are always going to be business ventures that are bringing something unneeded, overpriced, or otherwise unattractive to market. (Any of you shopping for a wimple-tree for your team of draught horses? Or how about an 8 foot TV antenna you can lash to your chimney?) Business ventures rise and fall all the time. In this continuous process sometimes a whole sector of the economy, or the entire economy takes a dive. In the depths of a souring economy, investors begin to see where capital investment has lost its potential for profit. As the quote from Joseph Schumpeter at the beginning of the chapter puts it, such "creative destruction," is what clears out economic waste and inefficiency thereby making way for future progress. It is at such times investors can begin to get glimpses of the new opportunities for profit and potential growth that are to come. And come it will, just as sure as the sun will rise. The process of destruction and renewal that characterizes the growth of free market economies is documented everywhere. The role of government in this process can be positive or negative. The buggy manufacturers of the early 20th century either got into the new automobile business or died out. Think of the mischief that could have occurred if the government had tried to save the buggy makers.

Banking: For the conservatives, banking was already in the throes of unwanted government interference in the economy. The free market system of banking and credit had been put under government regulation with the Federal Reserve Act in 1913. With the goal of addressing periodic instability and financial panics, the act set up our system of large Federally chartered regional banks and local member banks throughout the country. These banks had authority to effect the overall supply of money available in the economy and they also regulated the percentage of deposits that the local banks had to keep on hand and not invest. It was the depression era policy of Andrew Mellon, the conservative Secretary of the Treasury (1929-1933) to have the large Federally chartered regional banks do nothing, and thus let all the weaker banks throughout the country fail. Sounding like Joseph Schumpeter, Mr. Mellon is said to have once stated his policies toward recovering from the Great Depression in these few words, "Liquidate labor, liquidate stocks, liquidate the farmers, liquidate real estate." by which he meant to emphasize the importance of letting all of the weak parts of the economy lose their value and fail under the pressures of market forces.[15] For our purposes here, this definitely included weak banks that could not protect their depositors funds. Banks don't just store depositors money in their vaults. They put it out in investments, to earn more money. If the investments fail, and a lot of the depositors come to withdraw their savings, the bank doesn't have enough reserves on hand to cover the withdrawals. The bank fails. By 1933, 11,000 of the nation's 25,000 banks were no more.

You cannot do much better than brilliant financier, Andy Mellon, to get the essence of this conservative approach. According to this view, government is not in a position to steer the economy out of the bad old investments of the past and into the profitable new investments of the future. The best practice for government in good times or bad was to keep out of the way of investors by not penalizing their profits with expensive taxes, their production with expensive regulations, or by bailing them out when they make bad judgments.

So to summarize, this conservative response to the events of the interwar years viewed both the communist and ethnic nationalist extremists as threatening not only economically but also to American freedom. While they were committed to maintaining our representative government, at the same time, they were also extremely suspicious of any attempts that democratic governments might make to increase stability in the economy or lessen the unemployment that many people experienced at the bottom of the business cycle. Patience was in order because free markets are always actively regulating themselves by rejecting inefficiency and rewarding improvement. In the long run economic difficulties work themselves out. In this context it is important to note that being against government intervention in market economies does not require heartless neglect and cruelty to the poor. Helping the poor was seen as the task of charities not governments. The US President at the time (1929-1933), Herbert Hoover, had become world famous for his earlier humanitarian work, distributing food to the needy of Europe during and after World War I. He is also one of only two Presidents who donated all of his presidential salary to charity (John Kennedy was the other).

Free Market First Aid

The urgency of the situation brought attempts at government intervention in the economy as early as 1930. Even President Hoover caved to the insistent pressure to do something. He worked against the conservative wage/price theory that recommended patiently waiting for wages to drop. He actively opposed wage cuts. He hosted industry groups with a goal of reducing price competition within particular industrial sectors. He also supported tax increases. All of these measures were clearly inconsistent with the prevailing conservative belief in government inaction and trust that the market economy was self-correcting.

> **Gloss Note:** Where Joseph Schumpeter is consistent with the way the conservatives viewed the Great Depression, many of the policies of the liberal response to this economic crisis fit with the theoretical writings of the British economist, John Maynard Keynes. Keynes's fundamental argument was that the government was always likely to be the biggest player in any free market economy. This was not only because it was overseer of the laws and regulations for business and the currency, but also because it was a very big employer and an all-around big spender. Consequently, government should expand this role in times of high unemployment by starting projects, hiring and getting more money into the hands of more consumers. He argued that this could go a long way toward smoothing out the rough spots that were plaguing the economy. In the quotation at the beginning of this chapter, Keynes was reminding us that even though markets might self-correct in the long run; people are actually living and dying in the short run.

As the situation got worse, an even more interventionist program was launched as Democrat, Franklin Roosevelt, campaigned and took office. This is where the modern term, "liberal" came into our politics. FDR and his Democratic supporters sought to differentiate themselves from the past generation of reformers whose anti-big-business policies had been labeled "Progressive." To do this they took the name of the 19th century advocates of free markets, and called themselves "liberals." These partisans wanted to be seen as a new breed on the left: advocates of free market economics, but not against wielding the power of government to intervene when the economy falters. In particular, this new liberal response brought policies intended to address problem areas directly thereby making the stalled economy work better so as to produce fewer economic casualties in the future. After Roosevelt's administration entered the White House in 1933, they named their approach to the economy, The New Deal.[16] Let's take a look at how their New Deal responded to unemployment, investment, and banking.

Unemployment: It might be argued that unemployment is the single most pressing political issue in a severe economic downturn. The masses of able bodied citizens without work, very soon exhaust the resources to cover essential costs of living. At some point, their desperation can easily become a threat to the civil order. It is not surprising that food riots and demonstrations immediately preceded both the French and the Russian revolutions. Consequently, the unemployment problem was bound to be a central issue in the politics of the US as one in four left the workforce for unemployment. The approach of the New Deal liberals was to have the government come directly to the aid of those workers who were being forced out of the free market economy. The resulting government policies took four main courses:

-Through numerous different programs the government hired hundreds of thousands of people and put them to work in projects we now refer to as infrastructure. These projects were operated by agencies such as the Public Works Administration, the Works Progress Administration and the Civilian Conservation Corps. Today we can still see schools, dams, rural electrification, reforestation, National Park structures, highways, airports, post offices, schools and other public buildings all over the country that date from the 1930s.

-Farmers facing low market prices were given supplemental payments and low interest loans to in hopes of keeping them engaged in agricultural production.

-Those unable to support themselves due to old age or disabilities began to receive payments from an insurance program we now know as

Social Security while those with jobs paid the insurance premiums to cover the costs.

-The Federal Government allotted funds to states and localities for direct distribution to millions as "relief."

Investment: The direct investments in the economy by the government were of course intended to make up for the lagging rates of new private investment. Private investment activity was stagnant throughout the market economy. Part of the problem was the fact that a huge portion of the stock market investments prior to the 1929 crash were of questionable value. At least half of these investments were bought and held on credit. Critics came to see much of the roaring economy of the late 1920s as borrowed money buying get-rich-quick illusions; a house of cards just waiting for a puff of doubt or fear to destroy it. Just as unwarranted confidence can soar in a rising stock market, doubt and fear can become contagious when that same stock market starts to tank. The New Dealers figured that facts are the best way to confront both false confidence and unnecessary doubt. Throughout the 1930s, they introduced several laws to require that stock sellers register and report essential information about their stocks to buyers and established The Securities Exchange Commission to oversee the practices of the dealers and traders of investments. Besides standards of disclosure for business ventures attempting to sell stock to the public, limits were set for the use of credit for buying and holding stocks.

Banking: The Roosevelt response to the epidemic of failing banks was to declare a "bank holiday," which closed the banks for several days in 1933. To help prevent future runs on banks New Deal legislation introduced regulations to segregate commercial banks (where Mom and Pop might have a savings account), from securities firms that issued and traded stock and corporate bonds. The Federal Deposit Insurance system was established under which commercial banks paid an insurance premium and individual depositors got their accounts federally insured for up to $2,500, (currently it's $250,000). In addition, commercial banks were limited in the degree of risk they could take in their investments.

In Summary:

The communist and ethnic nationalist extremes of the 1920s and 30s have subsided and no longer threaten world domination as they did before and during WWII, and after that, through the decades of the Cold War. The governments of the Cold War communist countries have converted to some variant of capitalism. The "us against them" parties of ethnic nationalism are still with us and still use self-pity and blame to justify terrorist acts and larger violent confrontations from time to time, but since apartheid was ended in South Africa, these kinds of partisans have not controlled major national governments. This might seem like progress were it not for the Israeli/Palestinian conflict, Hutu Power in Rwanda, Ethnic Cleansing in the former Yugoslavia, the 9/11 attacks on New York's World Trade Center and the terror of ISIS and Boko Haram. Instances of ethnic and religious inspired nationalisms like these continue to present vivid contemporary reminders that the political power of smaller movements based upon extreme hate and fear are not purely historical concerns. Within the United States, the Ku Klux Klan, and its successors and race based opposition groups, exist in the prison system, on the internet and as angry, armed, and dangerous people in the news, periodically. Try as they might, the anti-democracy extremists so far never came close to getting a hold on the reins of government here.

What has the United States taken away from the turmoil of the inter-war period? Now, as then, our political partisans agree to transfer power through elections, and the economic dialogue continues under the implicit assumption that free market capitalism is an essential part of our way of life which must continue. On the other hand, arguments about how to keep a free market going so as to produce its maximum benefits, and what to do when things go bad economically, remain hot, heavy, and central to our politics. The same two schools of thought, -- one recommending patience and elimination of government interference, --the other recommending intervention to smooth out the lumps people might experience, have taken some hits over the years, but they are both still alive and well. Unfortunately the scientific endeavor we call economics has never developed much beyond models of the macro-over-time economy that explain the last economic crisis in the same conservative or liberal terms which became popular in the 1930s. While the arguments rage, an industry of academic economists, and self-declared professional economists, come and go as celebrity talking heads in our politics. (It is in the childish name-calling of these fiercely partisan economy-celebrities that we continue to hear reminders of the extremists of the 1920s and 30s as they call one another communists, Maoists, Nazis or Fascists, and such. Be advised, in the United States, when you hear such name-calling in our mainstream politics, you can be justified in feeling like your leg is being pulled.

Insults aside, more important for us, this ongoing argument we are having about governing the economy, begins, surprisingly enough, with a broad basis of agreement between the right and the left:

-- Both sides agree that a free market economy is essential to the survival of our constitutional democracy.

--After that, they agree that almost everything we need to know about how free market economies work best and how they go into the tank, can be learned from a close examination of the Great Depression back in the 1930s.

--And that's not all, both the right and the left also agree generally that the blame or the failure of the 1930s economy to recover should be placed squarely on the Federal Government. In a debate that now sounds all too familiar, the left claimed that the government had done too little and the right claimed that the government had done too much.

After agreeing on those three points, the left and the right shake hands, go to their corners and then come out with fists blazing. Since the time of the Great Depression we have seen World War II, the dawn of nuclear warfare, gone to the moon, signed millions of cell phone contracts, and eaten billions of fast food burgers, replaced downtown shopping for Malls, Walmart and the internet, and we've Tweeted. But the popular political debate about economics has pretty much remained in the two ruts that liberals and conservatives dug in to back then. Our politics is literally obsessed with arguments about the triumphs or tragedies that attend government interventions in the economy. And furthermore the arguments seldom climb out of the deep grooves that the left and the right dug themselves onto way back in the 1930s. We are now in a position to close this chapter on economics by summarizing the two sides of this political debate about the economy. Starting with their take on the Great Depression, here are the main tenants of each side of the argument.

As liberals see it

The lesson of great depression for activists on the left is: when the economy goes bad, the government should use its power to directly attack the resulting problems. Furthermore, after analysis of the causes, the government should promulgate laws and regulations aimed at preventing similar economic failures in the future. Being as it is, the biggest participant in the economy, the government, can do whatever is not being done. It can spend. It can hire. It can tax. It can borrow. It can help ease the pains of unemployment. For liberals looking back at the 1930s, Franklin Roosevelt had it mostly right. He cast his administration in the role of the nation's number one economic problem solver. He almost did it, but not quite. According to the liberal case, by about 1937 a combination of political opposition and maybe a little loss of that Big-Spender nerve, set the recovery back. Only when Roosevelt could begin to spend, big time, in anticipation for World War II, did the economy finally take off again. For the left, with the Great

Depression came a realization that the free market was not capable of providing certain things essential to our economic life.

- The markets always have and always will go out of whack from time to time. And at those times, problems in the economy should be confronted by government action. First, there is the immediate pain from things like unemployment, hunger, and untreated illness

- But beyond the periodic malfunctionings of the economy, there are some things that the market economy can never be expected to do adequately. While liberals reject the communist idea of equality of wealth, they instead focus on what they refer to as equality of life chances. This perspective puts issues like educational opportunity, universal health care, and discrimination (based on things related to sex and physical inheritance) at the center of liberal concerns for all citizens. They sometimes refer to this goal of equality of life chances, as creating a level playing field.

- This is why they view even the doctrine of *caveat emptor* ("Let the buyer beware") as needing government intervention in the form of consumer protections like food inspections and drug regulations. And, in addition, they advocate programs of government support for those not able to fully participate in the economy.

- It is a fact that business for profit will always make every effort to minimize costs. This is not only the hallmark of the efficiency of free markets but liberals also see this as a source of overall inefficiency. If a business can escape paying for certain costs of its' operations, it is not always clear that nobody pays. Economists call this process of forcing costs on others, externalizing these costs. Costs and responsibilities resulting from pollution and employee injury, are examples where liberals have attempted push back costs that businesses seek to externalize,

- Rather than individuals, our main economic entities are corporations. Corporations are huge concentrations of economic power devoted to the goal of maximizing share value. Corporations view governments as either an obstacle in their quest, or a potential tool that might be bought off and used to their advantage.

• Last but not least, there is the doomsday critique of free markets. It goes something like this. Let's even grant that a perfectly functioning free market, with no government interference were to evolve worldwide. Since continuous growth is essential to prosperous free markets, a point is surely reached when population growth and economic expansion captured and utilized all resources, and the whole house of cards collapses.

As conservatives see it

When the economy goes bad activists on the right hark back to the non-interference policies of the administration of Herbert Hoover and his Treasury Secretary, Mellon, to point to a near perfect government response to the Great Depression. Hoover and especially Mellon recognized that the true cure for a bad economy is to allow it to correct itself. The mainstream conservative case says Hoover and Mellon had it right except for one seemingly small detail. By 1930 the Federal Reserve banking system was now exercising substantial control over some of the country's largest banks, and these big banks were doing little or nothing to come to the aid of the thousands of smaller banks as their depositors swarmed in to cash out. During the run on the banks, every time a bank had to close, the overall money supply in the economy was decreased by the amount of that bank's assets. The shrinking money supply during the early 1930s left a shortage of private investment capital that government spending couldn't possibly make up for. This was the problem, but nobody even realized it at the time. That ignorance was repeated with another tightening of the money supply in 1937, followed, surprise, surprise, by another economic downturn. [17] For conservatives, the legacy of the New Deal is that huge government programs mean little more than taxes, deficits, and prolonging the bad times.

In Addition:

• If left alone, with an adequate civil order, a sufficient money supply, and courts to enforce contracts, the market economy, over time will produce as much as the technology, resources available, and the population can produce. This includes: Full employment, (maybe not every single day, but maximized over the long run.) An unconstrained flowering of all kinds of naturally occurring innovation.

• Taxes and deficits rob resources from the places where they can be most productive ---in the free market.

• Conservatives see the very problems that liberals want to attack with government, as problems that the economy itself can solve.

• Government interventions are just about guaranteed to delay progress first by standing in the way of innovation and equally important, by making some participants dependent on the government and not the private economy.

• On the individual level, market economies are at the center of human motivation. They must be allowed to continuously present each of us with the possibility of great wealth and the threat of crippling poverty. If government action gets in the way of either of these motivators, the miraculous productivity of the free market is degraded. Life is not fair, and nothing government can do will change that.

And that's about it for the conservative view. Theirs is a stricter support of free markets that sees the dislocations and unemployment of each dip in the economy as the destruction of the un-wanted and the inefficient as capitalism continuously transforms the world, to make better use of its people and its resources. Admittedly, this view has harsher consequences, in the short run, but conservatives argue that it is simply a reality we all should face for our own good.

Gloss Note: You should be aware that in recent years a branch of the conservative post- Depression legacy called "Libertarianism" has gained popularity. The views of this faction derive in large part from the writings of Austrian social scientists Ludwig von Mises (1881-1973) and Friedrich Hayek (1899-1992) whose analysis actually predicted the 1929 market crash. Libertarians argue that almost all of what modern governments actually do can better be accomplished in unregulated free markets.[18] The political principles espoused by libertarians would restrict government to doing little more than maintaining civil order, enforcing contracts, and defending our national borders.

As we bring this discussion to a close, I want to give you three very general clues you can use to spot right and left leaning views as people talk about the free market economy. We will call them: 1. taking sides, 2. time perspective, and 3. the limits of rationality.

1. What I mean by *"taking sides"* may seem silly to you at first. Consider this. Artists who paint pictures work in two dimensional space, in lengths and widths. Right? What if I were to tell you that there were two schools of painters; one school who sees all difficulties with their paintings, as problems of width, and the other school who only sees all drawing problems coming from length. Silly, no? Well, free markets also kind-of have two dimensions, and those two dimensions are supply and demand. What if I were to tell you that partisans on the right have a bias that sees free market economic problems on the supply side and partisans on the left are biased toward seeing free market economic problems on the demand side? Well, it's true. When the business cycle dips down into slow gear, liberals stress government action like unemployment benefits, minimum wage increases and spending on infra-structure like roads and bridges; spending to stimulate the demand side, *consumption*. The New Deal and it's critics still remains the World Wrestling Federation equivalent for such demand side arguing. Conservatives, on the other hand, focus on things like incentives and tax cuts and tax breaks for investors and the

ECONOMY AND POLITICS

ventures they finance which in turn produce goods and services, *production*. They remind us that these are the "job- creators." The supply side argument is that we should help investors to do more of what only they can do, increase investment activity.

> **Gloss Note:** One of the most interesting supply-side assertion ever, came from conservative advocate and economist, Arthur Laffer. Professor Laffer contended that tax cuts are so stimulating in sluggish economic times that the increased economic activity that follows significantly lowered tax rates, can actually increase the total tax revenue those taxes bring in to the government. Of course, as we'd expect, this claim, and the data he brought out to demonstrate it, remain controversial politically.[19]

So, notice whether a politician or economist-spokesperson is concerned more about the buyer's side or the seller's side and you can just about bet you have figured out their politics right or left. In any case, economic bad times are when conservative supply-siders and liberal demand-siders get to argue most about what to do.

2. The *"time perspective"* in the politics of economics is a conceptual difference that comes directly out of the discipline of economics. Most conservatives view market economies as self-regulating. Granted, shedding the old and inefficient and bringing in the new, can be traumatic. Whole industries can get closed down and cast out all their employees. But in the long run market economies have delivered the goods (and services) to more and more people and brought increasingly higher standards of living; In the long run, and there precisely is the rub. The ups and downs of private enterprise economies are much more than statistics and numbers. Unemployment, discrimination and poverty are sources of pain and misery. And as Keynes reminded us, in the long run, we are all dead. Why wait? Why prolong the pain? Liberals, think that people experiencing hard times should get the attention of the government. They should be helped right away. But this impatience of liberals has a second target. Free market economies give us all kinds of things we shouldn't want and don't need. And such

things must be confronted on a timely basis. How about fake miracle drugs, or lead based paint pigments, or cigarettes, or maybe the earth is warming, (not bad enough?--then) why not import some slaves from West Africa? For liberals, that same urgency for government action in bad economic times, shows up whenever the markets are presenting us with harmful things like these. Historically, many business ventures have been astonishingly immoral when the focus of their very existence is simply profit for investors. For folks on the left, harm and injustice that originate in the economy are not just economic problems. Harm and injustice are, for them, urgent problems that must be addressed with laws and regulations.

Conservatives are quick to point out that they are not advocates of phony drugs, lead paint, or slavery. They agree that all such need to be actively avoided. But history, and their own personal experiences have convinced them that effective and lasting solutions to problems like these come from the foresight and intelligence of the people buying and selling goods and services in free markets. In a truly competitive setting, information about deceptive and harmful products must come to the attention of the participants sooner or later. Patience is needed. For example it has been persuasively argued that slavery would have ended in the United States without the Civil War as market forces and technology made it obsolete.

So once again when a politician or economist-spokesperson is claiming that some problem requires immediate action to confront injustice or harm, you are probably witnessing a lefty, a person who lacks the patience and confidence to trust market forces.

3. Finally, there is a fundamental difference in basic beliefs about the *"limits of rationality"* that often comes out in the political debate about market economies. Folks on the right tend to place limits on human rationality which people on the left often do not acknowledge. Given the fact that both conservatives and liberals call their economics a science, it might, at first, seem unlikely for them to differ about rationality. However, it is true. First the left: these people take a pretty

conventional scientific stance. Out of the facts of the operations of markets we can generalize. Out of such generalizations we can build models and theories that explain what is going on and even predict future states of affairs. They don't claim to know how to completely eliminate economic downturns but they think that they can reduce their frequency and severity.

The right's perspective tends to be far more wary about this ongoing scientific study of economics. The actual participants in a market economy are continuously reacting to the existing circumstances as they perceive them and thereby altering even the information base upon which the game is being played. The direction that the economy takes is the aggregate result of these countless zillions of responses. Who is so foolish as to think that they can size up these zillions of thoughts, motives, and perceived needs and lay their hands on the controls to intervene and do good things economically? From the standpoint of this brand of economics the very best that government and its economic advisors can do is not get in the way. This, not getting in the way, consists of two basic principles: First, Let the market economy make the investment decisions about resource allocation (minimal taxing and regulating). And second, make sure that the banking system supplies adequate money but keeps the supply just less than will bring inflation.

Concluding Observations on the Great Economic Divide

We now have dug into one of the two great divides in our politics; the endless debate about how to get the best out of our free market economy. But, with all this history and theory and generalization, I am probably putting you readers to sleep! Before cobwebs form in all of this, I propose that we apply the political distinctions we have just been going through to a specific issue, so that we might better understand how the two sides view things from their sides of this great divide. I have selected climate change, but by this time you might be inclined to skip what I have to say here and pick your own issue to pull to the economic left and right this way.

We can expect that the two sides are going to differ about climate change right out of the starting blocks. First, where do we look to determine whether or not there is global warming and, if it exists, whether or not it is caused by a build-up of human created carbon dioxide?

Those on the right begin with the question of whether there is really a problem right now. It is simple common sense. Free markets address reality's problems. The economy is where you look to find out what's happening. If global warming were a problem, it would show up in economic trends. People would be spending more money and investing resources in solutions. They would spend money and devote resources: 1. because people would be experiencing adverse effects from global warming; 2. Such people and their needs would create demands for solutions that would make investment in the problem, profitable. For most of us, aside from smog, there is little clear (Ooops, a pun) evidence, day to day, that climate change is an immediate cause for concern and action. To the right, the scientific evidence and all the predictions of calamity are just so much Chicken Little, "The sky is falling!" nonsense. You need only common sense to know that the weather varies from year to year, but is about the same as it always was. There may be a problem in the future, but for now, SUVs and coal burning electricity plants are what we've got. If things were to change, we would see demand for interventions in the market place. Self-appointed experts and scientists are not market demand. The Market place is where you look to understand reality. Besides all this, even if there were a fossil-fuel-created-global-warming-problem, US government action could do little about it but to make life more difficult and expensive for Americans, because Asian countries and especially China are the main polluters.

Those on the left tend to view the problem very differently. Polar ice core drillings show that there is much more carbon dioxide in the

ECONOMY AND POLITICS

atmosphere than at any time since animal species were first around. Science is where you look to understand reality. Where do we get the most credible factual information about our world? Science of course, that's just common sense. The scientific climate models behind current explanations of weather extremes and predictions of droughts and rising seas comes from painstaking peer reviewed research. These facts of global warming represent, for them, a mounting problem that is just too big for the free market to tackle all at once. Waiting to act might take us beyond a point of no return at which nothing will save us. They look to government to make the necessary commitment and deploy the vast resources necessary to convert us to a post-fossil-fuel civilization. Those on the left do not think that they can rely on the market place to pull this off because the fossil fuel producing industry that grew up in the last century is made up of some of the largest and most powerful corporations in history. And those giant corporations can be expected to use all means available to them to prolong their prosperous run. Governments throughout the world must ban together to combat this sector of their economies and convert the globe to renewable energy sources.

And so on...

But before we congratulate one another about how well we now understand how the left and right think about economics, I want to point out that both sides are made up of intelligent, striving humans who are always capable of rethinking any issue. As I hope is clear though, they approach the subject with very different assumptions about when and whether there might even be a real problem.

Part III: The Politics of Morality

Chapter 6 Moral Beliefs: Some Background

"The root conviction that underlies [fanaticism]...is that the central questions of human life, individual or social, have one true answer which can be discovered. It must be implemented, and those who have found it are the leaders whose word is law."

Isaiah Berlin(1909-1997)[1]

"What was [his ideology,]... his view of the way things should be"

Laurence O'Donnell[2]

In Part III, we will be taking a much deeper look into political belief, and to do this, we need to start with a more complicated idea of beliefs than the one we normally carry around with us. I know that this might be one of those "where is this going?" moments. I seem to keep wandering off the subject. Politics, issues, government, shouldn't we just stick to politics?" Ok, but since our aim is to get a basic understanding of politics, and basic to that understanding is that people seem to have fundamentally different beliefs that we commonly associate with the left and the right in politics, we need to take a closer look at beliefs generally. More specifically, we have been trying to get focused, not on everybody on the left and the right, but just those less extreme folks who strive to keep things going politically without advocating a lot of repression and bloodshed. Unlike those more extreme politically, these more moderate people on the left and right are committed to dealing with one another within a framework of representative government. But differences in beliefs are central to the way they relate to one another.

Let me take this up from a slightly different perspective. We will be getting into the subject of the deeply held moral beliefs that political partisans bring with them into the political arena. Think about times when you hear a politician say something that makes you upset; makes the hair stand up on the back of their neck. The judgment that she or he is wrong is not likely to be just a political judgment, it is probably a moral judgment as well. And it is the way that moral judgments find their way into our politics that we will be taking up in the next two chapters.

This chapter gets into two preliminaries to this moral dimension in our politics. The first of these preliminaries will consist of an examination of beliefs generally. Beliefs are central to any understanding of politics, but they are really difficult to pin down in other people. Yet, in spite of this difficulty, politics in modern representative government, requires that people act on beliefs that they think they share with others. So we will make a short digression into the realm of beliefs.

The second preliminary is a discussion of the way political beliefs are usually covered in introductory political texts. In these texts, political beliefs are typically referred to as "ideologies." Since our aim is to be able to follow the play, and pass as unremarkable among political activists, we have taken a more unusual approach. While there is nothing inherently wrong about the ideological approach to political beliefs, it is not very helpful for our purposes. Even so, we should all know what commentators are talking about when they talk about ideologies.

Once we've passed through these two preliminaries, we can go on to examine the great divide that dominates the moral landscape that separates the left and right sides of our ongoing political drama. Not to get ahead of myself, but the way I see it, we can think of all this political/moral talk as it swings to the left and right as though it was on a kind of a hinge, a hinge that exists in the basic everyday assumptions people bring into their politics in the first place.

Core Moral Beliefs: (almost) Everybody's Got' em

From the start, I have been taking something for granted with you, dear reader, something that really needs some attention. Representative government places a great weight both on what people believe and on what people believe that others believe. And I have been treating beliefs as though they are simple, objective facts. It is neither that simple, nor is it very objective. Thus it would be a mistake to proceed to the topic of morality in contemporary politics without a fuller appreciation of how complicated and awfully problematical this subject matter— what people believe deeply and what they believe deeply that others believe— really is. This requires that we first step back and consider some of the problems we are confronting. There is quite a bit of ground to cover but I think we can take it in a few short steps. Our subject is core moral beliefs. First some questions: do people we disagree with really have deep moral beliefs? Should we believe them when they tell us what they believe? Then again, how is it that we can get ourselves up for thinking that we actually share such deep beliefs with other people? And how can all this help those, like you, among the politically disinterested, to better understanding the kind of thinking that contemporary political activists seem to be so upset about.

To begin with, let me remind you that making judgments about things is something all of us are doing constantly. You do it all the time; make judgments about whether the movie was funny, or whether the food tastes good. Among all these judgments, some are about ourselves and other people. You think you are, or somebody else is, cool, or clever, or disrespectful, or selfish, or cruel. We cannot seem to resist constantly making all kinds of such evaluations. Among these people-evaluations we do, and of special interest for our subject, are judgments we make about whether people and their actions are good or bad.

Just take a minute to think about it. You and everybody else has this kind of mental activity going on all the time. Our senses give us things to consider and our thinking and emotions give us dispositions about such things all the time (our reactions of true/false, of possible/impossible, of love/hate/shame/pleasure/disgust, etc.). This activity applies equally to ourselves and other people. We never seem to tire of evaluating and judging whether people are being good or bad, just or unjust to one another. It's continuous. It's unavoidable. It's irresistible. And what is more, these evaluations of good and bad are not private individualized activities. They are not private in two ways, in the *sympathetic* sense and the *gossip* sense. They get us sympathetically thinking about how others think and how they should think. In addition we very often share our judgments with others. We share such judgments about good and bad with others all the time. This kind of activity is the very essence of what we refer to as gossip.

To illustrate how these judgments fit into our thinking, here's a thought experiment that has been widely studied and discussed by philosophers and social psychologists for over 50 years.

> *You stand on a foot bridge that passes over some trolley tracks. A runaway trolley is approaching, and it will soon pass under the footbridge: clearly its brakes have failed. Further down, on the other side, you spy five people tied to the tracks. The trolley will surely hit them, and they will surely be killed. But next to you on the footbridge stands a very fat man. You quickly realize that you can easily push him off and onto the tracks, and given his great bulk he would surely stop the trolley and save the five. There is not much time. What do you do?*

This is a moral quandary. Is saving the five worth the death of one? But then again, the death of the one means that you will murder a mere bystander. This is only a kind of game with words, or is it? In his fascinating book, *Would You Kill the Fat Man: The Trolley Problem and What your Answer Tells us About Right and Wrong*, David Edmonds recounts the literature and history of the trolley problem and other related moral/ethical dilemmas. He reminds us that "Fat Man" was the name given to the atomic bomb that was dropped on Nagasaki August 9, 1945.[3] The moral arguments in both cases are similar. Does saving many people justify killing fewer but different people? You no doubt have an opinion. Is it: Thou shalt not kill?. Or is it: Do the lesser harm for the greater good? Your opinion is probably part based on reason and, at least part, based on emotions; those feelings that you get in the gut.

We often assume that this good and bad stuff derives from the moral code or a religious doctrine we carry around with us. But it simply doesn't seem to work that way. After all, people who claim not to be at all religious make these judgments about what's good and bad all the time too. An entire academic specialty exists at the intersection of philosophy and psychology which studies the intuitive judgments that people make when confronted with situations involving moral alternatives. There is even a website, "The Moral Sense Test," where hundreds of thousands of people from all over the world have registered their intuitive moral judgments.[4] Not only is such activity apparently wired into our brains, but this activity might be even more emotional than it is rational. Psychologists, have actually hooked people up to MRI scanners and asked them to make moral judgments to see which spots in their brains light up with activity. Surprisingly enough, the brain areas associated with emotional activity are the ones being activated. What's interesting about this for the history of our species, is that the structures in our brains that seem to deal with emotional matters, are believed to predate the development of that gray matter we use for more logical reasoning. There is a whole school of thought and research that asserts that, what we think of as our core beliefs, are really merely rationalizations of our gut feelings and emotions.[5] If this is true, we apparently decide what feels right and wrong morally, and then figure out the more logical moral justifications afterwards.

Consequently, rather than being restricted to those with strong devotion to one or another of the major religions, everybody seems to have some intuitive sense of right and wrong: what I am calling "core beliefs." But wait. Let me qualify that. I should say almost everybody, because there is actually an extremely limited exception. According to mental health pros, there are, among us, a small number of individuals who are completely lacking in the "emotional empathy" essential to such moral beliefs. Take for example, Adam Lanza, the shooter at Sandy Hook elementary school, December 2012. Mental health folks think that people like Adam have little or no conception of the thoughts and feelings of others.[6] As a result, such people lack the concerns the rest of us have when it comes to living with others. This deficiency is of course most troubling when these people take to hurting others. Terms like amoral, sociopathic, and anti-social personality disorder are applied to these kinds of folks, who unfortunately are often given the benefit of the doubt, and get labeled or diagnosed only after they do great harm.[7]

To quickly summarize: except for a few psychotics, everybody makes judgments about good and bad in ourselves and in the behaviors and the imagined thoughts of others. We do this all the time. And there is pretty clearly an emotional charge to these kinds of judgments, which might even come to us prior to our reasoning about them. Having said this, if you are either one of those clinically challenged few, or one of those folks who believe that anybody who disagrees with you about what's good and bad is stupid, evil, or both, what follows will not make much sense. There are moral standards in play in each of us, all the time. We all live with core beliefs. And, of course, our concern here is with how these core beliefs are brought into our politics.

THE POLITICS OF MORALITY

Core Beliefs: The Beliefs of Others are Ultimately Unknowable

So everybody's got core beliefs. So far, so good, but consider this sad fact. These core beliefs are not concrete things. They are in no way directly observable. While we know from our own experience that such core beliefs influence our own behavior, we can never really get beyond the single case "me" and truly verify the core beliefs of even a single other person. The best we can do is rely on the skimpy evidence, of listening to what they say and watching what they do. And, as we will soon see, what makes things worse, is that this outside observer strategy is plagued by a number of difficulties. In the final analysis, it becomes clear that even torture does not reliably yield the true beliefs of those who would not want us to know them.

Let me offer an example to emphasize how shaky these kinds of assumptions about others beliefs can be. We come across public opinion polls almost daily. They tell us things like that Republicans are quite a bit happier than Democrats[8], or that 15% of people world-wide believe that the world will end during their lifetimes.[9] I want to focus on the example of religion for a moment. Religion is, for most people, undeniably identified with their core beliefs. But religious beliefs are also beliefs that people are convinced that they share with others. It certainly, might be tied into their political beliefs and besides, a lot of survey research has been done about religious beliefs, let's take a look at what polling can tell us. In 2009 Gallup researchers asked people in146 countries, "Is religion important in your daily life?" This seems straight-forward enough. Among the reported results, 65% of Americans said yes, compared to 16% of Estonians, 26.5 % of the Brits., and 98% of Egyptians.[10] While ours is not the most or the least religious country in the survey, these results show what has been persistently revealed to pollsters: that a clear majority of Americans acknowledge the importance of religion in their lives. But what does this mean? What does survey data like this tell us about what people actually believe, how this affects them, and those around them? When somebody says something to a survey interviewer, we have no way whatsoever to verify it. In fact, there are lots of times when we suspect that people make statements about what they believe, and they are not even being honest with themselves.

Sticking with this example, we can logically peel off a number of categories of less-than-true-believers. Start with the fact that most people will straightforwardly acknowledge that they believe in God. But philosopher, Daniel Dennett, makes some interesting observations about this. He begins by pointing out an important difference between the belief and belief in that belief.[11] Think about it. There are those who take account of the fact that such a belief exists and that others believe it, but do not themselves subscribe. Among these non-believing "believers in belief," we would find:

--People who reason that since they live among a majority who say they believe, it might not be wise to admit that they do not believe. Call them the "go along to get along" people. You don't have to go back centuries and have heretics burning at the stake to agree that this false claim of belief can be a practical personal strategy. After all, you only need to consider the fact that a 2006 study reported that atheists are Americas least trusted minority.[12] Another survey found that 54% of Americans (as compared with only 14% of people in China, for example) say that they do not even think it is possible to be a moral person if you do not believe in God.[13] Why would anybody choose to invite kin, neighbors, and coworkers all to view them with suspicion?

--Next, there are less casual believers in belief. They don't themselves believe, but they, at the same time, acknowledge that a world full of God-fearing people is a better world to live in. So we may have non-believers who think belief is good, so they purposefully promote belief.

--Then there are the nonbelievers who purposely take advantage of the predictability that believers provide for them. Call these the hucksters and con artists of religion. "God will be good to you, if you send me money."

THE POLITICS OF MORALITY

By peeling away these go-along-to-get-alongs, promoters, opportunists, cynics and hustlers, we start to get to the folks who may be real believers. But what can we say about the beliefs of those who truly believe? Can we say that they have the same beliefs? Let's focus just on Christians, (though we could take Hindus or Rastafarians). Right away we are confronted with all kinds of sub-sets who claim differences in their beliefs: Russian Orthodox, Roman Catholic, Seventh Day Adventists, the distinctions go on and on. And it doesn't stop there.

Consider all the people who really believe they are Baptists. Believe me, I am not picking on Baptists. For our purposes here, they just represent a lot of folks who appear to share the same deep beliefs. But for the heck of it, I just checked and discovered that there are hundreds, maybe even over a thousand, Baptist churches listed in online directories for the metropolitan area where I happen to be writing this. Many in easy walking distance of one another. For instance, you can leave the bus or park your car and stroll to Baptist congregations at the Freemason, the Shiloh, the Jerusalem, the First Baptist, the First Calvary, the New Calvary, the first Baptist Annex, the Queen Street, or the Garden of Hope. Maybe the reality is that these Baptist don't seem so convinced that their beliefs are quite the same as all the other Baptists. In actual practice at least, they don't get together with each other much at all, and in fact many of them don't even get along very well. Maybe I shouldn't make too much over how Baptists in a given neighborhood congregate. But we've divided and sub-divided and further sub-divided Christian believers, yet even when we get down to a number of people who might swear that their religious beliefs are identical, we have to acknowledge that some of them, perhaps even many might either be mistaken (how can they be sure?), or not be telling the truth (how can we be sure?). So I'm simply saying that when it comes to beliefs that people may or may not share, if we take a closer look, the sharing may not be as great as people claim it to be.

To recap, so far we have it that everybody but a few loonies are guided by core beliefs. But the actual beliefs of others are not really knowable. Using religion as prime examples of core beliefs, even if we could consistently get honest answers, (and we cannot), attempts to lump people together by the beliefs they share, can be pretty tricky. These same cautionary points apply to all kinds of core beliefs. Consider for instance, when people say they believe in "liberty" or "human rights" or "freedom," just what rights and liberties might they have in mind?

> **Gloss Note:** Analytic philosopher, Ludwig Wittgenstein (1889-1951), is said to have really nailed this same point about how limited belief sharing can be. Here is how: Instead of "God", or "liberty" or "freedom" he took a simpler example: Imagine that each one of us has a small box, say a match box with a sliding cover for instance. Inside that box is something that each of us refers to as a "beetle." But none of us are ever allowed to look inside of another person's box. Consequently, everybody knows what a beetle is, however the word "beetle" cannot possibly refer to a particular thing. [14]

In Spite of this, Humans Want, Need, and Have to Believe that they Share Beliefs

Now that the complexities of belief and sharing have been pointed out to the point of beating the proverbial dead horse, it is time to look at the curious flip side of this core belief thing. Actual belief sharing has severe limitations. Of course it does. We all know from personal experience that, even the most intimate and long term relationships are sometimes fraught with mistaken assumptions and misunderstandings about core beliefs. Funny thing though, when it comes to how we think about it—and how we navigate our way through our days--all of these reservations, all this skepticism, seems to fly out the window. Amazingly, we somehow manage to convince ourselves and keep right on assuming that we fundamentally share and agree with the core beliefs of some people and fundamentally disagree with the core beliefs of others. Judging from the forgoing, this might seem irrational, a mental flaw, a weakness, that's bound to get us in big trouble.

On the contrary, this ability to stubbornly ignore all these uncertainties and subtleties about belief sharing may, in fact be critical to our existence and our survival. Social psychologist Jonathan Haidt suggests that this ability may be essential to our evolutionary success as a species. He points out that, without being able to continuously make assumptions that at least some other humans really have the same beliefs that we do, we could never enter the richly meaningful group life only humans can experience. Thus, our example, religion (and its moral teachings), becomes a kind of glue that allows people to adhere to one another in a uniquely human way. He sees this as nothing less than the evolutionary advantage that humans had, first in their initial survival as a species, and then in their successful efforts to dominate the entire planet.[15] Again take the example of religious beliefs. Religion can give us deep personal meanings about the universe and our lives in it. When we can feel confident that these are the same beliefs that others have, we feel somehow bonded to them. Such bonds are among the most powerful connections we humans can have with one another.

These belief sharing feelings are really special. Animals show emotions; pleasure anger, fear. A bear can get aggressive protecting her cubs. Those fire ants I mentioned can become suicidal warriors when faced with threats to their queen. But we humans can get ourselves together and worked up over things that we just make up out of whole cloth. Forgive the sneaky segue, but I am introducing a particular example that is actually made of fabric. Take for instance, a rectangular piece of cloth with a particular pattern of colors. If it happens to be our flag, it is far more than its presence as a mere physical object with many possible meanings and uses. It is a deeply meaningful object, evoking strong emotions and corresponding assumptions about a whole series of shared beliefs. So far as we can tell, other species cannot use their thoughts and the materials at hand to create this kind of whole other level of shared reality.

Flags are literally emblems for nation states. Ours dependably invokes in each of us what The United States of America means. In order to get us thinking on a more general level, I've been using term "core beliefs," that sense of morality and justice we carry around with us and keep at the ready. When people start assuming that they share such core beliefs, there emerges something that is literally greater than the sum of the beliefs of individuals who participate. Every time somebody uses the word "we" to refer to themselves and others whose core beliefs they assume to be similar, (whether they are talking about two people or 200 million people), they are in fact assuming the existence of a kind of overarching community where certain standards of humanity, morality and justice are shared. It is thus a whole other level of reality.

This process is truly amazing. Throwing caution to the wind, people everywhere cultivate the certainty that they share all kinds of emotionally charged yet quite abstract core beliefs. To emphasize the unique quality of this level of relating to one another, writers have often applied the religious concept of the sacred. In this way of looking at it, the material world, the objects and the creatures we identify and the everyday thoughts we have about them, are the realm they call the profane. Studies of history and anthropology tell us that experience of this sacred level of reality is a universal characteristic of human groups. And it is important to emphasize that it is, in its very nature, an experience of sharing beliefs, a group thing, their "we"ness, their oneness. In sum, the sacred is that "we glue" I mentioned earlier. It bonds people together both rationally and emotionally. It tells us what it means to be one of "us", where we have come from and where we are headed.

I hope that this talk about flags and "we glue" might be a helpful short-hand way of understanding the importance of the way we can be bonded together with others through feelings that we share deep core beliefs. It should be emphasized though that the central character of what we are calling sacred is not to be found in symbols and objects. It exists in the individual feelings; those emotion filled experiences of cohesion with others that accompanies the sense that they all share certain core beliefs. Such feelings of cohesion can be among the strongest and most fulfilling which are available to us humans.

There you have it. Everybody (almost) has deeply held beliefs that they think they share with others. There may be no good reason for them to think that others share these beliefs, but they seem to love to do it anyway. They often do it so intensely and emotionally that they really get caught up in feeling part of various "We" groupings. It is not unusual for such "We's" to be so compelling that they are literally to die for. Notwithstanding this, the truth about what others believe always remains a mystery, and what is more, it is a mystery that can be confounded with intentional lies. So much for beliefs as objective facts.

I have tried to add doses of irony and skepticism to this discussion not merely to have my own fun with it (though it was that). My aim was to demonstrate just how overwhelming our desire to experience belief sharing is. Our physical and mental health necessitates that each of us bond with all kinds of groupings, pushing back on doubts and fears. This is serious business. The political beliefs we will be taking up in the next chapter are only a particular variety of the kinds of core moral beliefs which can have this effect.

Ideology

Before moving on from this look at beliefs I want to remind you that other writers often approach this subject in a very different way. They strictly focus on beliefs about politics and neglect the complexity of how political beliefs relate to perceptions, judgments, core beliefs, belief sharing and such. The result is that they typically end up treating any individual's political beliefs as one or another of a bunch of formal political doctrines that are out there to be considered and either rejected or accepted in total by a person. They do this by relying on the word ideology. But just because I personally don't see it that way, there is no good reason that you should come away from this without a fair understanding of this "ideology" stuff. That being the case, I think it can be helpful for you to at least be familiar with the two main perspectives that this word ideology conjures up. Consequently, we will first consider ideology as a label given to various political doctrines, and after that, I'll try to approach the term the way it is used, often in a critical sense, to describe the subjective experience of extreme believers. While this discussion might not be central to our quest to follow the play by play of politics, the fact that writers and activists are making use of ideological concepts, and using the labels of political doctrines in their name calling, makes it worthwhile for us. Let me stress that neither of these ideological approaches to political beliefs is incorrect or useless, but as I hope you will see, in their way, each of them can oversimplify and thus distort the way the vast majority of people actually believe and act in politics.

As background, the origins of the word ideology takes us back again to France at the time of the Revolution. In that Enlightenment era of limitless, untested, optimistic, theorizing, the term, ideology had its beginning. A student of politics named Destutt de Tracy (1754-1836) used the term as he was proposing a new field of scientific study which would take up ideas, sensations, and their consequences: A science of what ideas are and how they work. In his optimism, de Tracy envisioned a new rational era. Once ideas were understood scientifically, we would be completely free of prejudice and fractious political argument.[16]

De Tracy's belief that we might end political argument by studying ideas scientifically, or studying them by any method, must seem kind of ridiculous. Well you are entitled to that opinion but new de Tracy types still surface from time to time to announce that we are nearing the end of our age old political differences. Two such cases in the past half century are Daniel Bell, who in 1958, and Francis Fukuyama, in 1992. Each proclaimed that an end of all substantive political argument was about to arrive. Note their timing, Bell just predated the politically divisive and turbulent 1960s and Fukuyama somehow missed both the rabid polarization of US politics in the 1990s and the rise of Al Qaeda and Isis and their plans for our total destruction.

Now for the two common uses of the term ideology: 1. a way of classifying political ideas in a formalized/scientific way, and 2. a way of classifying political ideas that you disagree, as the extreme, simplistic-hogwash-beliefs of idiots.

Ideology, Comprehensive Political Doctrines

Political scientists and other commentators apply the term ideology to any coherent system of political beliefs and principles that presents a comprehensive explanation of the shortcomings of current government and envision a political program which would bring things to where they should rightly be. The quote from Lawrence O'Donnell at the beginning of this chapter is consistent with this use of the term. As I took it, though he asked about a person's view of the way things should be, it is just as if he'd asked, "What was his ideology?" Many writers who approach ideology with this way of thinking have cataloged, labeled, and defined a number of distinct systems of political ideas. Conveniently for us, they almost always tack the letters "ism" on the end of the names that they give these doctrines. If you are interested in finding out about the doctrines of fascism or feminism, or fabianism, we now know that we have little helpers like Google, and Yahoo, to help us get into them. But I am going to take exception to this ideological doctrine approach to political beliefs. Here's why.

Besides all the qualifications we have gone over about how hard it is to know what people actually believe, I would argue that it is nonsense to pretend that actual human partisans, apart from maybe a handful of political philosophers, truly live and act in terms of a comprehensive, coherent and complete political ideology. We humans tend to live with contradictions in our beliefs and between those beliefs and our actions.

This is of course not only true for political beliefs but for deeply held religious beliefs too. Some of these contradictions we recognize some, not so much. Maybe you noticed how I used qualifying adjectives back when we were going over the left and right positions on various issues. I tried to avoid even using the words conservatism and liberalism. I said that people on the right or left "tend to" believe such and such, or that I was offering "typical" responses from each side. In just talking about left and right, I was ignoring the immense variation of opinions there are out there so that we could start to understand the differences between left and right ways of thinking.

In order for writers and commentators to come up with such comprehensive, coherent and complete statements of a system of political beliefs, these ideological doctrines have to leave the minutia of issues and forces in the actual arena of ongoing politics and enter the realm of abstraction. So what? you say. To make my point let me introduce you to a German fellow named Max Weber (1864-1920). Weber was very interested in politics and he was convinced that it would be helpful to develop abstract concepts in order to remove very general ideas from the complicated reality of history. But he was clever enough to spot a potential problem when we draw abstract concepts out of the messiness that is reality. He called such abstractions "ideal types" as a way of pointing out that though such abstractions might be useful in an analysis, they purposefully over-simplify the realities of the real world. What is worse, in using these abstract, ideal types, we can sometimes forget that they are not real and go on to make assumptions that are just plain wrong.[17] And removing politics from reality and history is just what we want to avoid.

Just consider a quick example. Take one of these ideological doctrines and use it to try to predict what a person will do. Say we have somebody who we think believes in "Libertarianism," say a congresswoman, (or just a "Libertarian" voter, if you prefer). At issue is a proposed law limiting access to abortions. Is our person going to be for the bill or against it? It should be simple. They just rely on their

Libertarian doctrine manual, (or maybe they have to go to their Libertarian cell phone APP) and the message is clear—"government intervention in the personal lives of citizens is an assault on the liberty of all, and therefore should be opposed." But wait, what about that nagging religious belief she picked up somewhere in the past that says that abortion is never right, and must be aggressively opposed. Then again, what about that high school friend who she admired and respected, and who got pregnant and had the child, and both of them slipped away from her, into grim lives of poverty and government dependence. And don't forget the poll that she just read about that says that her constituents support the bill two to one. But then there is that feminist organization that is warming up to a nice donation for her upcoming reelection campaign. What is her mother going to say about this?…It just goes on, and on, and on.

Maybe ants can live ideologically consistent lives. One might be a soldier ant, another, a nurse for the infants, and neither ever stray from their assigned motivational path in the colony.[18] The point is that, in reality, we always find layer upon layer of details that sometimes conflict and sometimes align among the beliefs of real people. Unless we are novelists and can make the whole thing up, for most of us, we just don't have consistent, dependable ideal type ideologies that we can rely upon to live by. Real life is more complicated and challenging to the beliefs of most of us. I hope that you can appreciate that it is folly to imagine politics as groups of lots of people, masses of people, carrying on while they are sharing whole doctrines of coherent, comprehensive political beliefs, and that these systems of beliefs can be found articulated somewhere in a textbook or at a website. Sure there are exceptional people out there but if you want to observe ideologically consistent lives, the surest place to go is to fiction.

Note that I am not saying that ideologies as political doctrines are altogether useless. They just aren't central to our appreciation of the way politics works. Now let's look at the other main use of the term.

Extremist Ideology: The Gift of Absolute Clarity

The second use of the term ideology focuses more on the believers than on their beliefs. They can be smart or they can be the opposite. In either case they fit the label ideologue. Getting back to our guy, de Tracy, by the time that the French Revolution had run its course, the term ideology got picked up by Napoleon and his supporters, as a label of ridicule they applied the to obviously confused thinking of those who opposed the Emperor. The next major use of the term also had this negative connotation. Karl Marx and Fredrick Engels appropriated the term to criticize German writers on the left who they thought were misguided. The critical connotation has stuck. Following this tradition, don't be surprised if you come across the term ideology being used to characterize the way people think about political matters in extremist and simplistic ways. In contrast with the comparative political doctrine use of the term, I'd suggest that an understanding of extremist ideological beliefs can be useful if only because you are likely to actually encounter people who seem to believe this way as you mingle with partisans on either the right or the left.

Let's begin our look at this use of the term ideology in this way, with a question. Ever wish that you were really a whole lot smarter? Not just better at crossword puzzles and math, or video games, but really super-smart, able to effortlessly make sense of the complicated chaos that life often seems to present to us. I'm not talking about merely understanding things well enough to successfully get through your days. I am talking about the kind of clarity that recognizes the underlying cause of all of this world's problems, combined with the kind of self-assurance that comes from knowing just what to do about it. What if it all made perfect sense? What if you could clearly see just what makes things tick?

Now you know that there are really people who are like that. Problem is that for every one of the few true geniuses who possess the ability to come up with elegant simplifications that increase our understanding, there are legions of zealots and crackpots who live and thrive on a

THE POLITICS OF MORALITY

whole range of simplistic theories that make sense of almost everything for them. When used in this way ideologies are political world views which suffer from three shortcomings. Namely:

- They depict events in the context of an extremely simple system of causation; we can call it a blame game

- They are closed systems; all-inclusive, not just limited to one or a few aspects of government or society.

- They make use of assumptions, and values, as though these were facts

Let's take a closer look at each of these defining characteristics.

1. Simple Blame Game: Some friends of mine attended a high school class reunion. At the end of the night they found themselves in conversation with a former classmate and her husband. They'd been out of touch with the classmate since high school, and they had never met the husband before. As the talk continued, my friends spoke less and less as the other couple launched into a long-winded analysis of the history of the Western world, concentrating on the 20th Century and especially the two world wars. The detailed brief my friends were presented with was that WWI and WWII were simply the latest catastrophes civilization has suffered at the hands of an evil group among us, and that evil group is the homosexuals. Think of it. gay people were actually around. Those great wars did actually happen. Through a deep and rich series of detailed explanations my friends were enlightened with the theory that if homosexuals had not exercised their awful power in world history, those horrible wars would never have taken place. Who'd have thought?.

My friends had gotten an excellent instance of that simplicity which is characteristic of what I mean by extremist ideologies. As this example illustrates, ideologies play a fundamental blame game. They chart a giant melodramatic struggle between us, the good and mostly naive folks and those bad (evil, demonic, etc.) folks who have victimized us.

Beliefs like these don't have to be intellectually rigorous or theoretically elegant to gain adherents. What they need more is to be simple and emotionally satisfying ways of understanding. This example is a particularly apt one as concerns how emotionally satisfying it might be to aggregate all sorts of things with a single cause. Lots of people have hang-ups about sexual matters and lots of them are on the lookout for ways to adjust. Blaming the two world wars on people with particular sexual preferences may seem both absurd and dangerous, but for the couple in this story, it was just simple and satisfying. It worked for them. What is more, I hardly have to call attention to the point that verifiable fact takes a back seat in this simplicity. The beauty of the simplicity is in how it brings a kind of clarity to gigantic quantities of otherwise complex and confusing information.

Extremist ideologies bring an otherwise chaotic reality into sharp focus; give it clear meaning, and give us as potential believers the feeling that actions, and especially our own actions, can be meaningful and purposeful in the struggle against those who are at fault for our plight. However, to become at all popular, such a system of beliefs must make sense, and bring similar clarity to large numbers of people. To state it differently, extremist ideologies simplify by refracting all reality against one or at most a very limited number of factors. In effect, they assert that it is only complicated before you realize that everything is connected it's all connected.

2. Closed Systems: By closed and all-inclusive I mean that extremist tend to have a way of explaining almost anything that comes along. Whether it is a recession, a sex scandal, harsh words from a foreign leader, a crime wave, a terrorist incident, or the infant mortality rate, the extremist ideologies that are popular at a given time will offer a thorough explanation of the causes, the implications and the "what is to be done. Nothing that happens escapes explanations from them for long.

It is almost like that bumper sticker that says, "Shit Happens," If you live by the wisdom of its slogan, whatever happens you can just say,

"See, what did I tell you." With actual extreme ideologies their advocates spend a lot of time and effort jamming new events and facts into their simple casual framework. And if something just will not fit, they can always discredit it or ignore it. Let me explain. First why do we think of facts as true statements? Consider statements like, when you buy a dozen eggs, you get twelve. Or the incidence of lung cancer is higher among people who have worked with asbestos. Or grass appears to be green to animals with cone cells on the retinas of their eyeballs. Or the population of the United States is now well over 300 million. In each of these cases, we consider the statement a fact because you can bring information up which will support or demonstrate its validity. We depend on such verifiable facts in everything we do. But extreme ideologies offer us a way to get around such demonstrated facts by denying the information that supports them. One of the main reasons for this is because one of the critical tenants of many of these perspectives is that where the true facts are concerned, most conventional sources of information are not to be trusted. This denial of the veracity blankets most government officials, most politicians, most so-called experts, and most media outlets as information sources. For the adherents of extreme ideologies, only very selected sources are believed to be truthful, and have credibility. For example, the Holocaust denying beliefs of many anti-Jewish extremists have had to cordon off mountains of substantial historical documentation and discredit its sources.

3. Assumptions become Facts: This brings us to the third feature of these extreme ideologies. Beyond the realm of demonstrated facts, we of course have beliefs that cannot be demonstrated to be true or false, but these perspectives make use of such assumptions as though they were facts. The example of confusing assumptions with facts that comes to mind, illustrates the point even though it may not come out of extreme ideology. Several years ago, I sat on a jury in a murder trial. Many days after considering the case, we were dismissed as a hung jury. In the hours and hours of discussions, we jurors got to know each other quite well. All but two of us were for acquittal, but two

maintained that they could never agree with the rest. What was interesting was how both of these jurors came to their judgment. Each of them stated clearly and repeatedly that they simply could not look at the defendant without knowing he was guilty. As one of them put it. "I knew he was guilty when he first walked into the court room." The weak case of the facts, the testimony, the evidence that the rest of us were relying upon was of no importance to these two.

As I have said, most of us confuse assumptions with facts from time to time. But extreme ideologies seem to rely on this all too human tendency. As you will no doubt discover, if you confront one of these kinds of believers, simply pointing out that they are basing their belief on factual error or assumption won't get you anywhere. What they assume to be true is no less true than demonstrated fact.

So much for our short detour into the uses of the term, ideology. In the chapter which follow, we can now get back to finding how differences in moral beliefs feed the contemporary political conflict between the left and the right. In the chapter which follows that we will try shed some light on why these same moral arguments of the right and the left could be working to completely turn off millions and keep them away from contemporary politics.

THE POLITICS OF MORALITY

Chapter 7 The Moral Divide in Contemporary Politics

"If all values are relative, then cannibalism is a matter of taste."

S. Jackson[1]

"Society is produced by our wants, and government by our wickedness…"

Thomas Paine (1737-1809)[2]

"Liberals are people who think that cruelty is the worst thing we do…"

Judith Shklar(1928-1992)[3]

"There are two new generations in this country now that have no morals."

a friend

The contemporary right and left disagree fundamentally on strictly moral grounds about many things. The discussion of beliefs in the preceding chapter should help us prepare for the intensity of that disagreement. The sincere people among the partisans on either side, each side holds core beliefs, and they are convinced that they share these beliefs with others on their side. What is more, each side holds these beliefs as part of their common sense and yet so fundamental, so basic to their humanity, that they consider some of these beliefs to be sacred. At the same time they are convinced that those people on the other side of the political/moral divide must be stopped because they are people who reject those beliefs, and if given the opportunity, those people will desecrate the things they hold sacred, and destroy any influences those beliefs might have in our politics. As an example, this is the state of play right now, as concerns the fact that modern medical technologies have made it quite safe and easy to terminate pregnancies. The moral divide on this issue is perhaps wider than on any other, so vast, in fact that neither side can even begin to comprehend, let alone appreciate, the opposing view as having any moral standing what-so-ever. According to one side's beliefs, the care, commitment, and resources necessary to carry a pregnancy to term and raise a child with even faint hopes of a chance in life do not automatically emerge at the place and time of every conception, and as even the pro-lifers know in their hearts these matters are among the most private and personal concerns a woman confronts in her lifetime. Forcing women to give birth is immoral and inhumane. According to the other side, when we truly focus on the fact humans reproduce sexually and that life; precious human life, begins precisely when an egg is fertilized, and as even the pro-choicers know in their hearts, any subsequent intervention that halts the natural process which follows, constitutes homicide. Abortion is immoral and against human nature.

This is just a single example. The same intensity combined with disbelief about the sincerity, and also the morality of the opposition carries through issue after issue. Was the United Stated justified in its invasion of Iraq in 2003? Will the Affordable Care Act (Obamacare) make American citizens more fit, secure, and productive, or will it sap the moral fiber of the people while it bankrupts the nation? Should undocumented immigrants be deported as criminals or should we assimilate them after screening out the serious criminals among them? A basic understanding of core beliefs, shared beliefs, and the sacred should make it far easier for us to identify with the intensity of the beliefs and commitments of the partisans in their many struggles over the various issues. Even if you, yourself, don't have beliefs that align with either side on an issue, you can understand what's at stake for the partisans. Just because you might wear boxers or a bikini depicting the stars and stripes of the American flag, is no reason that you can't empathize with people whose sense of the sacred has made them supporters of that proposed Constitutional Amendment to protect the flag.

You will recall that I promised to get us right to that place where people's thoughts begin to veer to the right and the left. I called it a tool, a hinge on that gate that swings to open to the right and to the left. This is probably not the not the first time and will probably not be the last somebody tries to offer a simple way of distinguishing left from right. When I was in high school, I was taught that the left wanted to change and reform, and the right wanted to protect the status quo. Maybe you got the same pitch. If this ever did make any sense, it doesn't make any sense now. After all, if activists on the contemporary right had their way, a lot of the status quo would be history. Among their prime targets are the public education system (which dates back to the 19th century), income taxes, (which began with a Constitutional Amendment back in 1913), and early term abortion, (legal since Roe v Wade 1973). At the same time people on the left are just as determined to protect these same elements of the status quo.

What we want is a simple tool to help us navigate through the moral landscape. I am not saying that we are out to discover the one true key to the problems that partisan politics brings us, just an easy way to make sense of the moral confrontation of the partisans, conservative and progressive.

Others who have approached this question, sometimes take the tempting route we'll call reductionism. Generally speaking, reductionists take their analysis of a subject down to a different level of facts and information. Say that someone is interested in plants but insists on talking in terms of bio-chemistry. The reductionists in political writing leave the realm of political issues and beliefs and dig into the psyche for their explanation of political preferences. When we come across this kind of thing, we need to be careful because, when you get right down to it, a lot of these reductionist folks are just using psychological and psychiatric jargon to tell us that people who disagree with them about politics are just some kind of nuts: name-calling, with or without clinical language, is not what we are after.

I say, a lot of these reductionists, but not all of them. George Lakoff, for example, uses psychology to make a more balanced analysis. His approach goes something like this: People tend to have trouble thinking about large scale things like government. To help them out, they model the big things by using metaphors that call to mind stuff that is more familiar and close at hand. In this way the nation and its politics might be understood as a blown up version of the family. And since there are two dominating conceptions of how families should work, there are consequently two dominant visions of how politics should work. In this way of thinking, conservative parenting (governing) is typified by the strict father (leaders). His objective is not necessarily to be loved or even liked, but by maintaining strict discipline he strives to raise self-reliant children (citizens) prepared to make their own way in a dangerous and threatening world. By contrast, progressive parenting (governing) is typified by the nurturing parent(s) (leaders). Think of a loving mom. The objective here is to cloak the children (citizens) in the warmth and support that they need to undertake rewarding relationships and realize their potentials as individuals.[4] While Lackoff's approach is insightful, I am afraid that it doesn't quite hit our mark. It doesn't quite give us what we are after. Our personal beliefs about parenting may align with our politics but wouldn't it be better to stay in the realm of moral beliefs to get to those moral beliefs that surface in our politics?

Another research approach that reduces politics to the psychological level comes from John Hibbing and his associates who have found evidence that folks on the right react more emotionally to potential threats. "Compared with liberals, conservatives tend to register greater physiological responses to such stimuli and also to devote more

THE POLITICS OF MORALITY

psychological resources to them." [5] Hibbing's research seems sound, but it is difficult to avoid the impression that it is labeling conservatives congenital scaredycats. The day may come when psychological profiling gets used to isolate the political opposition, but until now our politics has worked best with reasoned argument in an atmosphere of mutual respect

So instead of climbing into people's heads, perhaps we could simply catalog the right and left positions on various areas of disagreement: affirmative action, Obamacare, the death penalty, food stamps, income taxes, voting regulations, abortion, the United Nations, school prayers, immigration, campaign finance, foreign aid, stop and frisk, benefits for vets, the liberal lock on the media, nuclear proliferation, education policy, farm subsidies, enhanced interrogation, the Second Amendment, homeland security, too big to fail, food stamps, the Dreamers, unions, preemptive war, equal pay, stand your ground, the federal deficit, greenhouse gasses, the institution of marriage, the war on drugs, pornography, clean coal, minimum wage, to name but a few. Then we could try to summarize all of it in a simple phrase. Try it. Maybe you'll get further than me. Besides, if we were to do an exhaustive inventory of all the major moral disagreements in contemporary politics, I seriously doubt that we would be very much further ahead in our ability to predict how the two sides would come down on the next new issue that comes up.

No, what we are after is more straight-forward; we need to get closer to what people might be thinking in that place within their core beliefs. That place where people on the right and left fundamentally and reflexively sort themselves out. Partisans don't have some elaborate philosophical matrix they keep going over in their heads all the time. For them it is just simple common sense; common sense and not much more. It is that same common sense that people seek and find at hundreds of politically slanted websites. It is that same common sense that some can plainly hear when conservative, Rush Limbaugh talks to them. It is the same common sense that some others can plainly hear when progressive, Rachel Maddow talks to them.

At first, any attempt to discover the differences between what is common sense to partisans on the right and those on the left doesn't seem to give us much to go on. Unfortunately, when people talk in terms of common sense, we are often left with shallow, ambiguous statements, for example, statements like, "That's the way people are," or how about "Boys will be boys?" As we gathered from o'l Ludwig Wittgenstein in the previous chapter, these are a lot like statements about the beetles people have in those little boxes they carry around. What we need to do is open those boxes a bit. After all when somebody says, "That's the way people are." Their words stand for no less than an implied theory, of morality. What we need is to dig into people's common sense so that the underlying morality of their politics is revealed. If this sounds like a tall order for a primer, it is really not. Political writers and philosophers have been digging into this stuff for millennia. Remember, we are not out to discover some kind of moral/political secret of the ages. We are simply looking for a tool that helps us understand the politics that is going on around us.

To be worth-while for us, this tool, this hinge, has to be a clear and straight-forward way to make sense of the political debate. There must be a difference in point of view that pretty much exists for everybody; a fundamental difference in the way people think of themselves and the way they think of all human beings existing within the sweep of history.

Of course I wouldn't have brought this up if I didn't think I could present something you'll be able to use. I do think that there is such a simple point of view difference that comes from what people are thinking when they say things like, "That's the way people are." It works like this. While everybody recognizes that they live amidst history and change, when some of these people think and talk about "the way people are," they look at the world and see one thing that remains: HUMAN NATURE IS UNCHANGING. For these people, there is a permanence in human nature. Human life, for these people, is, and always has been, a continuous playing out of the same drama, where a constant, unchanging set of human appetites, is confronted by the constant, unchanging gifts of human thought and reason. Sometimes things get better. Sometimes things get worse. But the same ageless drama goes on and on.

By contrast, when others think about "the way people are," they see an entirely different human drama. For these people it is a grand drama of universal change, a drama in which human nature itself is changing, and is changing for the better. For these people, history is, and always has been, a human confrontation with a succession of transformative challenges and changes. When the challenges are successfully confronted, there is HUMAN PROGRESS: We, as humans, have actually been getting better at being human. We improve and the world becomes a better place. The good in the world can increase.

There are a couple of things about these two common sense perspectives we can notice right off. First, they both exist in the realm of pure assumption and speculation. They are equally immune to anything even remotely close to being provable. I recommend them not as the basis of some kind of politics litmus test for whose right and whose wrong politically, but as a good and practical tool for you to use in understanding the arguments and passions of contemporary politics. Second, you should notice that there is not so much as a hint of moral judgment or condemnation in these two formulations. They are themselves morally neutral, just two different ways of seeing "the way the world works;" "the way people are." Nevertheless, I think that I can convince you that this is a really good place to look if we want to see where the left and the right part company. Folks on each side could easily understand these simple assumptions even when they do not agree with one another. It is only further on that confusion sets in and understanding gives way. And, it is even further on they stop speaking and settle into suspicion and even hate.

Back in Part II we dabbled in some economics. I hope you are ready now to dabble in some philosophy. In the rest of this chapter I will first try to put more flesh on these bare bones I've just laid in front of you. Then, as the discussion proceeds, there will be opportunities to compare this formulation with some alternative ways that writers have tried to explain the left/right divide. Now, for a more detailed examination.

A Conservative View: Natural Law

The right swing of our gate hinge finds it's philosophical home in a tradition of writing called "Natural Law." Note that I am not saying that all the politically partisan folks on the right are up on the subject of this Natural Law stuff. What I mean is that Natural Law theory can help us understand their common sense way of thinking. This is because their way of thinking has a whole lot of consistency with this philosophical tradition. This may be more than a coincidence because Natural Law has figured into some major religious traditions.

Natural Law has a massive literature with many subtleties and differences of opinion. However, we do not need the subtleties and the differences to understand how Natural fits with the common sense thinking of folks on the right. Consequently, we will set our sights at achieving a general sense of this concept as it was developed by the ancients. To do this we go first to the ancient Greeks and get to know a couple of their conceptual tools: "essentialism," and "teleology." We will then spend a few moments with some early Christian writings. With this as background you should be prepared to take on Natural Law as it appears in the contemporary writings of prominent political conservative theorists and see how it mirrors the common sense way of thinking that folks on the right employ when they think about life, their fellow humans and their politics.

THE POLITICS OF MORALITY

Let's begin with the ancient Greeks. I said that the conservative view holds that human nature is constant. The ancient Greeks tended to think of it that way as well. In fact as part of their discipline of metaphysics when they set out to understand things in the world, they tried to discern the definitional characteristics of each thing; that essence that makes a thing what it is and not something else. In this way they contemplated, what is the essence of a fish, a brick, a man? We refer to this way of thinking about things as "essentialism." Such contemplations may be careful speculations, but they are nothing more than assumptions that they, and we, might use in hopes that this will help us later on in our thinking. With their essentialism, these early philosophers were saying that things have unchanging essences which can be known and understood.

These Greeks built on their essentialism by paring it with a second kind of assumption, "teleology." By teleology they asserted that things are naturally designed for a purpose, an end, and all other things being equal, they are disposed to realize or advance toward that end.[6] When applied to any object, these assumptions, essentialism and teleology encourage us to consider an object's unique nature and its end; the purpose of its existence. Applying these ideas to the subject of humans, what do essentialism and teleology do for us. The task of the philosopher was to discover the true nature, and the end to which man is destined. Beginning with two seemingly simple assumptions we arrive at quite a task to contemplate, no?

Maybe you think that I should have put this essentialism and teleology into one of those Gloss Notes so you could skip over it. Let me defend what I am doing. That these assumptions have a long philosophic past is something we need to acknowledge. It is equally important to realize that you don't have to be a long-dead philosopher to make the statement that humans have a true unchanging essence and that true essence has its rightful destiny. You may agree with this way of thinking about things or not, but it is definitely a view that has lots of contemporary adherents. In any case, this view of human nature and its ends is our first step in getting to understand Natural Law, the position of our metaphorical hinge, when people on the right go through that left/right swinging gate I spoke about.

Building on essentialism and teleology Natural Law is a tradition in thinking about morality: right, wrong, good, and bad. It asserts that we humans, as part of our essences, are pre-programmed to reach our end, our destiny. In particular, by our very natures, we have some understanding and a striving for what is good and just. It's part of our essence; our hard wiring. It should be easy to see that the religious traditions that hold to Natural Law think of these essential moral characteristics as being created in all of us by God. But the Greeks we inherited these ideas from were not particularly religious by modern standards. Religious or not, the point to remember is that this moral code is essential to each of us as humans, and it is ageless and timeless. To put it in terms of the vast scope of history, this view considers humans walking around today as having the same moral code built in to their heads as people did in ancient times. Just as nature follows regularities that we refer to as laws of nature, when we talk about Natural Law, we are talking about a subset of these laws of nature that has always been true of us as a consequence of our powers of human reason. Now let me try to amplify two of the most important characteristics of this essential human characteristic: 1. That they are capabilities unique to us humans, and 2. As human law, Natural Law is law of a unique variety.

• A Uniquely Human Capability: To get at the exclusively human quality of Natural Law, it might be helpful to think of the difference between other seemingly intelligent animals and humans for a minute. Take another mammal species like deer or dolphins. Deer and dolphins behave as though they must be aware of their needs as animals; their hunger, their need to avoid pain, their need to mate and leave successful offspring. Humans have a similar awareness of their animal needs. But in addition our awareness includes the power of reason, which takes human awareness much further in important ways. As a consequence of our ability to reason, we have the capability of recognizing what's good and what's bad for us all. Other species show no evidence of this capability.

• Unique Kind of Law: Besides being a uniquely human capability, this knowledge of an overall humanness allows us to recognize a special subset of the laws of nature that apply specifically to our species. These are not like the written laws, (rules that governments invent and impose on us). Nor are they the same as other kinds of regularities we humans have discovered in nature, (i.e. science, for example has discovered that, at sea level water will always boil at 212 degrees Fahrenheit). As we move ahead a few centuries from the ancient Greek writers, we can get a vivid example of this special variety of human law. The Christian New Testament writer, Paul, was among the first writers in that religious tradition to appeal to the unique character of Natural Law. While considering good moral conduct and discussing such conduct among non-Jews in particular, he asserts that, "They can point to the substance of the Law engraved on their hearts — they can call a witness, that is, their own conscience"[7] Given the ethnic/religious diversity of the first century C.E., for Paul, the non-Jews he is referring to were most likely pagans and other peoples with very little in the way of written laws or similar religious rules. Yet they have laws, "engraved on their hearts!" Paul's notion of conscience; the better angels of our nature, remains with us even today. Who isn't familiar with that little Disney character with a halo that sits on our shoulder and whispers to us all the time. But what do our hearts, and more broadly, what does reason tell us humans to do?

A formidable attempt to answer this question surfaces in the writings of an early Catholic philosopher, Thomas Aquinas. His formulation, written at about 1270 is representative of much subsequent Natural Law theorizing both within religious traditions and outside of them. Accordingly, it is worth our while to see what Aquinas had to say. Contemplating the way people everywhere acted and treated one another, Aquinas inferred that they seemed to behave most of the time, according to a simple set of principles or rules which they evidently found reasonable. As testimony to his intellect and the timelessness of these principles, his assessment remains quite reasonable even today. To begin with people everywhere seem to recognize things like greed, lust, envy, hate and a whole bunch of other human tendencies as obviously bad. He noticed that people try to keep these bad behaviors under control, and instead, do good. Furthermore, they evidence a strong desire for preservation, not only of themselves, but of others as well and even the human species as a whole. He also pointed out that people everywhere seek truth and knowledge, and they seem to strive to get along with one another by living in organized social relationships.[8]

Sure, there are other ways it has been stated and there are some disagreements as to what the essence of Natural Law might be, but Aquinas's formulation still remains reasonably authoritative and persuasive today. One corollary to the Natural Law way of thinking should be mentioned. During the 17th and 18th centuries as world exploration brought news of all kinds of hunter/gather and subsistence agricultural peoples the ageless constancy of Natural Law got challenged a bit. Several writers used this early anthropological reporting to speculate that Western civilization must have been predated by a time when all people lived a less human, beast-like existence in what these writers came to call "the state of nature." These writers emphasized this world as a violent place where fear of being killed and self-defense were first and foremost among natural human concerns. An example of these writers is Thomas Hobbes, whose path we crossed earlier, with his, "solitary, poor, nasty, brutish, and short," description of this supposed pre-historical time. Along with this corollary many of these writers reflected the politics of their time by preferring to use the term Natural Right instead of Natural Law. By doing this they took the focus away from laws and duties consistent with human nature, and instead emphasized the natural rights individuals had to defend themselves and their property.[9]

THE POLITICS OF MORALITY

> **Gloss Note:** John Locke (1632-1704) probably took this farther than others. Grounding his argument in biblical references, Locke claimed that governments were empowered mainly to protect life, liberty, and property. Property, in turn, consisted of the wealth and possessions that people acquired and used in "pursuit of their happiness." Sound familiar? Yes, Locke is obviously the writer who Thomas Jefferson cribbed it from when he drafted our Declaration of Independence. And there is more, John Locke also authored another of the Declaration's bold assertions: that a government that does not protect life, liberty and property is illegitimate. [10]

I hope that you will find this ancient history and background helpful. I didn't go through it because I thought you'd find it fascinating. Nor do I want to give the impression that it has somehow been brought together into a cohesive set of axioms that all partisans on the right subscribe to. All I am claiming is that the common sense perspective that a whole lot of people have; their reflexive way of sizing things up and making moral judgments, assumes that there is a kind of constant, changeless quality to human nature. While people don't have to read philosophy and religious texts to have this perspective, philosophers and religious writers have, for millennia, been elaborating a substantial foundation for this way of thinking.

Natural Law represents a series of basic principles to use for understanding life and living together, principles that our God, and/or our human reasoning, have revealed to us. Furthermore, Natural Law is widely viewed as no less than the principles that comprise the true and most fundamental basis for all just governing.[11] Consequently, the principles of Natural Law can be appealed to as standards that take precedence over any other laws that might be promulgated by governments of any kind. Again, we need only go to very first paragraph of the Declaration of Independence to see this assertion in action. The signers declared there that they were rejecting government by the British by appealing to "the separate and equal station to which the Laws of Nature and of Nature's God entitle them." For them

Natural Law simply trumped any and all contradictory laws passed by Parliament.

To summarize, there are three points to keep in mind: 1. Both the common sense and the theorizing of the Natural Law perspective begin with improvable assumptions, the assumptions we identified with essentialism and teleology. 2. In the conflict between good and bad that goes on in each of us, the bad can sometimes become completely dominate. As a result there are truly evil people in this world and so we must be on our guards. 3. Both the common sense and the more elaborate theorizing about Natural Law, (and later Natural Rights) present human nature as absolute and unchanging. Historically I guess this brings us up to nearly 1800. This is about the time that we start to see our hinge twisting so that the gate swings open to the left. So the time has come to examine the common sense perspectives of contemporary partisans on the left. As we will see, things operate the same way on the left as they do on the right. Starting with unprovable assumptions, the left's perspectives are the subject of a whole school of philosophical and religious writing. However, once again, for most adherents, it is nothing more or less than unexamined, reflexive, common sense. And once we are up to speed on this moral bases for the left, we will be in a position to see how these two perspectives function in contemporary politics.

> **Gloss Note**: I don't want to leave you with the impression that this conception of Natural Law is somehow inexorably a part of the core beliefs of all Christians, or for that matter all religious people. Many variations of religious belief differ radically from this view of Natural Law. Just as an example, at a great many popular sects that were flourishing in America and England at the time of our War of Independence, held to the radical belief that the era of morale law, as recorded in the Old Testament, and all other laws, had ended with Jesus, and that thereafter faith was all that mattered.[12]

THE POLITICS OF MORALITY

A Progressive View: Grand March of History

As our hinge opens to the left, it is all about Progress. Let's begin our look at ideas about Progress by considering its absence: no progress. There are times when nothing seems to change. A writer on diverse topics, John Lanchester, sees the civilization of ancient Egypt as just such a time and place. The entire civilization was dependent on the annual flooding of the Nile River. Depending on the extent of the annual flood there was either starvation, or plenty. In other years the floods brought massive destruction. But through feast and famine their political situation remained unchanged. The thing is, their religious elite had figured out how to exercise effective control over the people, because they had secretly developed techniques that could predict each year's Nile flooding in advance. They could literally tell the future. Better stay in good with the priests… No progress for these folks. Not very much changed there as the elites went on ruling this way for thousands of years.[13] With the Greeks we escape from a static world into one that slowly changes. But for them, Natural Law seemed just fine. What we might see as change they viewed phases in an endless cycle of rise followed by decline, followed by rise followed by decline…Things got better things got worse. Wars were fought. Governments cycled through aristocracy, democracy, and tyranny, and back. After the rise and fall of the Roman empire historians even have a name, "the Dark Ages," those 1000 or so years when a lot of them don't see very much changing.

It took a really different era to create a backdrop for the idea of historical Progress. We refer to this era of tumulus change as the European Enlightenment. What set things going were the intellectual advances in physics and astronomy in the 1600s and 1700s that we identify with Galileo, Copernicus, and Newton. This revolutionary knowledge had resulted from a series of stark discoveries about the universe that we have come to appreciate as that powerful way of knowing we call science. By ignoring the teachings of the past and focusing on careful observation and precise logical reasoning, new verifiable knowledge emerged. This period also brought with it major innovations, in politics, art, commerce, theology, engineering, economics, warfare, publishing, agriculture and just about every other area of human activity. Dramatic changes were happening all around.

Advances in navigation and ship-building had brought with them contacts with diverse habitats world-wide. The world that Europeans related to was expanding rapidly with all the new discoveries. By the late 1700s such discoveries had created an immense store of new facts about the diversity in animal and plant life, peoples and cultures. These were heady times. The human possibilities seemed all but limitless. In addition to abundant new facts about the world, and the new scientific observation and reasoning brought a remarkable new ingredient into the picture: optimism. To many it was clear that in spite of setbacks from time to time, human existence had been getting better and better. Science and the changes it had brought would likely build upon each other. This was a promise of more of the same for the future. Progress seemed to be a new fact of life. Let me stress that this new perspective, like Natural Law, can only be an assumption. It requires that we assume things have been and will continue to be changing for the better. Observable change is not necessarily observable progress. Right?

While the modern idea of Progress doesn't have the long history that Natural Law has, it is no less influential. Central to this human Progress perspective is what has been called the universal emancipation of humanity.[14] The believers in Progress, from the beginning, saw in the sweep of history, as a unidirectional expansion of human equality and freedom. As scientific and economic developments run their course, things can get better materially for large numbers of people. However, the very concept of what it means to be human is expanding along the way as well. To make this idea of emancipation clearer, I'll emphasize two of its main components: 1. The distinction between traditional and modern societies and, 2. What can be called the expansion of "we."

THE POLITICS OF MORALITY

Traditional vs. Modern: With the distinction between traditional and modern societies believers in historical Progress perform a bit of a trick on the Natural Law conservatives. But that's OK, because the Natural Law folks have already dismissed them for being hopelessly naïve about the human nature's capacity for evil and for their shallow optimism to boot. Ignoring these criticisms, the historical Progress folks put the conservatives in their historical place, so to speak. Let me elaborate. In the historic sweep of human Progress that they perceive, a good part of the universal emancipation they perceive is a rejection and casting aside in modern times of all kinds of restrictive and oppressive traditions. Many of the traditions and beliefs that the conservatives find most consistent with the unchanging nature of humans, the progressives see as disproved myths and superstitions of a passing phase of history. They label this passing phase, "traditional," or "pre-modern."

Here is how the argument goes: Pre-modern perspectives have dominated the human communities throughout most of history, and they still prevail over most of the world's populations. The characteristic feature of pre-modern thinking is that it encourages (and also coerces) people in any given community, to make sense of things by interpreting their lives and the people and events in them in terms of a set of established traditional beliefs. However, it is important to note that the term traditional as used here, isn't intended to refer to just anything that happened a lot in the past. We are talking about those traditions which are taught and enforced by those who have power and authority. Power and authority in turn are exercised in two different ways. Those who can enforce their will with power, use coercion and threats. Those who enforce their will by authority only, exercise control through their control of what the community considers sacred. In most traditional entities with any stability, those with the power and those with authority, (the political and religious authorities, in other words) support one another. These traditional authorities appeal to a particular set of core beliefs, and discourage any questioning of these beliefs. What is more, they insist upon behavior consistent with those core beliefs. These beliefs are said to be central to the knowledge and teachings which define the community. Access to positions of authority is most often such a slow and deliberate process, that only older folks, the elders occupy these positions. The core beliefs often reside in sacred lore and written texts which are in turn in the exclusive custody of these elders.

> **Gloss Note**: The controversial concept of Sharia Law actually presents a great example of this idea of traditional authority. Understood in simplest terms, under strictest Sharia Law the government has no legislative body. New laws are unnecessary since governance relies only on courts where religious elders apply the precedent found in the sacred texts and past rulings. It is thus no accident that some of the most radical advocates of Sharia present themselves as inerrant authorities on the Koran often pursuing their claims with even violent means. What gets scary is precedents like the one that tells the elders that since virgins cannot be executed, young girls sentenced to death must first be raped. It is ironic to imagine a switch of sacred texts and being governed by elders claiming inerrant understanding of the Bible. Lots of our Sharia-fearers might feel quite cozy in some small American town headed up exclusively by a government based on interpretations of the Bible by their elders.

So according to the Progressives, Natural Law conservatives are caught up in a nostalgia for traditional society, either because they are under the control of those with traditional authority or because they are advantaged by those traditional arrangements.

They contrast this pre-modern perspective with modernity. Authority in modern society is based not on tradition but on science and the pragmatic facts that it has brought with it. What is true and what is not true can is not a matter of tradition. Most everything we see, hear, taste and touch, and smell in the modern world is probably created or at least substantially modified by the application of scientific knowledge.

So where pre-modern thinking is synonymous with tradition, modern thinking is synonymous with the progress science and innovation has brought. At the center modernity is the principle that real knowledge requires objective proof. By comparison pre-modern beliefs do not require objective proof. They are accepted on the basis of the fact that they have been asserted for a long time. They rely on the authority of tradition and/or the authority of the powerful. The switch from traditional to modern ways of looking at things can be a heady experience, one of casting off superstition and confusion and embracing what seems a far more disciplined and powerful way of thinking. Among other things, modernism has brought us self-governing republics, germ theory, and steel reinforced skyscrapers.

Once again you should note that we are talking about the way some people think about history. It is a way for us to get at how people on the left do their historical thinking. People don't neatly sort themselves out into traditionals and moderns. After all, we actually live in circumstances where pre-modern and modern perspectives coexist. A fair amount of pre-modern thinking persists simply because it is considered unimportant or inappropriate to question it. Many contemporary religious beliefs are good examples. Just because the word of God and his prophets comes to us from the past and cannot be proved by science does not mean that it cannot offer deep and rich understandings to people living today, and give these same people usable guidance for their lives. But in modern times we pick and choose a bit. For example believers in the three Abrahamic religions (Judaism, Christianity, and Islam), popular in the United States, accept tons of scientific facts every time they answer their cell phone or board an airliner, but these same people no longer subscribe to the ancient teachings that adulterers and willful children should be killed or that a man might have as many as 700 wives.[15]

But the key to the perspective of human Progress is the overriding belief that the scientific way of thinking has brought, and continues to bring, tremendous improvements. Furthermore, these improvements go far beyond germ theory, air travel, and cell phones. The idea of human progress goes much farther. This new way of thinking has actually been making us wiser, and more understanding of one another and of how we share our little planet. We are making progress at becoming better at being human.

Expansion of "We" Perhaps the easiest way to understand this universal emancipation idea is to think of it as a series of changes in what people mean when they use words like "we" and "us." Think of these words as a simple way we have of putting boundaries around those who we fully accept as our kind of folks. We understandably push back on those who seem threatening, strange, suspicious, those not to be trusted. The emancipation idea reflects an expanding "us" and a contracting "them:" an ever smaller category consisting of those who might not be quite equal in their humanity and not quite worthy of our trust. Racial and ethnic distinctions limited the expansion of "we" for centuries. During those centuries the expansion of "we" focused on the mutual acceptance of rich and poor. The universal emancipation of the progress-minded, worked on wearing down distinctions of class and status within various countries.

Then in the early 20th century, progressives, especially here in the US heralded the inclusion of some Latinos, Asians and people from Eastern and Southern European countries into the inclusive "we." They called this expanding society, our melting pot. More recently African Americans, and Muslims, have been expanding the Progressive "we," along with folks with other differences in identity like women and people who don't subscribe to majority notions of sexual preference. This expanding emancipation is a source of great emotional satisfaction among Progressives so deeply emotional that it can only be appreciated as sacred belief. The object of this sacred belief is their concept of "humanity." It is the genuinely emotional pleasure of being part of (or glued to, if you prefer our cruder term for sacred bonding) a grander and grander thing. Some Progressives see no logical reason to stop at the limits of the species. They are pulling in research animals, livestock, dogs and cats, and dolphin, and elephants, and frogs, for starters.[16]

While for a large segment of the US population their "we" might very well still be two legged, white and own property, the interesting and varied "we" that is our subject is that of the Progressives, and the emotional attachment that they feel about it, needs to be emphasized. For lack of a better term, think of it as a kind of "comradeship,"(or at one time could have been called "brotherhood").

This idea of comradeship is critical because with it comes the emotional investments of concern, sharing and, mutual obligations. Furthermore, there is evidence this comradeship with an expanding concept of humanity has, for some Progressives, all the qualities of what we have referred to as the sacred. Some Progressives now acknowledge "Humanism" as a kind of religion.[17] However broadly a Progressive individual conceives of his/her "we," that category of people (and other creatures) represent all those one needs to do right by. Yes, you now live in a country where some folks can't sleep at night because they worry not only about young girls missing in the northeast Nigeria, but also about whales in the Western Pacific.

To summarize once again, the universal emancipation that Progressives see in history: 1. Continuously breaks away from here-to-for unquestioned beliefs and ways of the past, by replacing tradition based reasoning with justifications based upon facts and science. 2. By doing this, these folks are becoming aware that the numbers and varieties of individuals deserving our respect, our concern, and fair treatment by everybody, is, and should rightly be, expanding in these modern times. 3. However, as with Natural Law, both the common sense and the theorizing done about this universal emancipation we call Progress, rests on non-provable assumptions.

Implications

These two common sense ways of perceiving that we have now identified as Natural Law and Progress reside within the people around us. Though they may come to the surface only rarely, they influence judgments and actions all the time. However, there is one way in particular that the Natural Law/Progress distinction does surface in arguments from time to time. And for that reason alone, we should address it. Perhaps you have come across it. This is because even though one can have different understandings of just what Natural Law consists of, it is absolute and unchanging. It always has been and always will be with us in the very nature of things. Adherents to a beliefinan unchanging human nature often take considerable comfort in this kind of enduring certainty about right and wrong and express a corresponding uneasiness with a morality that is historically changing. In the extreme, they question the very possibility of a progressive morality. Think of it. How can what is right be something different at different times and different places? How does one distinguish such a situational, relativist morality from pure rationalization—a kind of moral license that could potentially justify anything?

For their part, those on the Progressive side of the argument stake their claims in trends and examples that comprise a sort of learning theory of history. For them, in spite of mistakes and exceptions, we humans have become increasingly less barbaric and more tolerant of one another. We come to the aid of those hit by epidemic and natural disaster. For the most part, we no longer slaughter or enslave those we defeat in war. And both in word and deed we take far more account of human rights than people once did. As has already been mentioned, adherents to the Progressive view of morality take considerable comfort in their sense of the expansion of human understanding and mutual concern.

To put it another way people with the Natural Law point of view, operate with reference to a notion of "we" that is going to be quite a bit more restricted than those who greet their world as a swelling multitude of good and worthy creatures. This is reflected in positions people take on all kinds of issues. How much is it fair to pay in taxes that might ultimately benefit others? Is the death penalty still good and valid institution? Is it good common sense that we should all own and carry

THE POLITICS OF MORALITY

guns? Should contemporary medical technology be used to allow all women to dissociate sexual behavior from childbearing etc. etc?

Perhaps the place that the Natural Law/ Progress difference shows up most clearly is in US foreign policy. Natural Law freely acknowledges the immense and continuing problem of evil in the world. Evil ain't going away, it must be recognized in whatever new form it might take and confronted head-on. By comparison, the human progress perspective actually allows that we are getting wiser in our dealings with one another as humans, with the result that threats from evil peoples can actually be diminishing throughout history. Biologist, David Sloan Wilson gives this idea of progress an evolutionary support. He tells us that, there is such a thing as cultural selection both planned and inadvertent whereby cultures/societies which are successful in competition with other cultures, restrict the survival of certain genes in the population of the unsuccessful opposing cultures. If the successful cultures/societies owe that success to altruism, (their ability to cooperate and coordinate with one another), those altruistic characteristics survive when those without them may find survival more unlikely.[18]

People on the left are much more likely to believe in the power of diplomacy in international relations. The post WWII establishment of the United Nations was in many ways a progressive attempt to create an international institution where diplomacy could prevail and eventually end war. Since the conservative perspective is more concerned with evil in the world, it places far less trust in diplomacy and the UN. Instead, the right recognizes the central importance of military threats and military preparedness in international relations. Because of this, the right favors mutual defense treaties such as the North Atlantic Treaty Organization (NATO) which was established at about the same time. For NATO members, a military attack on one, is supposed to be treated as an attack on all member nations. People on the right are not just talking this threat talk. They are also more likely to see the necessity to attack militarily and expand operations once conflict is happening. Thus we have come to call folks on the right, the "hawks" and those on the left, the "doves."

> **Gloss Note:** This dove and hawk distinction is often brought up by conservatives with two historical references in which the weaknesses of diplomacy are illustrated. The first is *Munich*. In September 1938, British Prime Minister, Neville Chamberlain, met with Hitler and others in Munich, Germany to negotiate over Hitler's claims that a portion of what was then Czechoslovakia should be part of Germany. After Hitler's claims were agreed to, Chamberlain returned to Britain claiming that he's negotiated "Peace with honor...it is peace for our time." Yah right, WWII soon followed. Chamberlain's diplomatic gift to Hitler has even been given a label. Giving in to an enemy prior to a war that is inevitable, is called "Appeasement." The second reference is Yalta. In early 1945 Roosevelt, Churchill, and Stalin met at Yalta in Crimea to arrange for the reestablishment of governments in various war-torn countries. Following this conference, the soviets established dominance over the block of countries in Eastern Europe that became part of the Soviet Union's sphere of control. Yalta is sighted as a huge diplomatic loss throughout the Cold War era that continued until the late 1980s.

With our understanding of this moral gulf between believers in Progress and those who believe Natural Law try to imagine a liberal trying to convince conservatives that we will all do much better once they learn to be more trusting and bring down their fear factor a few notches. Or imagine the conservative trying to convince the liberals that their comfort and optimism about humanity are, at best, only rare and very temporary experiences, and at worse, childish illusions. However it is approached, the task would consist of arguing against common sense: against what they mean when they say "that's the way people are." None of us can make sense of ourselves or our world without our own rendition of "that's the way people are." These Natural Law and Progress assumptions are central to this "that's the way people are" common sense. People carry around their own version with them and use as they cope with their world. It is thus not surprising that the political messages that are tailored to dependable voters play in harmony with one or the other of these two different versions of common sense.

By calling this the moral divide I do not want to suggest that everybody has to pick one of these two alternatives. There are all kinds of alternative ways of conceiving of "that's the way people are." The two we have been considering are simply the ones that seem to be dominating our political right and left at the moment. What is more, it just might be that this very domination plays a large part in turning a lot of folks away from politics

In the next chapter we will explore a popular moral perspective that is not important among our activist political partisans at this time. It is not important because politicians and the folks who help craft their messages to us, systematically avoid appealing to this moral perspective. On the other hand it is important because some politicians and many of the folks who help them craft their messages to us, consider this moral perspective as their own common sense way of thinking about, "that's the way people are." That's right. I am saying that our political world is an argument between traditional and modern ideas, but the people doing the arguing abide in neither of these worlds. For the most part, theirs is what we will call the "postmodern" perspective.

Chapter 8 Beyond the Divide

"We Tell Ourselves Stories in Order to Live"

Joan Didion[1]

"Nihilists! [Expletive] me. I mean, say what you want about the tenets of National Socialism, Dude, at least it's an ethos."

Ethan Coen and Joel Coen[2]

In earlier chapters, when we were trying to understand the perspectives of contemporary voters and other political partisans, we identified and dug into the background of two main points of diversion: 1. An Economic Divide: between unfettered free markets and government assisted/regulated free markets, and, 2. A Moral Divide: between those who see government as part of the dynamics of hope and human progress and those who see it is best when government clings closely to the support of Natural Law. These are the moral and economic perspectives that can help us understand most voters and a lot of the folks who run for office. You may yourself identify with one side or the other between these competing perspectives. It is my guess that the older and the more established you are in your style of living, the more likely you are to identify with one or another of these perspectives. But if you are one of those people for whom this politics stuff is a mixture of the boring with the incomprehensible, I doubt that these political perspectives can have much personal attraction.

Remember my reference to that point about national defense that the generals are forever planning for the last war? For many of you, these mainline political activist perspectives have that same musty last war quality. Yes, that's right, I am saying that our politics is in large part trying to settle arguments about contemporary problems with outdated perspectives from the past. Consequently, in this chapter we will trace the path that brought some among us past the old reliable common sense notions of Enlightenment era moral arguments to arrive at entirely new set of beliefs about how we should perceive our world and its politics.

The set of beliefs I am referring to came out of an intellectual movement in the arts, in philosophy and science, that began to emerge in the late 1800s came to maturity in the latter decades of the 20th Century. This way of thinking has most often been called postmodernism. So as awkward as that label might seem, we had probably better stick with it here. Since postmodernism is kind of hard to pin down for those unfamiliar with it, we will take the time to flesh it out as best we can. There is quite a bit to cover here but I am convinced that it is essential to your understanding of the outdated impression many people get from contemporary politics. I am confident that we can keep it simple. The postmodern perspectives we will be getting into probably span a portion of the American public that includes a huge chunk of the fifty percenters who continually opt out of politics.

Make no mistake, this postmodern stuff has been a radical intellectual shift. With one hundred years plus in the making there are still lots of folks who are not even aware of what it is. If you remember my aversion to textbook definitions and you think you are familiar enough with postmodernism, then by all means push on to the next chapter. For the rest, we will first take a look at several new and sometimes shocking ideas that loosened things up. These precipitating ideas came out of philosophy, science, and even commerce. We also need to recognize several major historical occurrences that contributed to this radical shift. From this we will have the makings of a working understanding of postmodernism. With this understanding we will be prepared for the curious fact that informs the chapter which follows. No need for surprises. That curious fact we will confront is that even though radical, postmodern ideas and techniques permeate every aspect of the thoughts and approaches of contemporary political pros, the messages they craft for potential voters, carefully avoid and censor even a hint of postmodernism, and cling to the time tested perspectives of Natural Law tradition and the modern optimism of Progressive emancipation. But let's not get ahead of ourselves.

The Emergence of Postmodernism

The postmodern way of thinking was not some clear-cut reaction to a single historical event. It was at least 100 years in the making. Nor was it the invention of some clever writer. It arose out of many thoughts and trends. To get beyond a shallow definition and to a practical understanding, we will cover three sources of the postmodern way of thinking, some radical scientific and philosophical ideas that came out, some revolutionary developments that took place in the field of commerce, and in addition, a number of disturbing historical events. Let's now look at each of these.

Challenges from Science and Philosophy

What follows is a description of several of the radical challenges that laid the groundwork for postmodernism. In each case I'll begin with a term or concept that can summarize the challenge, followed by a short summary of the ideas associated with one significant writer. In each case we are being challenged to see that things are definitely not what they have always seemed to be.

Open-ended Evolution: The ideas of Charles Darwin (1809–1882) remain quite influential today. After two decades of delay caused, in part, by the controversy that was all but guaranteed, Darwin finally published his *On the Origin of Species* in 1859. When people consider the significance of this theory, they most often focus on the past, and see it as an explanation of how humans and all the other existing life forms came to be. The controversy about this explanation has had amazing vitality because it contradicts religious teachings. At least in this country it might be argued that the debate about origins is even more intense and wide-spread today than it ever was in Darwin's time. But from the standpoint of postmodernism, this raging debate about the past pales in significance compared to what Darwin's theory suggests about the future. If the way species are constituted is defined by the mechanisms of reproduction and chance circumstance, then the future can be no more than an open-ended prospect "guided" by blind chance events. The meaning of life, its purposes, its ultimate goals, take a really big hit, if you accept this notion. If that makes the hair stand up on the back of your neck, it is because you are harkening back to when we were hairy beasts who could fight against a chill that way. If this is so, what, besides reproducing, could morality be about? If, in reality, there is no set future direction to life on earth, maybe we are just making up this morality thing as we go along. You decide what's right for you, and I'll decide what's right for me.[3]

Unconscious Motives: Sigmund Freud (1856 –1939) attacked the accepted knowledge about us humans from a very different angle. But for the legions of practitioners, patients, and other followers, his teachings were no less radical. Freud insisted that the familiar conversation that each of us conducts in our head to make decisions and recognize our reasons and motives for action, were but distorted reflections of the actual way we make determinations about our morality and our actions. He discounted consciousness and turned rationality into mere rationalizations for what we are actually motivated to do. And as for these true motivations, they were primarily about sex! His theories were equally challenging to the traditions of sacredness in the major religions and to that same role of the sacred that reason played for the writers of the Enlightenment. If the true motives for our choices are unconscious, rational arguments must be of limited value. To be really convincing, an argument needs to somehow tap into the unconscious. You could not possibly be surprised when I tell you that one of the recognized pioneers of the US advertising and public relations was Sigmund Freud's nephew, Edward L. Bernays.[4]

Cultural Relativity: The third of these theories might be less a radical conceptual breakthrough and more about a dramatic change in methods; the methods we use to make sense of what others think. Prior to this new approach, it was generally thought that human communities existed on a kind of continuum of progress, from simple and primitive, to more complex yet still barbaric, to civilized. The theorist Bronisław Malinowski (1884-1942) was nowhere near as famous as Darwin or Freud because he was just a part, a significant part though, of a larger movement of all kinds of social researchers. As it happened, he was studying trade practices among peoples of the islands of the Western Pacific when World War I broke out. Being originally from Poland, a territory of Briton's enemy, the Austro-Hungarian Empire, Malinowski was prevented from returning to his duties at the London School of Economics, and thus he was left stranded in the Pacific islands for the duration of the war. During this extended engagement he perfected his research techniques which we now call participant observation. You may be more familiar with his approach when I remind you of the slang expression "going native."

Anyway, the idea is simple but it's also time consuming. In order to get to know how people think, you really have to get to know them, sharing in their everyday existence.[5] You need to look with them and not at them. With this heightened level of observation Malinowski and legions of other researchers made it clear that there are an almost infinite number of thriving, self-sustaining cultures and societies out there. In each, there are beliefs that people assume they share. And in each there is some kind of common sense, a morality system, and some acknowledgement of the sacred. What makes the way of life of other human groups appear to be simple, could actually be our own ignorance. In the ongoing political debate, we identify this theoretical challenge as cultural relativism. By the way, this insight not only covers cultures at the level of nations and language groups but it can be applied to help us to understand subcultures, like, for instance, people in organized crime, skateboarders, or even activist political liberals or political conservatives in the United States, to mention just a few possibilities.

Nihilism: Much of Fredrick Nietzsche's (1844 –1900) writing has remained controversial, but his use of the concept of "nihilism" is pretty widely understood to refer to the situation which he found at his time in Europe, where core moral values, namely Christianity, had become devalued. These values had thus lost their power to bind society together and give life meaning for individuals.[6] He expresses his concern that this was happening with his declaration "God is dead." By this he seemed to mean a couple of things. For the masses of people in Western civilization, religious observance had become nothing more than ritual, a going through the motions without real belief. In addition, for elite thinkers, doubt and out and out rejection of Christianity had created a void of meaning in their lives. The challenge that nihilism brought to the political right and left should be obvious. Anybody granting plausibility to Nietzsche's nihilism would recognize the urgency of reestablishing values that would again bring us all meaning and purpose.

Reality as a Linguistic Construction: Another challenge came from group of writers who focused on a rather narrow question: what do our conscious experiences consist of? Common sense and much of philosophy had it that our senses are our windows to the reality of the actual world outside of us. Thus our thoughts correspond to real things out there. I'll cite Martin Heidegger's (1889–1976) approach to illustrate the kind of challenges to common sense we are concerned with here. Language comes first, not perception. Whatever may or may not be out there, can have no meaning for us without language. "Language is the house of Being. In its home man dwells."[7] Scrap essentialism. Rather than placing the essence of things in the things themselves, Heidegger and linguists and other researchers that followed him pointed out that what we call the nature of an object or a person exists in words; in the language we use to give all things meaning. (I'll pause here for a moment while I challenge you to think about something non-linguistically...Oh, you can think in pictures you say. I say "pictures of what? Things we have words for? Do you have any pre-language memories of your childhood?) So for Heidegger, the source of essences is not in the objects themselves as the essentialists would have us believe, but in the way that language and culture organizes our perceptions. Or to say it in starker terms, we live in an undifferentiated chaotic universe, but for the fact that through social interaction and culture we can take regularities observed over time and construct and live in a shared, linguistic reality. I think this is a fair sampling of the radically challenging ideas that helped shape postmodernism. At least it is sufficient to prepare us for our look into postmodern politics. But these are primarily intellectual factors and as such they probably didn't have a very immediate or broad impact on the everyday lives of most people. To do justice to this subject we have to see that postmodernism also emerged out of enormous changes in the world of commerce that transformed our way of life and the way we think about it.

The Challenges from the World of Commerce

For most of history it was assumed that the simple requirements of food clothing and shelter were for most people the basic requirements of living. Modern marketing awakened us to the fact that our wants and needs, far from being a settled matter, can be added to perhaps endlessly.

Marketing: The modern discipline of marketing developed out of an avalanche of careful record-keeping and scientific research on businesses that accumulated through the 20th Century. As you are probably aware, marketing is not the same as mere selling. Selling is what farmers hope to do with their tomatoes when they tend to their stalls and at the Saturday produce market. There is little more to it than posting prices and hoping for buyers. The practice of marketing takes things further. It aims at making selling into a science by studying the ways in which potential consumers can be influenced so that they think they desire and/or need particular products and services. At their most impressive, expert marketers can assist consumers in realizing value and creating demand for a product or a service where previously there was none. (For instance, without really good marketing, people might never have suspected that they really needed to buy lots of water in little plastic bottles.) These ideas and the methods came into wide use in the post WWII economic boom. Just as a growing middle class of consumers were experiencing substantial pay increases and levels of credit previously unavailable, modern marketing took off. In time a huge segment of business decision-makers in this country came to accept the idea that trained marketing experts could create and shape consumer demand. These, then became the ideas behind how goods and services are developed and brought to us.

To get a feel for how it all started, think of this situation. You make soap. And you sell soap to just about everybody who doesn't save up fat from table scraps, get the lye at the hardware and make soap for themselves. That's about how the soap business had always been. Then you start thinking, "What if we were to bring out several new soap products, say for different purposes, or even for different kinds of people?" You have your people survey customers and then try to develop diverse soap products that match up with the various customer preferences that came up in the surveys: strong soaps, mild soaps, soaps that smell real nice, soaps that burn the inside of your nose, fancy soaps for the well off, cheaper soaps for the masses, and so on. To get things moving you assign a person to specialize in making and promoting each kind of soap to its intended customers…And, as they say, the rest is history. The soap business for example grew and grew until now it takes up more than a whole isle in your local Kroger or Safeway. And each offering boasts special ingredients, special purposes and targets a particular segment of the buying public. There is more than fat and lye and perfume now. We have all kinds of solvents and anti-bacterials, and artist-created packaging. Researchers are now familiar with how different people from different walks of life think about, feel about soap, and how they decide to buy soap. There is an extensive litigation based system of trademarks, patented production compounds, and processes.

> **Gloss Note:** To give credit where it is due, the history of marketing and branding really starts something like this. Many track its source in a couple of brothers-in law named Proctor and Gamble who had started a thriving soap and candle business in Cincinnati in 1837. Partly because candles were going out of use after oil lamps and the electric light bulb came into use the secretive P & G operation diversified by developing numerous competing cleaning products. More products lines were added by acquiring other companies. Now food store isles display a dazzling array of P & G brands including: Biz, Bold, Camay, Cascade, Cheer, Coast, Comet, Crest, Dash, Dawn, Denquel, Dreft, Era, Head & Shoulders, Ivory, Joy, Lava, Lestoil, Mr. Clean, Oxydol, Pantene, Pert Plus, Prell, Safeguard, Solo, Spic and Span, Tide, Top Job, Vidal Sassoon, and Zest, not to mention their non-soap products, a very few of which are: Attends, Bounce, Bounty, Clearasil, Charmin, Cover Girl, Crest, Crisco, Downey, Folgers, Formuls 44, Jif, Max Factor, Metamucil, Noxzema, Old Spice, Pampers, Pringles, Scope, Secret, and Vicks.[8]

Of course we are not just talking about soap. Chrysler, Ford, and GM had gotten out of the same-one-size-fits-all mentality long before World War II. By the time of the 1950s boom, the car companies were conducting psychological research on cushiness. What a scientific breakthrough. They could now measure the minimum perceived difference in softness that people can sense with their butts! Cadillac seats had to feel more cushy than the seats in Buicks, Buicks more cushy than Chevys, right? This way of researching the pool of potential consumers went hand-in-hand with product development. Notice that it is critical to divide potential customers up in terms of their preferences and ability to come up with the money to pay at different prices. These demographically similar groupings are referred to as market segments. If properly researched a market segment contains only folks who can be expected to make purchases from the perspective of similar values. Representatives of these demographics sometimes get called in to participate in "focus groups" so that their assessments and reactions to the minute details of products can be studied.

I want to emphasize this demographic dividedness because it often goes much further than Lincoln Navigators vs. Rangers. Each product or service offering that is introduced continues to divide and subdivide into tighter, more well defined market segments and an entire production organization is likewise shaped to target each. Go to the food store and grab a jar of pasta sauce. Search among the music styles at your favorite on-line or phone app for recorded music. Buy some new clothes for the upcoming change of seasons. Get your eye exam prescription filled. Go to a movie. Order a new cell phone. Buy a car. Shop for furniture, or maybe you need to shop for an apartment or house first. Choose an investment advisor. Whenever you approach a marketplace, you confront a dazzling array of options, only a few of which are targeted for you.

To reiterate, the objective of market research is to specifically address the values, the tastes, the hopes, and the fears of each of the groupings which an identifiable portion of the general population (with spending money) can be subdivided into. The impacts of marketing science have been truly transformational. To get a feel for the tremendous success that marketing science has been, just consider this. Marketers have made us want and then desperately need so many things that, just to make room for all the stuff, we have, in recent decades, given rise to a new want: a growth industry consisting of rental storage spaces to put the old stuff out of the way and make room to buy more new stuff.

THE POLITICS OF MORALITY

Branding: But there is more to it than just marketing things. When the idea of branding gets in play, it can almost seem like the marketplace ends up producing you. Let me explain. Branding is a set of concepts and procedures that builds upon what marketing has done. It takes what start as demographic market segments and transforms them into self-conscious belief sharing groups. Brand is a Norse word for the practice of showing ownership of livestock by burning marks on their skin. You know, with a hot iron. When speaking of branding, marketers are not just referring to product labels. To appreciate the remarkable, even revolutionary developments that branding has brought to commerce, we need to understand it from its sources in psychological theory. Scott Bedbury and Stephen Fenichell, in "*A New Brand World*," do just this by taking readers back to the theories of psychologist Abraham Maslow.[9] In the 1940s Maslow theorized that human motivation operated as a kind of hierarchy of needs. Humans seek to satisfy all these needs but the fact is that our lower level needs like for breathing, food, and water have to be satisfied before we can go on to address higher and higher level needs. Maslow identified five need levels in this hierarchy. At the top of the heap, after physical needs, safety needs, needs for belonging and needs for respect are met, people are prepared to take actions that will actualize themselves. Self-actualization is that level of activity that is peculiarly human. Self actualized people are the ones who know themselves and are comfortable in their own skin.

Maslow's theory had a relatively short run in the discipline of psychology, but his ideas had great play in popular culture for decades. Branding is just one example of this enduring popularity. As many authorities on branding see it, brand choices have little to do with label picking or comparisons of product features. For them, brand choices are behavior at the top of Maslow's needs hierarchy. Thus brand choices become self-actualizing behaviors. We are not talking, "I-am-hungry-so-I-will-eat-something," kinds of personal decisions. The decisions that involve branding are more to the tune of, "It's-dinner-time-and-I-think-am-I-an-Appleby's-kind-of-person---or-wait---don't-I-actually-feel-more-myself-at-the Cheesecake Factory"? "Yes,-I-fit-in-with-the-people-there-and-the-food-is-my-kind-of-food -too." In other words, these are decisions that we make to define ourselves, to ourselves, and to others. We put our feelings into them. Let's take another look at those examples of shopping I just mentioned: for music, clothes, glasses frames, movies, cell phones, cars, furniture, pasta sauce, houses, investment advisors, branches of the military to enlist in. Advertising for these things and all kinds of other stuff addresses pitches to us on this self-definitional level. Sure the choices we make reveal practical considerations. They are also about the level of our financial resources. But in addition, they allow us to testify as to the priorities and values that make up our unique persona. Branding is so critical to how we present ourselves that it is not unlikely that many of you readers are right now wearing clothing which has brand labels on the outside so as not to confuse anybody. It's in all kinds of details. What kind of ball cap will you wear? What kind would you never wear? How do you wear it? Straight on? Cocked to one side? With the beak in the back? This stuff is important for the kinds of people you want to take you seriously.

Whether Maslow was really on to something or there is another better explanation, this branding thing has real and profound consequences. It had potential way beyond loyalty to particular trademarks. With these brand choices people are investing mere objects with special meanings that go beyond their material presence. People who believe that they share these same meanings can come to identify themselves as self-conscious groups. With branding, people who may choose to ride motorcycles are not simply a segment of all the motor vehicle travelers. They, and we, think of a whole way of life we call "bikers." (Though the hot irons of the Norsemen have given over to tattoo needles.) If all this is starting to have a familiar ring to it, it should. When we are talking about objects that that hold special shared meanings, we are just brushing up against what we have been calling the sacred. Marketers discovered that they could develop a kind of sacredness about things they worked with. We can only imagine the thrill that these marketing practitioners experienced upon first realizing they were in touch with such awesome powers.

> **Gloss Note:** This practice of bringing special shared meanings and emotions to common objects was not the sole invention of the world of commerce. Artists like Andy Warhol (1928-1987), e.g. soup cans, and Robert Rauschenberg(1925-2008), e.g. trash, among many others, were successfully applying similar techniques in the art world. Later artists like Banksy literally took to the streets bringing graffiti to a significance never before known. Then there was Thomas Kinkade (1958-2012) whose paintings introduced a world that his followers could take on as an imagined wholesome place to dwell in.

Before branding really took hold, we purchasers made selections among the available alternatives primarily on the basis of our place in the economic hierarchy; we usually bought the best that we could afford. These days branding selections don't merely communicate economic class, they bestow individuals with character, making it clear to others exactly what kind of persons we are. Those making similar branding selections are the people who, we imagine, share deeply in the same perspectives about how to best live ones life. As purchasers, the internet has made this sorting out of people by brands a whole lot easier. Wherever I might find myself, I can now use my PC or a handy phone app to connect me with the precise props (goods and services) that a person of my character finds essential.

Historical Changes and Events

Mediated Factual Knowledge: For most humans throughout most of history most all of what they knew to be facts were obtained from direct observation. Accordingly, most of the knowledge that they possessed about their fellow humans was from face to face encounters and second hand through conversations they had. Increasingly, during the past couple of hundred years, this is no longer true. For those in modern circumstances the facts that they must rely upon are, for the most part, mediated by third parties: individuals and organizations who bring information to them and present it as facts about things and people in other times and places. Think of it, apart from coworkers, family and close friends, everything you know is mediated. Might this be important?

Let's do another little thought experiment:

Step1: Pick a place in the world where you have never been. Now for just one minute, imagine being there. As you imagine it, what is it like there? Make some mental notes. What does your imagination serve up to you about the place? How is it different from where you actually are now?

Step 2: Now go back over your images and mental notes and think about their sources. List these sources of information. Write them down if you can.

Here is mine. I picked Reykjavik, Iceland. Never been within 1,000 miles of the place, but I came up with imaginary pictures of a sizable city, rugged landscape, mostly white folks, cold outdoors but cozy inside, McDonald's, but no Walmart...etc. As for sources, why should I be so sure I have anything right? My list of sources includes high school geography, a few news articles, a Nova episode about a volcano, maybe a magazine article about harnessing deep-earth thermal energy, an American Express commercial, and of course, Bjork back in the MTV video days.

I mean, really! What do we know about any of these places we just happened to pick? Yet I am somehow confident that I had quite a bit of it correct. Even no Walmart, (at time of writing, it seems that the UK subsidiary of Walmart was in the process of buying a chain of stores in Iceland.)

THE POLITICS OF MORALITY

Just think of it. It is like this with almost everything we know about this world. We don't just make this stuff up. That would mean hallucinations and serious mental illness. With almost everything we think we know about this world, we pick up these bits of information here and there, put them together with generalizations and some reasoning, and there we have our notion of something that we have never experienced directly. Time was when all but a small fraction of a person's knowledge was based upon direct experience, face-to-face encounters. Now the sources are completely reversed and most of what we know, we know second, third or fourth hand. This indirect way of knowing has two important implications. First, since this indirect knowledge can easily be obtained without directly experiencing what it refers to, many can possess it. In fact, the same indirectly obtained facts can be shared among millions of people. Second, no matter how certain people might become about such mediated facts, there is never going to be the same degree of confidence and certainty about such facts when compared to facts that come from direct experience.

Our little exercise involved a picking a place about which all that we know, we know from indirect sources. What works for places works even better for people, and politics. What do you know about Mitch McConnell, for instance? Beyond the unlikely possibility that you are reading this sentence and by some odd set of circumstances, you have met the man or know him personally, everything that comes to mind when you consider Senator McConnell derives from mediated sources some of which want you to think highly of him and some of which want you to think poorly of him. The same is true of the issues, the actions, and of course the scandals that make up the day to day content of political news. By comparison, for much of human history there was scarce little to know about the world that didn't come from what I just referred to as face to face encounters.

It is in this rapidly expanding universe of indirect knowledge and fact that distortions can thrive. Information whether true or false can be accepted or denied by huge numbers of people. The very numbers involved seem to offer support for accepting or rejecting the truth of any given proposition. Think about how people have had to cope with this torrent of information. Each of us has to sort it out and negotiate a configuration of sources that we trust or at least feel reasonably comfortable with. This process of evaluating the many sources of information being directed at us is essentially aimed at determining for ourselves, what is fact and what is not fact. We'll have more to say about this later but for now the point is that there is a justifiable level of skepticism and fertile grounds for controversy that comes with this new world of mediated facts.

The Cataclysms of the Twentieth Century: Whether a person was trying to maintain a belief in a changeless human nature or a glorious universal emancipation of humanity, the unprecedented violence that unfolded during the 20th Century was challenging to say the least. Think of it. World-wide economic collapse; two World Wars that routinely targeted and bombed cities and non-combatants. The grand promise of science delivers atomic weapons. Political purges that consolidated power in various nation states and their colonial possessions by labeling thousands on the right and left as extremists and executing them; the massive human exterminations we have more lately come to call genocide; weapons of mass destruction, these are parts of the very fabric of the century that has just past. The unprecedented scale human violence in the 20th century was not only crushing to the idea of human progress, its magnitude defied any conception of human evil that the Natural Law perspective could have previously prepared us or.

The survivors did their best to tell us that this destruction and brutality was purposeful and meaningful within the prevailing perspectives on each side of the moral divide. But OMG. Might all this be a bit too much? I mean, really. Where is the progress and human betterment in this mess? Or, if you are inclined to the perspective of Natural Law, when have the evil and selfish appetites of God's rational creatures gotten even close to this far out of hand? There emerged a widespread contention that none of the existing systems of moral teaching were adequate to take in the magnitude and novelty of all this 20th Century violence.

Summary: factors and causes

Before describing the postmodern perspective that emerged, it might be helpful to take a moment to summarize these contributing factors:

From science and philosophy:

- The history and future of human life on earth is most likely without clear direction or purpose. (Darwin)

- Our own conscious purposes and motives are probably just distorted rationalizations of real intentions we can never quite know.(Freud)

- The ideas we all share, about what is right, what is wrong and what is sacred; are not fixed, but vary from people to people and even from time to time. (Malinowski)

- The ultimate values that Christian religion has provided for people of Europe and the Americas are beginning to look empty and meaningless, and this is a threat to Western civilization.(Nietzsche)

- Our consciousness does not perceive the outside world directly but instead it senses phenomena that are being filtered through the lenses of language and culture. (Heidegger)

From commerce:

- Human needs are not static. They can be manipulated and even created anew through the use of persuasive messaging.

- People use the objects around them and the persuasive messaging associated with those objects, to select and project their own identities and to interpret the identities of others.

From historical events:

-A transformation to a world where virtually all knowledge is not direct but mediated

-The human capacity for brutality and violence has been vastly underestimated before modern times. Consequently, existing systems of belief about life and its ultimate meaning come under question.

In the previous chapter I made the claim that perspectives on morality in the West had fallen into deep grooves by about 1800, with the right assuming that human nature is changeless and the left assuming a progressive emancipation of wiser and more humane creatures. Let me assure you. Both sides of what I have called this moral divide are alive and well. However, in this chapter, I have been cataloging all kinds of threats that these two perspectives have come up against since 1800. (If you are already among those who are: 1. stunned by the historical setbacks of humanity in the past hundred years or so, 2. credit the awesome powers of science to transform things both for the better and for the worse, and 3. can manage to stay centered in spite of the constant blast of bias mediated messaging that is directed at you in these times, you are probably already thinking in terms of that view of the world we will be calling the Postmodern perspective.

The Postmodern Way of Thinking

Here are some of the ingredients of what goes into a postmodern perspective:

Ultimate reality is unknowable: If we are creatures of culture, language and unconscious motives, what we call reality is merely a kind of fabrication. We humans are continuously putting it together and then continuously revising it. Essential to postmodernism, whether in art literature or, philosophy or even, science, is a belief that what we call reality is something that we construct. This is an acknowledgment that the "out there" world that we perceive, and grasp, and try to understand, only seems to be "out there." It isn't only a fantasy. Sure there is a universe beyond our brains. But much of what we take for granted as being part of an objective reality is, and always has been, not out there but part of our human thought processes and especially part of our abilities and talents with language. Our version of reality is constructed with the very words we use to parse up the world in a particular way. As we choose the words we use to think and talk, we are modeling that world through our choices of symbols, stories, myths and metaphors. This is what novelist, Vladimir Nabokov was pointing out when he wrote, "'Reality' (one of the few words which mean nothing without quotes)."[10]

Skepticism: If we assume: the absolute truth about reality cannot be pinned down; things are hardly ever what they seem to be; the course of evolution is open-ended subject to pure chance, then, any assertions about wisdom or knowledge should be met with skepticism. This skepticism is called for with respect to any claims anybody makes about reality and truth. It is the ultimate postmodern irony that we live in the midst of so much information, so many claims, and so many facts from so many sources, and yet, we can view it all with so little confidence and so little certainty. When it comes to knowledge about our world, postmodern thinking views all kinds of authority with suspicion. All grand theories are to be questioned. The wisdom from the past that we know as traditional authority is suspect. Don't traditions mainly perpetuate inherited advantages? Rational/scientific authority is suspect. All too often we see that intellectuals and scientists seem to be for sale to the highest bidder. Even our direct observations seem unsound, since we discovered that things are seldom what they first appear to be. (This particular skepticism has been supported by the demonstrated fact that eye witnesses are among the least reliable for evidence at criminal trials.)

A New World of Possibilities: If reality is so elusive that extreme doubt and skepticism are required, we must be in for sad times, right?

No, not so. This lack of certainty about any ultimate truth, instead releases a diversity of possibilities in postmodern thinking. Let me put it another way. If all grand theories are to be approached with suspicion, it doesn't mean that they are all complete hogwash. After all, any way of looking at things might be the correct one, and several ways of looking at something might be useful and productive. Consequently, there is a kind of leveling of possible validity among ways of looking at things at different places and different times, and with that leveling, we become more open and even playful with what might work for us. One might realize that a particular idea is questionable, or untrue, or even pure zany fantasy, but act on the belief in spite of this. The entire range of ways of seeing the world becomes a storehouse from which we may choose our frames of reference. This richness of possibilities for meaning is seen as a positive feature of postmodern life.

At the same time much of postmodern humor makes fun not so much about particular beliefs but with the certainty people have about holding those beliefs. This especially includes the opinions of people on either side of the political divides who are convinced of the truth of very questionable "facts." TV programs like, The Simpsons and South Park and formerly The Colbert Report frequently contain examples of this kind of humor. Postmodern art emphasizes the reality of our symbols that we can know for sure over the reality of the elusive world "out there," that these symbols are supposed to represent. In paintings, there is a stream of Postmodern work featuring borrowings of unlikely and discordant combinations of subjects, genres, and even different historical and cultural references. (We are being invited to draw meanings (which are called out from the total symbolic pool that consists of the entirety of culture and history globally). If words make the point, put those words in the painting. Many artists are continuously pushing hard against that very elusive line between what is called art and what is not. Postmodern literature and films give us the same juxtaposition of styles genres and characters. Think, of Blade Runner.[11] Or even Animal House; anyone up for a Roman toga party, one featuring a 50s R&B band?

Believing: But extreme skepticism combined with a playful attitude, does not automatically point postmoderns in the direction of a purposeful, richly meaningful existence. How do people who think this way manage a meaningful and effective postmodern existence? Or to put it the way the ancient Greeks would, how does one live the good [postmodern] life?

The postmodern perspective fully acknowledges that without any beliefs, meaningful action is quite unthinkable. We humans must have some convictions about the world in order to care enough to act. So people adapt to their postmodern skepticism by relying on more limited personal beliefs. You don't have to have the perfect theory of everything to appreciate logic, love, power, cruelty, and countless other things that make life and action meaningful. Just because your skepticism rules out adherence to a universal religion or ideology like Catholicism or communism, it doesn't mean that you cannot set certain big questions aside and devote your thoughts and energies to the Sierra Club, or to restoring 1950s pick-up trucks, or raising decent kids. However it is addressed, we might say that the art of living in a postmodern mode consists of forging a meaningful path through profound and seemingly overwhelming ultimate uncertainties.

> **Gloss Note:** French writer Jean-François Lyotard (1924-1998) is often credited with coming up with one of the best explanations of postmodernism. He characterized it as an incredulity towards metanarratives. If we give this a kinder translation Postmodernism is simply an enormous doubt or suspicion, (incredulity) about sweeping stories (metanarratives) that claim to explain the history, and nature of humans. It was his belief that certain more recent events, that we have recognized and named, have invalidated these narratives.[12]

Belief-sharing: Just as we have belief-sharing groups of people on the left and right sides of the moral divide, belief-sharing postmodern communities exist. But they are held together by similarly more limited and compartmentalized beliefs. It is more than a coincidence that a whole lot of such postmodern communities might look a lot like the branding market segments we came across a few pages back. In contemporary society, self-consciously postmodern people are coalescing into communities which are acting on the basis of a great variety of different and even opposing beliefs. Consequently, postmodern culture can be thought of hodge-podge of belief-sharing sub-groups and niches of like-minded people. Some are face to face, some are creatures of the long established media like newspapers, television and radio still others exist exclusively on the internet.

One thing these diverse groups share in common is that they do not fit into the mold of either side of the great political divides between the metanarrative of natural law right and the metanarrative of the march of progress left. Nor do the two sides of the tired analysis of great depression economics fascinates them. However we shouldn't take this to mean that these groups do not share in those rational and emotional bonds that we have been calling a sense of the sacred. Strong believers in the rights of women, for example, can, and do, share *their* beliefs as fundamental to their own very sense of humanity. And, strong advocates of the Second Amendment also can, and do, share *their* beliefs as fundamental to their sense of humanity. But even with their beliefs there is no reason to think that they identify with one or another side of the great moral and economic divides. Strong supporters of the right to own and use firearms, for example, may identify with conservative politicians for their positions on the Second Amendment and care nothing or even oppose the same politician's traditional stand against gay marriage or welfare reform. Similarly, committed advocates of equal pay for women, may not ever give a thought to the universal emancipationist sentiments that advocate immigration reform with amnesty for undocumented residents.

Above all, postmoderns live in a world where they fully realize that between them and whatever the ultimate reality is out there, lies a rich world of all kinds of meaningful ideas and symbols. They may address their world with a healthy dose of skepticism, but they address it with the raw material of the entirety of accumulated history, ideas, and symbols, which have been built up over the expanse of human existence on this planet; an impressive bag of tools.

A Note on Nihilism and Relativism

Before moving on, there is an important criticism of postmodern thinking that we need to get past. Critics from both the right and the left cite this way of thinking as morally reprehensible. They label this way of thinking with terms like nihilism and relativism. From the right folks from just about any religious perspective would obviously view it as an untenable departure from their theological explanations of all things. But there are also serious misgivings from other points of view. Noam Chomsky, who we encountered in chapter two, is one of postmodernism's fiercest critics. For him the apparently light and even playful view that postmodern thinking has created, isn't much more than a diversion from a much more sober reality. Much like consumerism, he thinks that it has diverted the serious attention of both intellectuals and others away from essential issues and efforts for progressive change.[13] The thinking goes like this. These critics would have us think that all postmoderns are either nihilist who believe in nothing or relativist who have no enduring moral beliefs and consequently change their morals from situation to situation. It would be easy to dismiss such critics as biased from their religious or ideological vantage points, but I want to question such criticisms. Let's take this up in two different ways.

As the examples we have just considered should illustrate, people with postmodern perspectives can and do possess moral beliefs that guide them through their days without subscribing totally to any all-inclusive religion or ideology. Recall that back in chapter 6, I mentioned a line of research that is finding that gut feeling of right and wrong come to us even before we fit them into existing moral teachings. Beyond that, in more commonplace language, a person can place profound significance in "the Golden Rule," and do onto others in his daily life, as he would have them do onto him, without believing that this teaching came from Jesus, or that it requires pacifism, or a vegan diet, or that it requires any other beliefs. A different person might perceive that there is an incredibly powerful dominance of the wealthy individuals, in the way the world works and dedicate himself to resisting that dominance, without subscribing to Marx's theories of history and revolution, or being a progressive, or an advocate of the welfare state. A third individual might be convinced that the existence of great fortunes motivates the economic efforts of millions who are less well off, without subscribing to the free market ideology that claims that unregulated free markets solve all problems that can ever occur when humans live together in large numbers. As I said before, just because such beliefs fall short of indorsing a world religion or political ideology does not mean that they cannot serve as a moral guide that remains stable and constant through events and time.

Perhaps a simpler way to refute the nihilist/ relativist criticism of postmodernism is just to imagine what the consequences would be if, from this very moment on, you were able to force yourself either to believe in nothing or simply to infer what is right and wrong strictly from your perceptions on a situation to situation basis. As we experience the continuity of ourselves as persons through time, an existence without continuing beliefs makes no sense. A life without enduring beliefs seems meaningless. And though people sometimes do things they consider wrong, this is a far cry from proving that they don't have a continuity in their moral beliefs. Consequently, critics of postmoderns from either the right or the left can probably be better understood as just accusing people they disagree with as being less moral or less intelligent than they are.

For our purposes, we can still make more sense of things by maintaining the assumption that only those rare few psychopaths among us lack an enduring moral compass. Having said this we want to leave this subject with the realization that unlike others, postmoderns are able to construct a moral compass by drawing from diverse sources.

THE POLITICS OF MORALITY

While there is no reason to believe that postmodern views represent moral progress, there is, by the same token no reason to believe that these perspectives signal moral decline either. Since we've already noted that all of us are making all kinds of judgments constantly, it shouldn't be difficult put all this together and imagine a postmodern's morality.

In the chapter which follows we see how the postmodern perspective has infiltrated our politics not so much among the voters and low level partisans as among the legions of career professionals that help to research write and produce the political pageant we see before us.

Part IV: The Contemporary Political Scene

THE CONTEMPORARY POLITICAL SCENE

Chapter 9 The Facts

"Everyone is entitled to his own opinion, but not to his own facts."

Daniel Patrick Moynihan (1927-2003)[1]

"It is difficult to get a man to understand something, when his salary depends on his not understanding it."

Upton Sinclair (1878-1968)[2]

"In an information-rich world, the wealth of information means a dearth of something else: a scarcity of...attention...Hence a wealth of information creates a poverty of attention and a need to allocate that attention efficiently among the overabundance of information sources..."

Herbert A. Simon (1916-2001)[3]

"Science is just somebody's opinion."

a friend

In the Part III we first examined the differing assumptions that underlie the moral perspectives of those who are politically active on the left and the right. Then we got an introduction to a third perspective which I referred to as postmodern. In Part IV we will be taking up the subject of how the information about politics is produced and presented to potential supporters on the right and left. Starting in this chapter with a discussion of the facts of the matter (all the available information about our nation and our government), we continue on in the next two chapters to look at the messages and their messengers that make up the public discussion of our politics. I have used the word "Facts" in the title of this chapter only to emphasize that it can sometimes be difficult to distinguish reliable and useful information from information which has been manipulated one way or another by partisan interests. In the titles of chapters ten and eleven I have used the theatrical terms "Script," "Audience" and "Actors" to emphasize the degree to which both the messages (information and issues) and the messengers (politicians and office holders) have increasingly taken up styles and methods which are strikingly similar to those we find in the drama of theater and the movies. Granted there are still people with true, heart-felt, messages for us, but these messages must now reach us through the special kind of "reality TV" that our politics has established for us.

As we turn to the factual basis of our politics there are two things that confront us immediately. First the sheer magnitude of available information out there and second, the absurdly low standards which often seem to apply to what partisans sometimes are referring to as facts. To help you become more comfortable with your understanding of this aspect of our contemporary political scene, let's take up each of these in turn.

The Raw Data

The United States began in the era when there was a considerable popular press consisting of broadsides, pamphlets, newspapers, magazines, and books. By beginning with an insistence on freedom for speech and freedom for anything one might do with a machine called the printing press, the Bill of Rights acknowledges the critical importance of information to those who would hope to govern themselves successfully. In addition, our laws and customs that specifically recognize zones of privacy for individuals and corporations

THE CONTEMPORARY POLITICAL SCENE

do not allow any similar privacy zones for governmental agencies. If you question me, I can say, "That's none of your damn business." When a question arises, the government can only try to avoid an answer. It can sometimes stall, or at the national level it might make an appeal to the argument of "national security." But for all our governmental jurisdictions we insist on what we call transparency--a complete openness, for all the activities and records.

Actually, people being as they are, even government employees sometimes, don't like having people watching what they do too closely. As a result, we have a number of tools that we can use when confronted with arguments and delays from government officials. So-called sunshine laws, covering various levels of government require that meetings and other activities be conducted in public. Most noteworthy among these kinds of laws are Federal and state "Freedom of Information Acts," which require government jurisdictions to make their records "promptly available to any person," and allow those wanting answers a recourse to the courts if the government doesn't comply. You can even go to an internet site that will walk you through the whole drill for submitting a Freedom of Information Request to the Federal government.[4] Imagine the response you'd get if you wrote to your next door neighbor or, for instance, or to Citicorp asking for specifics about what they are doing and how they operate. Then there are the investigative powers of Congress and the state legislatures. I am pretty sure that most people have seen elected representatives holding public hearings where they grill officials and even corporate officials and individuals about their activities.

I once thought it ironic that some partisans on both the right and the left seem to exhibit enormous trust when it comes to huge corporations (the internal workings of which they know little or nothing about) while these same folks seem not to trust government at all. It is among these people that all kinds of conspiracy theories are hatched warning us about the sinister plotting of the government (about which they seem to know plenty). I now think that I have come upon at least a couple of important reasons this lack of trust exists. For one thing, call it a case of information overload.

Few would argue with the notion that successful self-government relies on an informed citizenry. Facts about our world and how our government operates in it are like the raw materials in that process by which citizens are informed. On the positive side, as far as raw information about our country and our government goes, the transparency and the tools that enforce it have yielded an almost limitless information resource available to guide both the politician and citizen. Just to get a sense of how much information we have coming at us, and to get a feeling for the sheer size of this mountain of government information, according to the Bureau of Labor Statistics, the various 90,000 or so government jurisdictions in the United States employed 21.3 million people in 2014, and this figure doesn't include the more than 1.3 million uniformed military personnel.[5] By comparison, Walmart, which is often identified as our biggest private employer, employed 1.4 million people. So government employs more than 16 times the number of people that Walmart employs.

Add to this 16 to 1 ratio the fact that as the growing size of government became an important political issue in the past several decades, more and more government work has gone to contractors and consultants. Estimates of this shadow government workforce are hard to come by, but the Federal government alone probably pays well over 7 million of them. It is said that some government agencies, like for instance, The Department of Homeland Security have fewer people directly employed than they do contractors. But this figure of 7 million for federal contract employment gives us only a hint of the total number of contractors for all levels of government. Part of the reason is that many federal programs that employ contractors operate through the states. For example, the federal government provides substantial funding for highway construction and repair, but the funds go to the states and the states do the actual contracting out. In any case, you can get the picture: the total number of government employees and contractors, who are supposed to be working under conditions of transparency, is probably way bigger than most people ever imagine.

But it only starts there. To those dozens of millions of people doing things in the name of our governments, we need to add the millions that the actions of government are intended for in order to get to a realistic idea of the state of the nation and its place in the world. When you take all this into account the concept of the informed citizen starts to seem impossible, practically speaking. This is what I mean when I say that it creates an information overload. Even so, I bet some of you are saying that I have just described a greatly exaggerated problem, or even a false problem. After all, nobody has to take all of this information in, analyze it, file freedom of information requests to fill in the gaps and then decide what they must do as citizens. The reality is that we have legions of observers, reporters and researchers to rely upon, who are producing information about just about every aspect of the state of the nation.

True, but a bit ago, I said that there are a couple of important reasons why lots of people don't trust our government. Besides having quite literally too much information to cope with reasonably, I think we can blame the way that a lot of this information gets selected and worked before it reaches us. Essential to that process is that thing we have come to call "spin." The fact that there are people out there trying their best to make their political arguments persuasive is probably nothing new. We used to call the skills and techniques for doing this, rhetoric. What we call spin has taken old fashioned rhetoric to a whole other level though. As with a number of other topics we've gotten into, a bit of history about spin will make for helpful background.

A Brief History of Spin

The First Amendment in the Bill of Rights was drafted to protect free speech and free press. It doesn't say anything about restricting these freedoms to true speech and true printed statements. Consequently, the Bill of Rights leaves the truth seeking up to us. When that group of men got together and designed our republic, they seemed, in some fit of optimism, to assume that the truth will naturally always rise to the top. At least it appears that they thought that way. Whatever they thought, it is clear that they never encountered the modern techniques of public relations (PR). Contemporary approaches to influencing political opinions are so closely aligned with the discipline of public relations that we ought to be more familiar with what it is and where it came from. Put most simply, public relations operates as a mediator, in the sense that PR specialists put themselves between the presumed source of information and the people who that information reaches. . Political parties once played a major role as such a mediator, but this role was gradually taken over by PR professionals working directly for candidates and politicians. It is generally understood that the goal of public relations is to intervene in communication channels between the public and a source such as an individual, or organization and once there manage the information that the public gets from that source so as to present it in particular positive or negative light.

That's right. In the nicest way I could, I just said that PR people purposely distort the information in one way or another. As a comparison, consider this. If somebody stands in front of you exaggerating and contorting the truth, we use terms like lie, falsehood and even perjury. We tend to hold people personally responsible for the accuracy of their statements. But if the statement comes mediated through one of those otherwise anonymous folks we call "spokespersons," things get more complicated for some reason. Whether the purpose is to enhance or degrade actual facts, the PR practitioners try to present the information from a different perspective than we might otherwise get it. Since much of the practice of public relations emerged during the same period that modern commercial advertising was developing, it is not at all surprising that we hold PR to similar standards of believability as we do advertisements.

THE CONTEMPORARY POLITICAL SCENE

Words like spin and propaganda certainly put public relations work in a negative light, but they are probably not very far from the heart of the matter. The standard for truth falls somewhere in the same ballpark as it does with the hype we get about commercial products. But let's face it. We all take this kind of thing in stride when it comes to commercial advertising. (Beer doesn't give guys headaches, it only gets the babes swarming around them.) Similarly, the President's Press Secretary or the spokesperson for the police union isn't soon likely to confess to any stupid moves or misdeeds of the person(s) they speak for. This legacy of PR has now infiltrated virtually every aspect of our public messaging. Not only do the spokespersons stretch the truth and spin in favor of those they represent, but we routinely assume that all the words of the primary players, like top executives, and office holders have been worked over by PR consultants. And sure, these public monologues of pre-planned vanilla flavored word confections are one of the main reasons that lots of people view many politicians and CEOs as habitual liars. It is no doubt also why occasional non-PR-processed tweets and off the cuff comments from these kinds of folks can sometimes go viral.

I hope that this will make for a sufficient wallow in the sea of PR deception. Now I will try to explain why this spin stuff is neither surprising nor sufficient reason to turn away from politics completely. OK, whether public relations practitioners are intervening in a scandal or producing a vast propaganda campaign bent on propping up the public's resolve to go to war, the purpose of spin is to achieve popular acceptance of a particular point of view on some subject. What is more, there is a long standing tradition in public relations circles that sees their work as good, noble, and even necessary. Remember our look back to the United States and Europe in the years following the French and American revolutions. There arose deep concerns about whether citizens now being asked to vote for those who would lead them were up to such a task intellectually. Out of this came the good and noble idea behind public relations on the right: the idea that the masses needed careful guidance to ensure that they understood proper the meaning of public figures and events.

But please don't get the impression that guiding the masses by use of spin is strictly a one side thing, with the right side spinning yarns for the masses and the left side proclaiming the truth and nothing but the truth. Spinners past and present have found plenty of jobs working for either side. After all, it was the avowed progressive, Theodore Roosevelt, who actually vilified the truther journalists of his time by naming them "muckrakers."[6] .If that's not convincing to you, how about Vladimir Lenin. He had so little faith in the brains of common folks that he insisted that an intellectual vanguard of Bolsheviks was needed to do the heavy thinking for his revolution and explain things to the masses.

In fact, this concern for the ignorance of the masses has even brought political partisans from the left and right together in support of PR practitioners from time to time. When both sides shared the same need to bend public opinion in a particular direction, like for example, with the fostering of pro-war sentiment PR was deployed. The US took pride in a non-partisan approach to war-making through most of the last century. A good bit of the reason comes from the fact that bi-partisan, and even government sponsored public relations efforts, went into getting the public ready and then sustaining public commitment to both World Wars.

> **Gloss Note:** One week after we entered the war in 1917 the federal government Committee on Public Information (CPI) was activated to put the existing theories of social psychology to work to help convince a wary American public of the necessity of going to war in Europe. This same kind of pro-war effort came with the World War II period which witnessed an avalanche of calculated pro-war material from Hollywood and official US government agencies. What is less well remembered is the fact that all this pro-war propaganda brought with it a realignment of conservative support for the previously hated liberal, Franklin Roosevelt. Lest we think that

THE CONTEMPORARY POLITICAL SCENE

> they over estimated their war time PR problem, remember that people claiming German ancestry still rank at the top of this country's diverse ethnic mix.[7] What is more, those same German-Americans were being targeted by a competing Nazi master race PR campaign throughout the 1930s.

Our concern is with politics. But whether in the service of patriotism, celebrity, or product promotion, the practitioners of public relations inserted themselves between the ultimate sources of information and the public. Once there, they were equipped with the best techniques that the emerging science of psychology could offer. As mentioned back in chapter 8, Sigmund Freud's nephew, Edward Bernays, applied his uncle's theories and became one the most renowned players in the early days of PR.

While public relations began as a single specialized field, it gradually evolved into a whole bunch of separate consulting specialties. These days corporations use specialized public relations consultants to burnish their public image (and promote their share price). Union consultants script union officers and write copy for TV spots that tell us of the invaluable contributions their organizations bring to the community. Government agencies and the branches of the military hire PR specialists to sing their praises to us. People embroiled in scandal hire different PR specialists who take on the role of defense attorney in the court of public opinion and attempt to explain all the known facts in the very best light. People who are famous, or who would like to be famous, hire PR types called publicists to get them in the news. And of course, politicians employ their own variety of these specialists to present themselves to us. But these political pros have long since split off from their PR heritage to become a separate profession and a separate industry.

Consider the Source

Thus it is for the would-be informed citizen: the problem of an enormous flow of far too much information from and about our government, much of it intentionally manipulated to pull our opinion and judgment one way or another. Oh no! What's the citizen to do? Of course, it turns out that each of us solves this problem by choosing certain information sources and ignoring others. These sources select, analyze and organize the information for us and turn it into the facts we rely upon. And this act of choosing our sources brings with it a second problem: a large percentage, (maybe not all, but a large percentage) of these sources are also very much committed to spinning the facts to comport with their political objectives. So I should come to the rescue here with a directory of all these sources of information and give each one a ranking of from -10, for extreme left through center left and center right and on to +10, for extreme right? Sorry but that ain't happening. I have too much respect for you readers. By now you are probably able to do that kind of thing yourselves.

Let's try an example and check for the right/left spin. Police force strategies. Over the past few decades there have been two strategies for city police forces that have been widely debated and publicized. One or the other of these emerges in writing and news coverage about police and crime all the time. In short form:

The Broken Windows Approach, under which city police officers are supposed to make efforts to seek out and apprehend people for even the slightest wrong-doing. According to this line of thinking, if you don't catch the window breaker, not only will he be emboldened to do worse in the future, but the neighborhood will be, to that extent, more blighted in appearance and seem more generally to be on the decline as concerns law abiding.

The Community Policing Approach, under which police officers are supposed to make efforts to really get to know the people in the community, with the objective maximizing police/community rapport.

According to this line of thinking, if police officers have deep personal ties with the locals, they are not only more likely to encourage law abiding behavior but they are also going to be far more likely to get citizens to report and assist them when actual law-breaking occurs.

(My apologies to actual law enforcement professionals, but the people who endlessly argue over these kinds of simplistic characterizations of your line of work are more likely to be running for office or supporting politicians than ever actually doing police work.)

OK. Did you figure it out? I doubt that anybody needs a hint, but: Which approach emphasizes the evil/bad impulses in people which must be controlled? Which approach recognizes the unifying power we achieve when we can expand what that word "we" refers to?

While, by now, you shouldn't really need that directory of political information sources with right/left scorings, there are a few points and clarifications that might be helpful if you find yourself trying to negotiate the landscape of all that political information without a GPS. With this in mind we can side-step the information which emanates from the parties and the politicians themselves and move away to some of the other sources of information that typically show a bit less bias, while acknowledging that a quest for politically relevant information sources that are objective and free of partisan bias isn't ever going to be easy.

501(c) Organizations: As we get past the messages coming directly from the politicians and the consultants they hire, we encounter a whole range of outfits that are literally in cahoots with them. The Federal Elections Commission (FEC) and the Internal Revenue Service (IRS), are the two government agencies charged with enforcing the laws and regulations on campaign financing. Under Internal Revenue Service Code, section 527, we have long had fund raising and spending by PACs, Political Action Committees. The tax code puts limits of $2,700 per election and $5,000 per year on individual political contributions to PACs. In recent years we hear more and more about Super PACs.

Under section 501 (C) 3 of the tax code, organizations are granted tax-exempt status to engage in activities that have the following "charitable" purposes: religious, educational, scientific, literary, testing for public safety, fostering national or international sports competition, preventing cruelty to children or animals. The same tax regulation specifically states that if these organizations are to remain tax exempt they "must absolutely refrain from participating in the political campaigns of candidates for local, state, or federal office..."[8]

Sounds like we might get some really useful, unspun information from these sources. Or conversely, how could this provision possibly be good news for politicians, political consultants, and the people who sell air time for the television industry? The answer is simple. Just because it is a 501(c) 3 organization that doesn't mean that it cannot have definite opinions about how you should vote, and then act on those opinions. This is because the IRS decided not to enforce this non-political restriction several years ago. As a result, along with all the other real non-political 501(c) (3) organizations devoted to causes which are "charitable," we now have all kinds of political advocacy organizations, and they operate without restriction so long as they don't coordinate directly with the campaign of a given politician. Groups and individuals operating under section 501 (C) 4 of the code, expressly devoted to "social welfare" and 501 (c) 6, "trade organizations" can do their politicking for candidates directly but they have to pay any taxes that are due. These are often referred to as Dark Money sources because they are a source of political funding without limits, and those sources don't even get reported.

These days lots of operations now run a "charitable" (c) 3 arm and a separate (c) 4 arm "social welfare". Separately or combined these Super PACs have brought tons of money into our politics. What has been lost is some of the credibility that people used to attach to information coming from organizations claiming to be devoted exclusively to charity and social welfare.

THE CONTEMPORARY POLITICAL SCENE

Newspapers, Print and Internet: Moving further out from the full spin zone we find newspapers and their internet equivalents. Traditionally, newspapers managed to maintain at least the appearance of partisan neutrality by labeling most of their content as objective reporting, or 'news," and putting their particular slant on things in a section called "editorial" or "opinion." This news VS editorial distinction has carried through to today's print editions and their internet counterparts as well. In this way both national distribution newspapers and even local community papers have been able to cultivate a readership that often includes people who respect their news reporting while they thoroughly disagree with their editorial positions.

Critics will point out that the pure news being reported can often be somewhat less than bias free. You can appreciate this criticism when you consider that the very act of selecting the material that is to be "news," can often be politically biased. For instance, when race is a politically controversial issue, the number of column inches a paper devotes to articles about racial conflict is itself a reflection of the particular bias of their publication. Beyond that there are all kinds of opportunities to spin the news in the way it gets written. Next time you read a police or crime story in the paper, see if you can tell whether the writer favors the "Broken Windows" or the Community Policing" theory. I bet it will not be difficult.

In trying to sell their news reporting to publications of many editorial stripes, the international news services like Associated Press and Reuters do seem to try to avoid some of this bias in both selecting and writing about the items they cover.

The internet has brought with it a flood of other sites that can appear as news but are actually staunch advocacy operations. Many of these are devoted to one cause or interest or another and troll for funding, petition signers, or support for particular actions by your representatives in government. While it is pretty easy to distinguish between sites that are strictly informational and sites that lure you into action, it is important to note that these internet activities have transformed the lives of your representatives by creating piles of appeals and petitions from constituents who have sometimes been recruited with false information but who nontheless must be addressed. When the time it takes to address such internet nonsense is combined with the time it takes to do fund-raising, many politicians complain that they have little time left for doing what their oaths of office require.

> **Gloss Note:** Your local newspaper or its internet version, often with the help of the League of Women Voters, is unusually an excellent source of the where, when and how of voting along with basic information on candidate backgrounds and issues up for a vote.

Broadcast Media: Unlike print, the broadcast media is regulated by the Federal Communications Commission (FCC). Broadcast stations have an assigned place in the airwaves that is licensed to them. Over the years much of this airwave broadcasting was replaced by a network of direct wiring with somewhat different regulations going to the cable companies.

In its hay day the regulated broadcast industry and its government regulators took great pains to limit the spin and bias of the political information it disseminated. Two of the standards used to ensure broadcast objectivity and balance are worthy of our attention:

The Equal Time Rule dates back to The Radio Act of 1927. It insists that a broadcaster airing one candidate must make equal time available to opposing candidates. Further, the broadcaster should offer that time at the same price and that this price should not be above that charged to the station's "most favored advertiser." If the broadcast time is free, the equal time is also free. One exception that we need to keep in mind is that when the air time is considered a news event, the rule does not apply. Another whole area of exceptions has to do with TV debates. Over the years rulings have resulted in the practice of excluding all candidates not representing the two major political parties.[9]

THE CONTEMPORARY POLITICAL SCENE

The Fairness Doctrine was of more recent origin. Starting in 1949 broadcast stations were required not only to present controversial issues of interest to the public, but to present both sides of the issue that the FCC held to be "honest, equitable, and balanced." If this seems strange, it is because the Fairness Doctrine was eliminated in 1987. Now days, it seems difficult for us to crawl back into the minds of people in the 50s, 60s, or 70s and even understand the idea that an issue might be considered one of general public interest.[10]

Once the broadcasters and the major parties cleared out coverage for lesser candidates from third parties, the business of selling broadcast time to political campaigns became a real money maker. Think about it. The candidates pay for all the production costs, and the stations just sell the time and bank the revenue. As we will see ahead in chapter 11, TV exposure has become the most critical ingredient in the careers of many politicians. This fact, combined with the virtual end of regulatory restraints on campaign financing, have resulted in a huge windfall of profits for television. For our purposes here, though, we need to note that these political profits has probably had an impact on the news coverage broadcasters direct our way.

Question 1: If you were a TV news executive and you got to drooling over potential profits from selling air time for political campaigns ads, would you decide to begin news coverage of the election and the candidates sooner or wait till just before the voting? Or maybe you'd see it in your interest to begin covering the "candidates" even before they announced that they were running.

Question 2: If you were that same TV news executive and you were aware that in a particular race there was one candidate who had the election completely sewed up a year before the voting, would you see that this news got reported or would you withhold it and for as long as possible cover this particular election as though it were a close horse race?

I'm just saying…

Sorry, I got carried away. I should not be speculating on the thoughts and motivations of TV news executives. Let's just note that the news coverage of elections, especially at the national level, has stretched out from being a season of events that cycles into the news coverage every few years to now become an almost continuous subject of news program speculation and coverage. I use the term speculation to point out that this political coverage has evolved into a whole new species of news reporting in which a broadcast anchor is not telling us what has happened (the traditional definition of the news) but instead is asking some pundit or expert what might or will happen sometime in the future. At the same time that old horse race imagery has become the conventional mode of coverage for many election contests that in retrospect were never even close.

The proliferation of cable channels has brought with it outlets that, for our viewing pleasure, are intentionally biased. Fox News maneuvers through what is happening to appeal to the tastes and objectives of the right and MSNBC tells us what the world should be looking like to good progressives. Comedy Central uses, what else, comedy, to lampoon the absurdity and irrelevance of the players and the postures of the political scene while that scene never seems to leave the comedy writers short for material.

Before going on we should at least acknowledge the existence of two other broadcast sources, Public Broadcasting (in particular NPR radio and PBS television) and CSPAN. As we began this examination of various media, I distinguished between the admittedly-biased, the based-but-not-admittedly-biased and those optimists who strive for objective facts. NPR And PBS are staffed by people of either the second or the third of these three types depending on who you talk to. Since they are criticized for bias more from the right than the left, you may be among those who score them with a liberal bias. These public broadcasters once relied on a good amount of public funding, but with these criticisms of bias and the more general trend to reduce the reach of government, that funding has given way to dependence on viewer/listener donations. CSPAN on the other hand is funded by the cable and satellite service providers. Its content escapes some of those criticisms of bias in large part because CSPAN specializes in gavel to gavel coverage of Congressional activities in all their boring reality.

> **Gloss Note:** AM radio is a niche in broadcasting that any politically knowledgeable person should probably be aware of. Besides those call-in sports shows and religious programming, outspoken political ideologues of both the right and the left are there waiting for us. After the FCC scrapped the fairness doctrine, these highly ideological talk shows became a staple of AM radio programming. At the time of this writing, the right-wing talk radio personalities include Rush Limbaugh, Glenn Beck, Sean Hannity, and Michael Savage. The array from the left includes Thom Hartmann, Randi Rhodes, Bill Press, and Alan Colmes. There are many more and since some of them are at the mic several hours every day, they are easy to catch. This comes with a warning. For many of your fellow citizens, this stuff seems to be addictive. Many of their listeners can't make it through a day without getting a fix.

Think Tanks: At the heart of the process of purposely converting the glut of raw information into politically actionable ideas, we find organizations popularly referred to as think tanks. In general, these organizations are tax exempt and devoted to in-depth study and policy advocacy in specific areas of our society. They recruit authors, scientists, and academics who specialize in their area of interest. As such, these research and policy institutions can be thought of as doing the intellectual heavy lifting in confronting the information overload we are talking about here. However, as available resources out there to inform you and me, the think tanks differ considerably. Some cultivate a public presence, and others are more private and even secretive. When it comes to questions of bias and spin, these organizations are all over the map, with some doggedly fitting the facts into their professed narrow ideological slot and others displaying far more political open-mindedness. As a result, the label, think tank, can apply equally to an impressive world class intellectual effort at study and problem solving on the one hand, and on the other hand, to a sham propaganda outfit trying to clothe itself in some of the trappings of intellectual respectability. It is probably of some value to understand the wide application of this term, think tank, even though this isn't going to be much help to you when it comes to the credibility of a given think tank. Wikipedia will give you a list of these organizations.[11]

Scientific Facts and Our Politics: Beyond this, maybe we can improve our skills in sorting out spin from actionable facts by moving away from the sources and focusing more on methods. If, as I would contend, sloppy governing decisions are most likely to come out of a sloppy understanding of the facts, then we could benefit here from going straight to a political controversy about knowledge itself that has emerged in recent years. This controversy is of course about science and the value of the scientific method as a way of understanding our world and what government can and should do. The science controversy is not that one side believes in the validity of scientific facts and the other does not (granted, there are certain politicians who bad-mouth science generally as part of their anti-intellectual shtick). What it often comes down to is politicians and political interest groups in disagreement about what the scientifically established facts are.

I will cite the example of where the science-based political debate is at its loudest: the issue of carbon burning and climate change. These days even petroleum industry executives seem to accept the finding that human created CO_2 is warming things up.[12] Yet some politicians continue to assert that the science they respect shows no relationship between burning fossil fuels and global warming. This 'my science' versus 'your science' stuff has become commonplace. It confronts us all the time. When corporate profits and liabilities are at stake, the left often rests their case on accusations about purely financial motives. But we need to go further. Since science is now quite often one of the determinants of government policy, we need to have a reasonably good understanding of what it is. What it is not, and how information that is said to be scientific gets to us.

THE CONTEMPORARY POLITICAL SCENE

Yes, I admit, with certain reservations, I generally support the scientific quest. My old friend, quoted at the beginning of this chapter, tells us that science is just somebody's opinion. This is, after all, a pretty widespread belief. Not only is it popular, but it is true; true for a whole range of things that are *misrepresented* to us as science. It is because of such misrepresentations that a basic understanding of what science is has probably become essential for any informed citizen. If you see this as another one of my detours, I can only say that I promise to keep it brief. Here goes:

When we were looking back at the glory days of the Enlightenment, pre French Revolution, science, the newly recognized way of knowing about the world, was a central feature of the unbridled optimism of the times. Human progress was revealing itself everywhere, and the very engine of that progress was science. Remember Destutt de Tracy? If he'd been right about the power of his new science of "ideology" you wouldn't have to read books like this. Science would have eliminated the need for all political differences long, long ago. What could possibly have prevented such an inevitable outcome? As the years passed, the methods and limits of science became clearer. Because of its prominence in political discussion, we will first consider how science is supposed to work, but just as important, we will look at how it can fail to live up to its promise. After all, science is a human endeavor very much susceptible to human failings.

First, the way it is supposed to work. Think of it as a kind of social networking thing that takes place among people with similar interests. It could be ants, or how police perform their duties, or the aurora borealis, or language learning among toddlers, but it does need lots of players interested in the same thing. There might be hundreds or even tens of thousands of them. They network mostly in writing so they don't have to ever get together in the same place at the same time. Each of them is looking closely at this thing going on that they are all interested in. It might be something that they have been fascinated with since they were kids, but whatever it is, they are sufficiently obsessed with their subject that they invest the time and effort to learn as much as they can about what has been observed and written about it in the past. Within the scientific disciplines, they refer to all this background material, with pompous sounding words like "the literature," as in "one earns the right to speak only after one has mastered the literature."

And speak up they do. In fact these knowledgeable people make speaking up into an important step in the whole science process. It goes like this. If one, or a group of them, thinks that they have observed something never before seen (new facts), or if they come to the conclusion that they have new information about how the verifiable facts relate to one another (theory), they write about it and explain their new findings. That is to say they write up precisely how they went about to observe their new facts or newly discovered relationships. Many times the write-up actually includes the data, and the observations which led to the finding. But rather than just posting it on their page at the network's website for all to see, they send it to a panel of recognized experts in the field to get agreement that they have actually discovered something new about their subject. If they make the cut and this panel of judges agrees that they have something new to offer to the rest of the network, their write-up is made public in one of the "journals," open forums specially dedicated to the particular scientific network. Just google "journal of" and pick one, if you want a look at one.

So far this all must seem pretty boring. You'd have to be really obsessed with a subject to keep up on it and stick with one of these networks and reading their fine print journal articles that hardly ever have any pictures. But here is where the tension begins to mount and the play can get bumpier. At this point in the proceeding, the entire network is free to—no, they are actually encouraged to—criticize and even invalidate the new finding. They are expected to try their expert best to do this. They might poke holes in the logic of the write-up or they might show that they repeated the same observations and got different results. This is the rough part of the game. And since there are no time limits, it can go on for years. If, for example, the finding comes from a single person, I like to imagine that it resembles a dodge ball game with only one player left from one team and everybody still up on the other team, all trying to knock that one player out of the game. In science they could call this the dodge ball phase, but instead they use a much dryer term. They call it "peer review." Yawn...

To recap, science is a process that produces a store of observable, variable facts and makes attempts to relate those facts to one another logically. It operates within a network of people studying a particular part of nature that the rest of us don't devote near that much attention to. Before any new facts or theoretical relationships are added, everybody gets a chance to challenge them. It is in this way that scientific knowledge builds up over time in these interest areas. As the base of demonstrated, variable facts builds up, participants are encouraged to work up generalizations or theories that explain how these facts relate to each other.

However, in the long run, all the facts and the theories always remain open to rejection if anybody in the network of people familiar with what has been discovered in the past can refute them with more verifiable facts and better theories. This last point is important. Science can never "prove' something is true, it can only show us what cannot be true and what might be true. A favorite illustration of this partial and tentative quality of scientific knowledge is the physics of Isaac Newton. Historians of physics point out that while Albert Einstein and others had taken their science far beyond Sir Isaac by the 1960s, applied Newtonian physics was still perfectly adequate for the calculations that brought humans into earth orbit, into outer space and eventually to their moon landing. Newton's observations and theories were just fine basic knowledge for these accomplishments.

OK so far. Let's see: devoted scholars, verifiable facts, theories, journals, peer reviews. Have I left anything out? I can think of two things missing right off: money and egos. But to fully reckon with these two factors takes us away from the way science is supposed to work and into how it can fail.

Here is what I mean. The network of interested people I mentioned above could very well be a bunch of hobbyists. In fact, early scientists were often just that. Contemporary science, though, often consists of expensive research projects. The researchers do their science as a career. They may receive salaries from universities, or they may work as entrepreneurs, financing their careers and their research from grants they receive from foundations and corporations. Thus success for these people often goes far beyond the satisfaction of obtaining new knowledge. Success also can bring fame and respectable levels of wealth. Also with success there is the potential to partially sidestep the peer review process and put out expensive textbooks and even best sellers..

Now I am not saying that scientists are a bunch of career obsessed money hungry hacks. They are just people of all kinds. Nevertheless, the temptations of wealth and fame cannot be designed out of the enterprise of science, and the possibilities for wealth and fame bring in two consequences that effect science directly and a third that actually attacks science from completely outside of its peer networks. These three problems are:

- Scientific research that has a commercial payoff often takes priority. In other words, what doesn't get funded so much, doesn't get studied so much. Just for example, if our governing process is to benefit from the best information voters and politicians can obtain which subject is likely to find us better scientifically informed; research on convict recidivism upon reentry, or relative excellence of charter schools. Charter schools are more likely to turn over a profit.

- The career success and institutional power that the scientific community can confer can entrench itself as a vested interest and become an obstacle to advances as new facts and theories immerge. Even biographers of Isaac Newton have noted as President of the Royal

Society of British scientists, he took great efforts to suppress intellectual opposition.[13] In the previous chapter and the one which follows this one, influences of commercial advertising far beyond the marketplace are noted. Science is unfortunately not exempt from the temptations of exaggeration and spin. Quite independent of scientific merit, a successful career in science and the funding it requires can be significantly enhanced by the distortions of fame, celebrity, and even crass self-promotion.

- Sometimes there are well established, peer reviewed, scientific facts that compromise commercial interests. When this occurs, the commercial interests have the option of creating the appearance of a significant scientific opposition. People are recruited and funded with the precise purpose of appearing to be scientists or to represent scientists who have findings that dispute the actual, peer reviewed, but inconvenient facts. The classic instance of this involved the tobacco industry back in the 1970s and 80s. The industry fielded invented experts to counter the research about the addictive and harmful effects of smoking. For a shareholder concerned with the value of investment, such fake science dramatics are a cost/benefit no-brainer when compared to accepting the actual scientific findings. It is relatively inexpensive to create reasonable doubt in the court of public opinion.

In short, science has for centuries now been a tried and consistently reliable method of expanding our understanding of the world and ourselves. Scientists, on the other hand, have been silenced and even bought off from time to time. When there is a lot at stake financially, science has been fabricated and scientists, impersonated. Even so, for the informed citizen concerned about pollution, or species extinction, or global warming, or food contaminations, science probably cannot be ignored. And like other facts that must be considered in our politics, science has developed its own media consisting of reliable science reporters who appear on TV, in newspapers, magazines, and popular books.

In conclusion, taken together these various sources of politically relevant material present an overwhelming amount of information, some trustworthy, some not so much. In the end you are the judge of it all. Now we move on to the people who put it to use, in the service of politicians and their campaigns..

THE CONTEMPORARY POLITICAL SCENE

Chapter 10 The Script: Creating the Political Messages

"[Propaganda's] effect for the most part must be aimed at the emotions and only to a very limited degree at the so-called intellect. All propaganda must be popular and its intellectual level must be adjusted to the most limited intelligence among those it is addressed to... As soon as our own propaganda admits so much as a glimmer of right on the other side, the foundation for doubt in our own right has been laid."

Adolf Hitler (1889-1945)[1]

"The [senior adviser to a President] said that guys like me were 'in what we call the reality-based community,' which he defined as people who 'believe that solutions emerge from your judicious study of discernible reality. That's not the way the world really works anymore. We're an empire now, and when we act, we create our own reality. And while you're studying that reality -- judiciously, as you will -- we'll act again, creating other new realities, which you can study too, and that's how things will sort out.'"

Ron Suskind[2]

"By 1968 you can't say "n---er" – that hurts you, it backfires. So you say stuff like, forced busing, states' rights, and all that stuff and you're getting so abstract. Now, you're talking about cutting taxes, and all

these things you're talking about are totally economic things and the byproduct of them is that blacks get hurt worse than whites."

Lee Atwater (1951-1991)[3]

People, throughout history, have made great efforts to influence and control the actions of others by influencing and controlling their beliefs. Even for a dictator, it is clearly easier to get people to do things willingly than it is to have to use force all the time. Popularly elected governments are held to a standard that is a bit higher since they can be criticized and removed from office if they rely on overt coercion and terror to carry out their policies. So influencing political beliefs is a much more important factor for elected governments.

The New Political Pros

To get their best impact, the political messages that reach us, whether from the left or the right, typically invoke beliefs that take positions within the dominant economic and moral perspectives we've been examining. As we have seen, these are deeply felt beliefs held by politically active people. I'd also like to believe that most of the people who commit themselves to elective office, probably hold such deeply held beliefs themselves. However, our task in this chapter is not to better understand the economic and moral content of the political beliefs of politicians and activists, but to appreciate how the professionals of political messaging ply their trade. In fact, I am tempted to say that from this point on we will need to set all considerations of morals and the economy aside. Surely they have political beliefs, but we will see what they do more clearly if we think of these pros; the pollsters, the legions of professional consultants, and campaign managers as a bunch of hired guns. These are the people who, for the most part, work behind the scenes. They are often more akin to marketers and brand managers in the world of commerce than committed political activists.

THE CONTEMPORARY POLITICAL SCENE

The moral and economic divides that prevail among voters and partisans are critical to political pros, but critical as the raw materials they use to work their messaging crafts. To survive in their careers, these pros have come to practice and see politics more strictly as a contest between winners and losers. Apart from whatever their personal political beliefs might be, these pros must compete in a political consulting market place where the folks are all out to win. Their livelihoods and their professional reputations are at stake. And many of them are very good at what they do. It is true that Republican strategist Dick Morris was hired by Bill Clinton to orchestrate his move to the right for his reelection campaign in 1996. But, as a rule, consultants are hired by folks from just one of the parties. Consultants work for Republicans, or they work for Democrats.

To approach this same point in another way, these political pros think about politics and practice politics on a whole other level from the way you or I ever will. If you are expecting that we are about to enter the world of deep, careful logic and reasoned arguments about policy, think again. These pros, themselves,function in an environment that is decidedly postmodern. Their efforts consist of using the popular currency of symbols, pieces and chunks of our language and culture, to move political activists and potential voters. And incidentally, if they are any good at what they do, the financial rewards can be fantastic.

Through good and bad times, theirs has been a growth industry. However, in 2010 the US Supreme Court virtually blew the lid off legal limits to wealth and riches for our professional political consultants. In Citizens United v. Federal Elections Commission, the court took a case involving political activity one of those 501(c) group mentioned in the last chapter. The majority of the justices ruled that restrictions on independent political activities of these groups violates the First Amendment right of free speech. Since then the political dollars really started flowing. Career Counseling Note: Regardless of whether this left/right political stuff attracts you. If you are interested in making lots of money, you could do far worse than political consulting in this post-Citizens United era.

Now let's take a look at some of the things they do. To do this we will get into polling, and the focus group research that message-makers now use to identify and understand the folks who they target with their messages. Once their target audiences have been thus defined, other specialist craft the messages intended to influence attitudes and behaviors (like registering, voting, signing petitions, making contributions, demonstrating, or just not interfering). Finally there is the orchestration of the ground game that gets out the voters.

Researching the Voters

Polling: As we take up opinion polling, let's start by asking ourselves a question. Which would we prefer, a political system where people aspiring to take, and hold, office tell you exactly what they think and what they plan to do, or one where they take great care and incur great expense to tell you what you want to hear? Most will say that they prefer the former. In fact, one of the more nasty ways to criticize an elected office holder is to say that their opinions and positions vacillate with the latest polls. Let me suggest that the relationship between politicians and opinion polls has both this bad side and a good side as well. Good reliable information about what citizens think is of course essential to every chameleon-lizard-politician. However, the same information can be a treasure to a sincere individual intent on perusing the will of the people she or he represents. The information itself is neutral. In the world of politics, opinion polling was a standard feature throughout the last century, with increasingly sophisticated methods bringing more accurate and useful results. Here are some of the features that contribute to effective measurement of public opinion.

Demographic Sampling: If you set out to find out what people think about something, the best way to do it would be to just ask every last one of them. To control their costs, pollsters have continually worked on ways to ask as few people as possible and still get a handle on current beliefs in whole populations. This process of limiting the number of contacts is, of course, sampling. Pollsters build their sample of survey contacts by including people with various characteristics, in the proportions that these same characteristics are found in the larger population. These are characteristics that they suspect, might make people see the poll questions differently, like sex, income, age, marital status, race/language group. They have become good at it. A reliable national poll can sometimes have as little as a few hundred people in the sample. Since polling done in connection with political campaigns is most interested in potential voters, pollsters take care to exclude people from their samples who cannot vote or are not likely to vote. One of the ways that only likely voters can be targeted is to rely on public records that are available which show who is registered and who has voted in past elections.

The Questions: Good survey results of course also depend on good questions. Experience has taught pollsters that people balk and just plain lie when confronted with certain questions. In the 1950s, pioneer sex researcher, Alfred Kinsey, found that he did best by moving his questions about income to the very end of his long interview. Subjects who could talk and talk about their intimate sex lives would refuse to talk about their finances and sometimes end the interview. The precise wording of questions can also be critical. If you ask people what they think of the institution of Congress, as it is defined in the US Constitution you will get very positive responses from most people. When asked about what they think of their own Congressional Representatives the responses will be a little bit less positive. When the survey question asks people to evaluate all of the politicians now serving in Congress, strong disapproval comes out.

Then there is a range of instances when people seem likely to tell lies. For instance, going into the Mid-term elections of 2014 there were at least a dozen Senate and Governor's races that the polls said were way too close to call right up to election day. When the actual votes were counted, Republican candidates won by large margins, prompting the unlikely speculation that, in spite of the highly polarized climate, lots of folks had changed their minds at the last second. German writer, Elisabeth Noelle-Neumann has a more interesting explanation of such serious flaws in political polling. As she sees it, people are not likely to publicly express opinions that might isolate them. As opinion shifts take place, people feel increasing pressure to hide their opinions when they think their views are unpopular. She has called this kind of event a "spiral of silence," since actual opinions are getting further and further away from what people are saying. She says that people's fear of isolation, is the ultimate cause of this polling flaw, and thinks such fears are quite characteristic of Americans.[4] If correct, this would seem to be a lot like the go-along-to get-along phenomenon we came across in chapter 6.

Access to subjects: Even with a good sample and good questions polling cannot succeed if the pollsters can't reach the subjects. This problem created difficulties when the cell phone became the telephone of choice. Over 40% of US households could not be reached by land line by 2013 compared less than 5% back in the late 1990s. Since cell phones first became more popular with young people, it is not surprising that, in the 2008 Presidential election surveys that also used cell phone numbers found different (higher) levels of support for Obama than for McCain. People do not necessarily cooperate just because a pollster manages to reach them. In fact, there seems to be a trend with an increasing number of folks taking a pass when questioned in a poll. In some forms of polling these refusals now come from a majority of those contacted, which leaves it up to the statisticians to come up with methods of speculating about what the majority think, while basing their findings on only a minority of their sample. And while we are on the subject we should note that when we get news reports of those "horse race" polls during a campaign, they normally refer to the opinions of "likely voters," just another reminder of how little nonvoter's opinions really matter.

Bogus polling: An altogether different set of difficulties has been threatening accurate polling in recent times. Some highly partisan websites poll their highly partisan viewers and present the results as though they are representative of *all* Americans. Other phony polls are actually after your money. So-called "push polls" that aim to spread false information may be undermining whatever legitimacy political pollsters might have had. Many of you have already been contacted for what seems to be a survey but quickly turns out to be a pitch for a check or a credit card number. Push polls ask questions that are made-up BS, questions like, "If reports turn out to be true that Candidate X has a record as a pedophile, not just in this state, but also in nine other states, would you be prepared to vote for him?" Besides these kinds of negative experiences generally, the increasing sophistication people have with polling may threaten accuracy. If you are contacted by a pollster, what would be your motivation to give honest replies (especially if you somehow suspected that they were working for someone you dislike)?

Tracking polls: A polling technique called tracking has now become a stable feature of most political campaigns. Tracking polls develop a small sample of potential voters that the campaign has confidence about and then goes back to this sample again and again to get running feedback on their reactions to the messages and events in the ongoing campaign. This tracking sometimes continues even after a candidate is elected and in office. The usefulness of tracking is thus obviously only as good as the sample.

Focus Groups: While innovations from commerce and innovations from politics led to increasing accuracy polling in both fields, we should take particular notice of one series of commercial developments. Whether commercial or political, the ultimate objective of all this opinion stuff is to sell people; to shape or shift their preferences, their desires, and ultimately, their behaviors. As we know, quite early on marketers realized that by choosing different ways of picturing their products and different words to talk about these products, they could actually affect marketplace demand. Out of the kinds of mundane market research that brought us tooth-whiteners and remote car starters, a whole new packaging and selling sub-specialty arose in political research.

The objective of focus group political researchers is not just to sample the opinions people have, but to discover ways to change those opinions. This not only includes getting people to accept more favorable impressions about their client/candidates, but also to get them to view opposing candidates more negatively. Focus group researchers, now routinely work on changing the way people feel about particular issues, policies, laws, and even institutions like the political parties, the branches of our government and the US Constitution. And let me emphasize the word "feel." As I've already mentioned, the going theory is that first we react with our feelings and then we work out the reasons. There is even some convincing social science that backs this up.[5] Thus focus group research is after discovering the quick reactions and gut feelings which presumably set us up for believing one way or another about people or issues, and putting this knowledge to work.

Focus group researchers vary in their methods. Let's take a look at how Frank Luntz, one of the more famous practitioners, reports on his operations. You may have seen him. He now appears pretty regularly on TV. And, by the way, just because Luntz has done most of his business with Republicans shouldn't suggest that the Democrats are focus group slackers. They also rely on focus groups. In his book, "Words that Work," Luntz describes some of the typical ingredients of this technique.[6] Potential focus group members are pre-screened by written questionnaires, so that the researchers are confident that they are representative of the kinds of folks they eventually want to influence, and also to be sure that they are likely to contribute usable input, (silent-types and loud mouths need not apply). The result is a group of just 10 or so carefully selected folks, who the researchers use to learn about the target demographic, whose sentiments and thinking they want to understand. The uniformity of the study group not only allows researchers to better generalize to the larger demographic they represent but it also helps assure an atmosphere in which members feel freer to fully express themselves.

The focus group subjects are presented material that they are to react to, and they are further encouraged to express their feelings in the group's discussion. All the while observers look on from outside the room, through one-way mirrors. Sessions can last a few hours. Sound like not much fun? Don't worry, if you ever get picked, you will probably get paid. Keep in mind, the goal is not only to find out what people think, but to find out the best way to present products, ideas and facts, so that the members, and more important, people in the target demographic group will be likely to accept them. Whether it be a product, a policy, or a politician, matters little. This is a kind of reactions laboratory, where the objective is to discover how to achieve the right reactions. I remember an instance years ago when I lived in Detroit, it was widely rumored that Ford executives put a stop to the release of the new Mustang model and replace it with a completely different car. Focus groups of Mustang lovers had apparently had their say. They made it clear that they wouldn't tolerate their macho-Mustangs with front-wheel-drive!

In a more high tech variation that Luntz calls "Dial sessions," a larger number of people take part. Conversation is unnecessary. Each participant is provided with a hand held, wireless device on which he or she can immediately register their reactions as material is presented. With the data thus obtained the researchers get a numerical measure of how positive or negative the focus group members are reacting.

Focus group research that has had a profound impact on our politics since it was introduced about thirty years ago. Beyond the specific tested words and stances that have been adopted by individual campaigns, there are some more general effects we might note. Since negative focus group reactions can be quite clear and intense, focus group research has taught politicians to never say things and revealed topics they should avoid. Thus it has made them more guarded, some would say less bold and even intentionally vague on a whole range of topics. By the same token, focus group research has tutored them in the opposite direction by allowing them to master those "hot button" words and phrases that make their base supporters drool and bark like dogs. At the same time, negative findings from focus group research have contributed to the growing popularity of negative campaigning. However this matter of focus groups might strike you, what is clear is that it is not likely to go away in the near future.

> **Gloss Note:** In his classic novel, 1984, about how totalitarian governments operate, George Orwell, used the term "newspeak" to describe how language was used as a tool of the government to control. Consistent with focus group research, part of the purpose of newspeak was to replace negative and controversial words with neutral, accepted ones. Critics on both right and left often cite weird word choices in our politics as focus-group- sourced instances of newspeak aimed at countering oppositional thinking. For instance, critics on the right cite the preposterousness of naming an extremely expensive law subsidizing medical insurance for millions of people, The Affordable Care Act. The history of this controversial law is a textbook case of newspeak. Initially designed by the conservative, Heritage Foundation, and passed into law in Massachusetts, when the Democrats took it from the Republicans and made it Federal law in 2010, conservative politicians disowned it and resorted to calling it "Obamacare" and attacked it at every turn. This tactic was extremely effective. For example in Kentucky, where this law was, implemented under the name "Kynect," according to polling, (NBC/Marist College, May 2014), when called, "Kynect," only 22% of Kentuckians disapproved of it. When called "Obamacare," 60% disapproved of this same law.

Opposition Research: If you are truly an outside observer to the struggles of our politics, there is one aspect that you are nonetheless quite familiar with; and that is the negativity that dominates our political conversation. Slanderous attacks, assertions of guilt by association, dug up dirt, and outright scandals are part of every day's TV and internet fare. One reason for this will come up in the next chapter. There we will see that politics has come to rely less and less on issues and more and more on personalities. This makes for a situation where personal attacks simply work better than they might have in the past. If you have ever made a political donation or if you have simply been mistaken for a potential political contributor, the relentless piling on of this trash turns up in your email and mailboxes as well. There is ample public opinion research that has brought consultants to encourage politicians to go negative. Even so, there are also instances where this kind of stuff has backfired. The point for us is that it is taken as common wisdom that negative messages against the opposition really work, and so long as consultants and candidates believe this, we are not likely to get a break from this sad stuff. Here, in summary are the main components of this current consensus that negative politicking really works:

1. If politician A's campaign consultants can discover and publicize bad things in the past of opposing candidate B, then candidate A's supporters are affected emotionally. Whether its fear, rage, disgust, or whatever, they not only become more emotionally committed to A, but they are more likely to contribute to his or her campaign and show up to vote.

2. If people who are indifferent to both candidates, get turned off enough by negative messages, they become less likely to show up to vote.

3. The negative messages can even register with some of the supporters of opposition candidate B and turn them off enough so they don't show up to vote.[7]

If there is any truth behind this consensus about negative campaigning, it looks pretty powerful. It helps the candidate by enhancing the turnout among supporters. It depresses turnout among those iffy folks in the middle. And it might even shave off some of the votes for the opposition.

With all this going for the negative side, it is no wonder we now have campaign researchers and think-tank people whose specialty is digging up, or out-right fabricating, and the dishing dirt. We will get to the dishing part momentarily. If you think about it, the task of negative research, even if the practitioner is completely committed to accurate reporting, isn't that challenging. Here is what I mean. Look back on your own life experience. Who is the most unsavory person you have ever known? What have you done that could have made the papers if you were a celebrity or politician? With the exception of those among you qualifying for sainthood, the negatives are probably there for the taking.

The negative researchers actually work on two fronts. They dig into the opposition candidates to get negatives and if they really hit pay dirt, they might even uncover the makings of a scandal. At the same time they screen the candidate they work for and all of her or his associations so that they can get the jump on the opposition research of the other candidate and have a serviceable response ready or even spin it out preemptively.

Political Messaging Making

Now that we've looked into some of the raw materials that inform the message makers, we can take up how such information is put to use to communicate with voters. As was mentioned in connection with the history of PR, virtually all of the communications from politicians are mediated or at least planned and practiced under the guidance of political advisors. Politicians and candidates hardly ever depart from this planned and guided communication path. And as mediated communications, the messages are narrowly focused on that minority whose support is sought, the potential voters, contributors and volunteers.

Focus groups, opinion polling, and opposition research make up most of the raw materials used in developing the messages that politicians and their campaigns deliver. As we turn to the messages themselves, we need to have perspective on the objectives they seek to accomplish. Of course, they are after campaign contributions and ultimately votes, but what does this quest look like in general terms? Let's look at an imaginary example. It's a "3 thirds hypothetical:" Granted, most of the time one side starts with an advantage, but for our hypothetical let's look at national campaign in which two candidates start out equal. To put this vote-getting in some kind of perspective, we can use fractions.

The actual percentages vary, but let's just say for the moment, that nationally, Americans who participate in elections can be roughly divided into thirds: one third with Republican leanings, one third with Democrat leanings, and a middle third who identify with neither party consistently. If people in this third in the middle can be brought in, they can potentially contribute and vote either way. (For state and local campaigns the concentration of partisans can be far more favorable for one or the other party making for an easier messaging effort.)

First, with the 1/3 leaning toward support. These are the base of supporters. The voter research is used to identify the hot buttons: the beliefs to appeal to and the words to use that will stoke their emotions and commitments so that they will volunteer, contribute money and turn out to vote. The messages crafted for base supporters articulate the importance of what the consultants understand as critical, and even sacred for these people.

The 1/3 that leans toward the opposition is addressed differently. According to the common wisdom among the political consultants, people in this part of the electorate are most open to negative messages and even scandalous information about the candidate they might otherwise line up behind.

The middle 1/3 thus becomes the essential target for all kinds of convincing messages. Do the math. If this 1/3, 1/3, 1/3 split were at all accurate, the objective is to peel off just another sixteen and two thirds percent, or whatever less it takes to win. The consultants use the research to address that middle third; not the whole third, but segments of it, that they might bring to their side. This is how commentators get to throwing around demographic labels like Joe six-pack (male working stiffs who might go for either party), soccer-moms (married females with concerns about their children's futures). More recently, campaigns have been focusing on the not-yet-party-aligned younger people and also the diverse nationality groups they casually lump together as either Asians or Latinos.

As the professional campaign consultants do their work, some simple ground rules apply as they draft and implement messages about candidate images and stances (on morals, economics, personal character, current events, and issues). They have to take care not to present messages for base supporters which might not appeal to segments they think they might peel out of that uncommitted middle 1/3. If the base is motivated by a candidate's anti-tax stance, there is going to be trouble if he or she courts uncommitted moms with a stance that educational improvements will necessitate expensive reforms. As we leave this 1/3, 1/3, 1/3 illustration notice, where you nonvoters fit in. No place! Sorry, the task of turning nonvoters into voters who can be dependably turned out for a particular candidate is both too risky and too expensive as a viable campaign strategy. This results in campaigning which ignores unlikely voters most of the time

Now for the messaging. There is a good deal of agreement among political consultants about how to turn opinion research into effective appeals. As an unwilling observer of the incessant political messaging that reaches us, you are no doubt familiar with many of these methods. Let me mention a few.

Low information content: The old admonition, KISS—Keep it simple stupid, has become common-sense wisdom that guides most of the

THE CONTEMPORARY POLITICAL SCENE

messaging that is presented in hopes of influencing voters. But the STUPID here refers to supporters and potential supporters. Now doesn't that make their ignoring you feel better? The dumbing down is, at least in part, inspired by a continuous stream of reminders about how clueless the public is out there. We are trying to talk politics here when, according to a September 2014 Annenberg survey, over 60% of the folks out there can't name the three branches of government defined in the US Constitution, and a third of them couldn't name even one branch, (It's no shame not to be a trivia expert—they are the Executive, Legislative, and Judicial).[8] Like it or not, the KISS idea has really taken hold. As a result, all we are likely to get from politicians and their ads is simple words, emotion evoking words and pictures, and short sentences aimed at the low grade levels. If you get a sense that politicians sound sophomoric you are right. A nonpartisan group studied the speechifying going on in congress and found that it comes in at about the 10th-graders' level, and has been decidedly falling in recent years.[9] Tenth grade! In the real world, even people who quit school at or before the tenth grade continue to expand their knowledge and verbal sophistication, but apparently our lawmakers never consider this. What is certainly ironic and maybe worthy of suspicion, is that the official written work of these 10th grade talkers, (the bills they sponsor, the rules promulgated to implement the laws they pass, and the court decisions that often follow), is expressed in a highly sophisticated language of lawyers and lobbyists that cannot easily translate into this 10th grade speak.

The same principle that instructs message makers to talk down to their audience also insists on their being brief. This is to take account of our assumed short attention spans. The main casualties of these efforts to avoid lots of words are many of the issues and problems that confront us as citizens. This stems from the fact that, in the real world, issues and problems are very often complex and multi-layered. Simplistic depictions can be down-right dangerous. But in practice contemporary political messages avoid complexity like the plague, and distill it into single words and short phrases that go after the desired impression and the emotion it calls up in us. The resulting brevity is sometimes just short of poetic. You don't have to understand the issues like government funding, health care cost inflation, or poverty; think of "Obamacare." Skip all that stuff about ethnic prejudice, citizenship and international relations; think "Dreamers." We are given what passes for an analysis, a conclusion and often an indictment in a phase or a few well-chosen words: War on Women, Benghazi Cover-up, School Choice, Open Carry, A fair break, The Israel Lobby, Media Bias. Behind each of these there may be an actual complicated issue that confronts us, but more often there may be just a few actual facts overlaid with bold yet fuzzy partisan assertions. There is nothing subtle in these short hand messages. The trick is to create a mental connection between a politician on the one hand and an emotionally charged value in the mind of voters and contributors. Any details, let alone the pros and cons of issues, are avoided. One of my favorites, "Special Interests" is a term that is almost perfect for politicians of either side to use. As near as I have been able to figure it out it means "Anybody who might be working against my best interests."

Aw shucks. In fairness, simple brief language is also preferred for a couple of other reasons. Heaps of research from the world of commerce supports the idea that consistent and repetition of simple, novel phrases, (the kind that comes from those old commercial jingles) can really bore into people's heads. And in fact, given the number and complexity of the problems our democratic traditions are probably facing, a detailed consideration would take up more time than most of us have. We might be happy with all this brevity and simplification, were it not for the immense distortion that comes with it.

Framing: When the messaging needs to change the way people think about something, the message makers sometimes resort to "framing."Consultants do framing when they make efforts to redefine an idea or issue by talking about it in a novel context; choosing a different "frame" of reference. By doing this they make the item a smaller part of a wider perspective within which it takes on a different meaning. This might sound a little confusing. Let me give you an example. Immigration is simply people from other countries coming into this country for long-term residence. When they discuss immigration, politicians and commentators on the left, dependably try to place it in a particular historical context; they frame the issue in terms of a "story of America." You know how this framing works: "We are a nation of immigrants." Leaving out the involuntarily African immigrants, the story goes like this. Each wave of new people, (the English, the, the Germans, the Scandinavians, the Irish, Asians, the Southern and Eastern Europeans, and now the Latinos and the Arabs and many other new-comers) meet first with some unreasoned hostility, and then at last gain full acceptance as part of the "us" that is the United States. According to this frame of reference, we are the most vital and creative nation because we are a racial, ethnic and religious "melting pot."

An alternative historical framing, while probably quite popular, is seldom as fully expressed. Let me take a stab at it. "We started as a nation of Anglo-European settlers who came here and put down roots and developed vast lands where only small numbers of wandering hunter-gatherers once roamed. After settling, the success of the Anglo-European efforts attracted numerous other groups of immigrants. Efforts to absorb these immigrants have continually put all kinds of cultural and religious strains and demands on the settlers and their descendants. You may be thinking of these two framings as naive Kumbaya in one instance and harsh racism in the other, but that's not the point. Nor is this a matter of true or false. In both cases the framing is putting--people from other countries coming into this country--into a larger context that gives it a positive or a negative evaluation. Depending upon how it is framed, immigration becomes a continuing national asset, or it becomes a chronic national problem.

When done effectively the new context that framing creates and the valuation that comes with it sticks and becomes a part of our culture. Years ago opponents of birth control and abortion adopted the frame of reference they called "pro-life." While there is no denying that favoring successful pregnancies and births can be pro-life, this frame casts those who do not agree with them into some hypothetical opposite, the "pro-death" camp. These are only words. Or are they? Aren't they evaluations of moral character? And the pro-life label has really stuck. In this game of words the alternative frame of reference, "pro-choice" is much weaker and it only begs the question. It connotes a choice between what and what, (is there a pro-abortion segment of the population who would like to see a lot more abortions)?

Another favorite technique of framing is to use the "war" metaphor to indicate extreme conflict, literally soldiers in a combat to the death. Sometimes it sticks, sometimes not so much. We have had this war framing for poverty, cancer, drugs, women, terror, and Christmas, to name a few. If we were to be keeping score, to date, none of these wars have been won.

One of the best instances of framing came from former Nixon speech writer, Pat Buchanan. Buchanan was asked to give a speech himself, back in 1992, at the Republican National Convention. In the polarizing politics of the two decades then just past, the nation had been through partisan debates about civil rights, the Vietnam War, drug laws, poverty, welfare, crime, immigration, and Presidential impeachment. In a highly effective speech Buchanan combined all these issues and many others, and explained to his listeners that they were at war, with enemies within, bent on destroying our country. He asserted that our politics had evolved into a "culture war;" a struggle for the very sole of the nation and everything his Republican listeners held sacred.[10] His framing has really stuck with us. Not only do people on the right frame their views as part of a cultural struggle, but a major proportion those on the left have come to see their politics the same way. Nice work Pat! For our purposes we need to remind ourselves that one of the defining features of our politics is that there is no war going on within this country. Civil War combat ended 150 years ago. Further, his framing, neglects the fact that our political disagreements involve a lot more than culture. We differ on all kinds of policies involving economics, the environment, foreign policy, justice, and the very size, and reach, of government. But the fact that all of this conflict doesn't neatly sort us all into two armies facing off, has not seemed to have dampened the popularity of this framing oversimplification over the years. Do you take sides in the culture war?

Negative Messages: This is where the negative research gets used. There are candidates and consultants who pledge to avoid negative campaigning. Some by the luxury of their lead or the strength of their character, actually do avoid it. What is closer to the reality of things is that politicians benefit most when they passionately oppose negative campaigning while effective negative messages about the opposition abound. To assure negative campaigning dependability, the negative stuff can emanate from outside the candidate's campaign organization. "Uncoordinated" 501(c) groups often fill this role. The messages that develop out of opposition research are, of course, crafted to turn people off. They can be very narrowly focused to shave off small numbers who identify with a single issue, or to reach a broader target. A fascinating account of this line of work can be found in *Blinded by the Right* a book by David Brock who started his career as a hired gun writing attacks for the right and now points his guns from the left side of our politics.[11] On TV, we call these, attack ads. Take a minute to recall some attack ads you have seen. Some of the producers of such ads are rich and famous because of the wide-spread belief that their TV spots have been so effective. As a result, the makers have become so confident that a lot of this material seems to follow a formula. You are forced to watch a series of grainy black and white shots of the opposition candidate or his or her dirty doings—the sad faces of the helpless people he or she has hurt so bad—all capped with an admonition that all this must be stopped. It is difficult to be sure that you aren't watching a movie trailer from "Sin City." What is even more difficult is to figure out if these attack ads were inspired by the new film noir, or whether it was the other way around.

Some of the messaging in the negative bag of tricks departs from the truth altogether. Examples from recent elections include mailing out fake mail-in ballots, the "push polling" mentioned earlier, and pamphlets and mailers containing false information about dates and places for voting.

If one of our messaging pros were to have their secret dream, it would probably be to hatch a scandal that is tied to the opposition's candidate. There have been political scandals in the past, but the contemporary scene is particularly well suited to them. This political atmosphere that is particularly ripe for scandal is part of the subject of the next chapter, so we can save the topic of scandal for there.

Summary

To bring this subject of messaging to a close, since the task of political messaging is to present the candidate or office holder in the most favorable light, it was probably inevitable that practitioners began borrowing their techniques from PR and commercial advertising. And as PR and advertising got more sophisticated with surveys and focus group research, so did the pros in the political industry. With these techniques they are able to tap the emotions and deeply held beliefs of the folks who are politically active. In good messaging work the practitioner has at her or his disposal the entire universe of human symbols and meanings and the postmodern sensibilities which allow them to creatively combine and present them to best and most persuasive/evocative effect. Good messaging work can literally buy votes and support. The fact that almost all that we see or hear from politicians is indirect and mediated through TV, radio, and the internet, has facilitated their work by allowing these professionals to carefully stage and even script a major part of what reaches the potential voters. As we will see, their objective is to present a media persona who people feel they know and trust, while raising feelings of incompatibility and mistrust for the opposition.

THE CONTEMPORARY POLITICAL SCENE

Moving forward, it is already clear that the funding bonanza that is now coming into our politics will finance more and more targeted messaging and direct contact with individual voters. The newest area of consulting expertise involves what's referred to as the "ground game". The map of your neighborhood and everybody else's is now in the hands of campaign operatives and your residence is marked for "contacts." Once they have you listed as one of their possible voters and have your cell number, you can expect at least three or four friendly contacts as election day nears.

But recall the previous chapter. The work of these political consultants doesn't exist in a vacuum. Their work has to be sufficiently durable to confront the mountains of facts and data that are produced outside campaigns and other activist organizations. In fact, to be accepted, their political messages have to be consistent with at least some of these outside facts and data.

The facts, the messages, **now for the audience and the actors**.

THE CONTEMPORARY POLITICAL SCENE

Chapter 11 The Audience and the Actors: How do we Know the Politicians?

"I refuse to join any club that would have me as a member."

Attributed to Groucho Marx (1890-1977)

"Celebrity is the advantage of being known by those who do not know you."

Nicholas Chamfort (1741-1794)[1]

"There are two things that are important in politics. The first is money, and I can't remember what the second one is."

Mark Hanna (1837-1904)[2]

Now that we have explored the vast information generated out of our self-governing and how political messaging has developed, we can take up some of the striking changes that have occurred among those presenting and receiving these messages. I am convinced that together these changes help to explain a lot of what has made our contemporary politics seem so unattractive to so many. So, in this chapter the politicians and their audiences are the featured subject. However, this is not just a simple matter of the men and women in public life speaking directly to us as we crowd around to hear them. It is my intent to demonstrate that a major shift has taken place on the political scene. On the surface this shift appears to be a change of the focus of our politics from issues that affect us to the personalities of the politicians themselves. While true as far as it goes, this recent emphasis on personalities is probably better understood as only half of the story, because, while this shift from issues to personalities was happening, there has also been a noticeable change in the way that each of us relate to one another as citizens. First we will take up the changes in how we relate to one another as citizens, and then go on to the shift in the way we understand and choose among our politicians.

The Loosening Ties Among Americans

Back in the 1830s, French travel writer/political philosopher, Alex De Tocqueville noted the high levels of public discussion among the people he encountered during his travels here. He became a firm believer in how essential this continuous conversation among our people was to the success of our new republic. He was positively enchanted with the extent to which this country's residents displayed their citizenship and their sense of equality by using their freedoms of speech and assembly to sustain a vibrant political discussion everywhere he went, "No sooner do you set foot on American soil than you find yourself in a tumult...a thousand voices are heard at once, each expressing some social requirements...If an American should be reduced to occupying himself with his own affairs, at that moment half his existence would be snatched from him."[3]

Following his lead, observers of our public life have generally agreed that free speech, assembly, and press are necessary enablers for the discussions, debates, criticisms, arguments, demonstrations, shouting and so on, which have always been recognized as essential to the success of our representative government. The rationale behind this view is, of course, not only that wide ranging dialogue ensures exposure, debate and testing of candidates and ideas but also that a true consent of the governed necessitates at least some degree of consensus among those governed. Not an agreement on every single law and

THE CONTEMPORARY POLITICAL SCENE

ruling but at least a general consensus on the overall representativeness or at very least the legitimacy of those in power.

These ideas about the importance of an ongoing public conversation have continued to make sense to observers of our governing system, and as research on our governing practices grew, scholars realized that this public political discussion could be formulated into questions amenable to research. For instance, what are the circumstances that bring people together to discuss things of interest to them? Are occasions where this happens getting more or less frequent? Is the general degree of consensus substantial? Is it increasing or declining?

There's a generic term researchers use for places where people get together and talk about things that interest them: "voluntary associations". This term nicely emphasizes the two most important characteristics of such groups. They are not compulsory, and participation is primarily a social activity rather than for pay, for instance. In an influential book about voluntary associations, researcher, Robert Putnam, reported on his extensive research.[4] Since several of his insights seem quite relevant to our topic, I'll try to summarize them here. In this book Putnam traces a clear decline in participation in all kinds of voluntary associations throughout the latter decades of 20th Century. He documented this decline by analyzing the membership records of all kinds of voluntary membership organizations. Just to get a feel for what he is looking at, I'll mention some examples of the associations he studied: PTA, League of Women Voters, 4H Club, AMA, the Kiwanis, (the social clubs named after animals like) the Lions, the Elks, the Eagles, the Moose(s), the Shriners, the Masons, Knights of Columbus. As you read these names I am sure you'll at least not question his data, after all, these are now mostly organizations that only old people belong to. But that's precisely his point, the membership of these voluntary associations is aging. It is literally dying off while at the same time, new members aren't showing up. For most of the organizations he studied, this has been going on since the 60s, with overall participation declines of 40-

50%. What is more, new replacement, get-together organizations like these aren't springing up either. But it doesn't stop with the kinds of organizations I just mentioned. The title of his book is *Bowling Alone,* which might sound strange until you hear that, at the time of writing, there were more people bowling in this country than there were people voting, and yet the once very popular, organized bowling leagues that brought teams together to bowl each week, were experiencing the same kind of decline in participation that he found in the PTA and the Masons. As a true fan of the movie, "The Big Libowski", the part about bowling was hard for me to contemplate.

This fall off in going to organizations where people get together was just Putnam's initial finding. People invite friends over for dinner or house parties less. They go to public meetings less. They get together to play cards less. What might surprise you is that, in an era of evangelical religious resurgence, overall attendance at religious services also declined. Putnam noted the same trend in political organizations and the political parties themselves. He identified reasons for these trends: longer commutes, families with two or more jobs and the electronic video screens which now take up the time that used to be spent in front of the live faces of other people. (He reports that, on an average, Americans were watching television four hours a day, even though he found that face to face socializing is actually enjoyable for most people, and also that, for relative enjoyment, people rank even being at work, higher than they rank watching television.)

Putnam's analysis goes on to point out that the linkages that emerge among people who hang out with other people are important connections that facilitate getting things done in a society. He calls this dynamic of connectedness, "social capital." If you are interested in knowing more, you might go to check out one of his lectures on C-Span.[5]

As you take some time to mull these findings over, you are probably beginning to ask yourself just what's so special about this face to face interaction stuff for our topic, politics? Consider trust for a moment.

THE CONTEMPORARY POLITICAL SCENE

Beginning with De Tocqueville getting all excited about how vibrant and open the ongoing public conversation was in the early years in this country, writers have seen this kind of activity as the basis of our mutual trust. It is not unlikely that causation here works both ways. The public conversation engenders trust and the trust facilitates the conversation. In contrast, levels of mutual trust are notoriously low in authoritarian situations. Imagine yourself dropped into East Germany, back in the 1970s. With a population of 17 million, the Stazi, security police, boasted 90,000 full time employees and another 170,000 collaborators on the ready to snitch on their neighbors and coworkers. But you don't have to imagine 1970s East Germany to get my point. Your employment experiences might very well have taken you into an authoritarian business organization where your survival required that you quickly realize that nobody could be trusted. On the other hand, trust facilitates talk, and talk facilitates trust.

Let's go at the same point from a different direction; consider a single individual's experiences with all kinds of people, over time. For those of us who aren't hopelessly naïve, I'd argue that feelings of trust emerge, for us, out of our face to face dealings with other people. Part of the importance of play among children is that it is an arena in which such feelings of mutual trust get negotiated and worked out. Through our countless encounters with others, we also derive a generalized notion of trust that we can apply even to strangers. Hence, it is a meaningful question when people are asked, "In your experience, can most people be trusted?" Low and behold, pollsters have been asking people questions like this one and other questions about trust for years. And sure enough, as Putnam reports, these polls show that levels of trust have been falling simultaneously with the declining participation in all those different face to face situations. If a vibrant public conversation is essential to self-governing, this is cause for concern. In any case, a growing lack of trust is consistent with the extreme polarization and acrimony that we see daily in our politics. Though the trend away from voluntarily getting together and the trend of decreasing levels of trust are reversible, there seems to be little evidence that they have lessoned or turned around since Putnam's book came out.

Some place high hopes on the internet and smart phones and the other new small screen technology, but others point out that these advances have only contributed to a decline in empathy, isolation and to the political polarization. If you contend that texting, blog sites, Facebook, Twitter, Instagram, and the like are now where people hang out together and have conversations, others are bound to argue that live, face to face spontaneous conversation has lots more going for it. These media put everything in a TV-like context. Besides the loss of visual expressions and the subtleties of intonation, a texting "chat" seriously limits the spontaneity of conversations. Yeah but, with Twitter, can't we really get to know the rich and famous? Besides, petitions, blogs, and comments abound on the internet. But most of the participants are virtually anonymous. For many, their web appearance is probably their own best approximation of what they think it'll look like when they finally hire the PR consultant and that personal trainer, that is, if they are not one of those 52 year-old males living on line as a 14 year-old female. More ominous, investigations following some of the mass shootings we've had, show us that a person can go on the internet and completely submerge themselves in all kinds or rare and hateful ideologies to the exclusion of anything counter-arguments…ENOUGH! Are these new technologies a political game changer? At this point both sides of the proposition are being argued. Only a few things are clear so far. The rapid timing and world reach of these new techniques have exponentially multiplied the sheer amount of world-wide information we get while at the same time all but eliminating our concern for our any local news except maybe weather reports. In the process we have also become immediately available to the theatrics of the most outrageous among our politicians and to the disgusting brutalities of demented terrorists at any time and anywhere in the world. We can be hopeful, that some good will come as well, but, all this electronic hanging out and social networking has yet to approximate the kind of robust national political conversation that so impressed Alex De Tocqueville. Rather than bring out that national conversation our internet activity has so far tended to divided and sub-divided us into narrowly focused groupings which often share little more than lifestyle and consumer branding choices.

To summarize, from our earliest days the United States was known as a society with a vibrant public life where citizens gathered and engaged one another about their interests. This characteristic has often been singled out as a significant factor in making our system of representative government a success. There are, however, clear indications that this vibrant public life has been declining in the last several decades as people withdraw from participation in voluntary associations and indicate a general lack of trust in their fellow Americans. These developments took place during the same period when our politics were becoming more polarized and acrimonious.

We should keep these trends in mind as we now take up the way our politics has backed away from the facts and issues coming to focus instead on the public personalities presented to us by the politicians.

From Issues to Personality: The New Politics of Trust

The central feature of our way of governing is of course that government is supposed to represent us. Let's examine this idea of representation for a moment. Traditionally, when writers take up the topic of this representation, they are distinguishing between two theoretical varieties. Elected officials are either representative because they carry out the precise wishes of those who vote for them (we might call this theory of representation, the proxy-holder). Alternatively, representatives should serve because voters consider them to be better qualified than themselves to make the difficult decisions that governing requires, (we might call this the wise leader theory). Interestingly, this proxy-holder/wise leader distinction is probably aligns reasonably well with the left or right orientation of the writer, with left thinking more in line with the proxy-holder approach and right thinking asserting that people should vote for the wise leader who will do what's best for them. But theories aside, in practice this distinction is probably a misleading one. It would be closer to the truth to acknowledge that these two extremes in representation are better thought of as the ends of a continuum. In practice a representative might operate closer to one end or the other. They may get their opportunities to show off their wisdom a little or a lot, but to remain in the game they'd better not stray too far from the desires of their supporters.

For our purposes though, this proxy holder/wise leader distinction might be useful for another reason, besides this choosing sides on how representation theoretically ought to work. Our concern here is with a transformation in the way politicians are perceived by their supporters. Here we will quite literally get into how they *look,* how they appear. What I want to show you is that as people replaced the printed word with pictures, the proxy holder view has been gradually losing out to a greater reliance on the wise leader perspective. As we shall see, the shift I am describing here was not accomplished through a series of rational decisions by political activists. It was more the subtle byproduct of changes in the way we do our politics.

From Print to Photographic: a Shift in Tactics

We have seen the way that politicians and their consultants have adopted new tactics from the world commerce. The same is true of new technology, and photographic technology in particular. I just said that the shift from a politics that relied primarily on printed words to pictures and video was a transformational change. This is a kind of before and after story for which I ask your patience. First we will look at the events in over a century of the innovations and changes that brought about this shift. After that we will be in a position to appreciate how much the adaptation of video magic to politics has transformed things for our politics.

THE CONTEMPORARY POLITICAL SCENE

Before TV: To get to the "before" part, 1858 will do just fine. Going back to 1858 it is not likely that anybody was asking voters whether they'd prefer to have a beer with: Stephen Douglas or Abraham Lincoln. And as for their famous debates, I'd think that most of us would be both bored and brought to tears if we had had to witness even the first 1858 debate between these two guys. Their first debate went like this, Douglas, who'd got the starting slot, spoke for an hour. Lincoln was allotted an hour and a half to respond. Then Douglas had a half hour for his rebuttal. I get sleepy just thinking about it. If this debate were to happen today, and YouTube's 15 minute limit were relaxed, how many hits do you think it would get? And remember, this was only one of the seven debates they did. And don't forget, Abe was probably not that great to look at, not that his shorter opponent was such a handsome guy. On this evidence alone, I rest my case that interest in the debates about the detailed content of the issues has seriously declined.

It is key to our understanding of what was happening in the time of Douglas and Lincoln to acknowledge that information most people got about both the candidates and the debates came from the print medium. Of course, besides print, people knew politicians by word of mouth, through political parties, conversations with family, folks at work, at church, and in the other face to face contacts in their social lives. But print predominated. Photography was just starting to supplement these sources with black and white still images. We have photos of both men, but darned if I can find a photo on the internet taken during the hours and hours that these debates went on.

Then in 1896, William McKinley conducted what they called his "front porch" campaign. The candidate made extensive use of photographs which now could appear in newspapers. Without pictures this front porch thing is almost meaningless. But you can still see the newspaper pictures for yourself.[6] There in the typical American mid-West town of Canton Ohio, we can see him on his porch, just like people in neighborhoods all over the country. He's like a neighbor, looks prosperous enough, but he's like a neighbor. Kindly face on the guy, and the (black and white) red, white and blue bunting's a real nice touch. It is equally important to realize that before McKinley candidates did very little campaigning themselves; maybe some letters to be published in the papers, a few speeches. But McKinley's chief backer, Mark Hanna, thought up this innovation in our politics as a way to give voters a photographic familiarity with his candidate that other candidates couldn't hope for. McKinley's campaign pronouncements can take on a face and a setting in our mind's eye. Immediately after McKinley, Teddy Roosevelt made himself known with plenty of photos and the rapid development of movies made him familiar to millions of Americans.

As movies technology was developing further, radio came into being. In the 1930s and 40s Franklin Roosevelt is known for a personal mastery of the new media, especially the seeming intimacy of his radio talks, as AM radio broadcasts had by then powered up to virtually blanket both the cities and the remote country side. With World War II, radio broadcasts from Europe, and the "newsreels" showed at movie houses introduced the voice, the gestures, and the bearing of Supreme Allied Commander, Dwight Eisenhower. People could "know" their General, Ike in a much fuller sense, a big step in the transformation to personality politics is clear for us to see. One could make the case that Eisenhower, the video media phenomenon, had transcended the political party system. In the years after World War II as the Cold War settled in, the immensely popular Dwight Eisenhower, known primarily as a military hero, could easily have run either as a Republican or a Democrat. In fact there was a period when his 1952 candidacy was appearing more and more inevitable yet as a General he remained officially neutral as to his political party preference. In the end, even though the Democrats had won five presidential elections in a row, the retired general was elected as a Republican, and served two terms as President. On an issue basis, and in hindsight, many view Eisenhower's actions as President more in line with the contemporary left than the right; like the Korean War cease-fire (anti-war), the Interstate Highway

THE CONTEMPORARY POLITICAL SCENE

System (massive infrastructure investment), and his ominous warnings about an ever more powerful "Military/Industrial Complex" (anti-corporate/anti-military).

Early Television and the Beginnings of the Decline of the Parties: Now let's skip to the beginnings of the age of television, and all the little black and white screens with fuzzy live pictures on them. Early television technology brought the next major turning point in our issues-to-personality transformation. Nineteen sixty of course brought the Republican candidate, Richard Nixon and the Democrat, John Kennedy debated on live TV. The FCCs equal time rule had to be temporarily suspended to allow these debates. Pundits and scholars have analyzed these televised encounters to death and what is most interesting about all their analysis is that most of what they have had to say almost completely ignores anything that either of the two men actually said. Virtually all of the analysis focuses is all on appearance, demeanor, and, let's call it what it is, the stage presence of these two fellows. Whether anybody quite realized it at the time, these 1960 debates pushed TV projected looks and TV projected character to the forefront as a basis for making presidential voting decisions. (What is more, a trip to the library or an internet search of the Kennedy presidency, before the assassination, November, 1963, will quickly bring you in touch with the huge video media coverage enterprise then known as "Camelot," in which pictures and film gushed over and mythologized about an idyllic First Family.

> **Gloss Note:** Ever since the 1960 presidential election candidate debates have been a featured event in national campaigns. If you are a latecomer to this 50+ year tradition, I would not be surprised to hear that you readers find them a waste of time. However those first debates between Nixon and Kennedy are often cited as a transforming event. Whether this is true is itself debatable. But it is hard to deny that in these debates brought the video sense that we know these people

into our politics. Polls of radio listeners thought Nixon did better than Kennedy. TV viewers may not have thought that Kennedy won but they at least thought he did just as well as Nixon. Over the years, these campaign lawyer and party negotiated rituals have come to replace actual issues discussions with focus-group-tested-slogans and with follow-up coverage that features gaffs and gotchas.

Political party influence didn't of course end with Eisenhower. In 1960 the political parties were still powerful. Some historians credit Kennedy's win to questionable measures taken by Chicago's heavy handed Democratic boss, Richard J. Daley. Though corrupt political machines did exist at various times, and Chicago's Daily machine got its share of notoriety, we need not throw the baby out with the bath. Traditionally, and at their best, the parties served as a different kind of mediator between politicians and their supporters, especially at the national level. Recall the previous discussion of voluntary associations, those face to face places where people hung out with others with similar interests. In their hay day a party functioned as an interlinking series of voluntary associations at local state and federal levels. Through party participation, politically active folks could talk face to face about candidates and issues to people with whom they shared interests, people who they trusted, people who could explain the issues and in some cases personally vouch for the candidates. The parties had an additional effect those days. Voluntary associations tend to recruit participants with similar backgrounds and interests. This usually meant that members were attracted from a narrow range of socio-economic circumstance. Before their decline in the later decades of the last century, this socio-economic homogeneity was true of the political parties as well, which meant that the Democrats tended to be lower class and working class, and the Republicans more from the middle and upper classes. In recent years the parties have not only lost their primacy and influence but they have lost this socio-economic alignment as well. While the nomination process remains based on obtaining commitments from party delegates the candidates campaign for most of these delicates in primary elections. At the presidential level, what remains of the old time party machinery now waits in the wings for the unlikely event that no candidate gets to convention time with enough votes to take the nomination (an event that has not occurred in 40 years.)

Currently, the two major parties still do some fund-raising and candidate support work. They also still manage the delegate system that formally nominates the candidates and structure the committees and agendas in Congress and in state legislatures. But the politicians themselves are nowhere near as dependent on them as they once were. Especially at the local and state levels, you often can't even identify a candidate's party affiliation in their speeches and campaign literature. It could be argued that the main work of the main two parties now consists of working together on a task they agree on: smothering the prospects of growth for any potential third parties.

Accompanying this decline comes the popularity of a statement that epitomizes the age of video based personality politics: "I don't vote for the party, I vote for the man (or occasionally, the woman)." As the media personalities of the candidates came to prominence, the parties, the platforms, and the noisy spectacles of the party conventions have all receded from their prior significance. Now let's consider why the political professionals have all but given up print, in favor of the power and persuasiveness that they see in video technology.

From Print to Photographic: Movie Magic

Photographically Mediated Celebrity, Exhibit 1: In the early 1900s, as movies gained popularity, the actors usually went unnamed. Movies were known by the companies that made them. One of these actors was young woman who became known by the name of her employer as "the Biograph Girl." In 1910 newspapers incorrectly reported that she had been killed in a street-car accident. A clever promoter saw the opportunity and announced that he would bring the Biograph Girl, by name now, Florence Lawrence, to two theaters in St. Louis on a given day. The huge crowds of fans who turned out were a media amazement. In their adoring admiration they even pulled buttons off her dress and trimmings from her hat. This is just stardom, as we now call it. It was something that had only become possible as a result of the movies.[7] Folks had been fans of stage actors in the past, but movies had now brought a kind of personal intimacy through close-up photography to the masses. These people felt as if they knew this young woman herself. Many wrote her letters. She got bags of fan mail. She was a sensation. She also battled with personal ups and downs that ultimately ended in suicide.

Photographically Mediated Celebrity, Exhibit 2: Later on, in the middle decades of the century Americans came to know and love a man named Marion Morrison. In a career of movie making he was transformed into the iconic American we know as John Wayne. As the world came to know this John Wayne, both on film and in his life, he was a man of few words, of firm beliefs, and heroic determination. Over and over again Americans watched Wayne confront evil and fight for what was obviously good and right. They watched him fight. Among others, they watched him fight hostile Native Americans, Mexicans, Japanese, Germans, Russians, Arabs, Vietnamese. He fought in the uniforms of all branches of our military service. The facts of Marion Morrison's life really don't matter that much. Apparently, our movie warrior never served in the military and even made considerable efforts to avoid such service during World War II. Critics say that his career took off in the 1940s as his leading man competitors joined up. Apologists sight an old football injury or his wife and four kids.[8] Our interest is not in Marion Morrison. It is John Wayne we need to consider. There is no reason for us to dwell on that nearly anonymous person, Marion Morrison. John Wayne is the public guy; our guy. I, for one, am a big fan. I must have seen Rio Bravo a dozen times.

In contrast to John Wayne, Florence Lawrence had a few promoters but was otherwise on her own. John Wayne and super stars that have followed him are group projects. He is a product created for us out of collaboration between a skilled performer and countless cinema and media professionals. We are intentionally reminded of this at the very end of every movie. As the credits run, we get the documentation, the footnotes, for this filmed instance of the entire created persona and his or her story.[9] We may not know who Marion Morrison was, but through these countless numbers of people and their work, we sure as heck feel like we just got to know the powerful character and personality of John Wayne.

Unfortunately this custom of running the credits, to give credit where credit is due, is just a convention that developed in the movie industry. For most all the other, larger than life public personas we are familiar with, nobody ever runs those credits for us. Of course, that doesn't mean that the Marion Morrison/John Wayne difference isn't there for them too. However, without ever seeing their credits run, we are even more inclined to accept the Photographically Mediated Celebrity as a real person who we think we know. Here's a challenge for you: think about some of the people, not in the movies, who we all think we know. What do you really know about such people? People like, for instance, Martha Stewart, Stephen Colbert, Taylor Swift, Miley Cyrus, Pharrell Williams, Justin Bieber, or how about Bill Cosby?

A Different Kind of Knowing: The modern celebrity that shows up in our politics, came out of this peculiar quality of the movies. The film industry didn't invent modern public celebrity. But it managed to discover it and tap its startling potential in a way that was previously unknown. As the quotation from Nicholas Chamfort at the beginning of this chapter suggests, celebrity has a much longer history. People could get emotional about characters in print. In 1841 crowds swarmed the New York docks beseeching passengers on docking ships to tell them what had happened to Dickens' Little Nell in his last installment of The Old Curiosity Shop. In its modern form, film, and after that television and the other electronic media, have taken things much further. With better and better photographic imaging and better and better sound reproduction technologies there came the possibility for billions of people to have both visual and then auditory information about single individuals; and from this they can each get the genuine sense, that confident feeling they "know" these individuals, when perhaps they really don't. This process of mediated familiarity is no less than a new kind of knowing. Furthermore, it is clear that this felt sense of familiarity that we can have with distant strangers we will never meet, is for most people on the planet, an inescapable feature of modern life. And it's effects have profoundly changed the way people relate to their world. Whether we are talking about entertainers, criminals, athletes, politicians, or just ordinary people in unusual circumstances, we don't seem to have any problem in taking close up images and speech out of the media that surrounds us and developing the sense that we know these people. Without much thought, we do it all the time.

I hope that my two Photographically Mediated Celebrity exhibits are enough to get us to thinking about how very different this way of knowing somebody is, compared to the old fashioned face to face way. Think about it. As a culture, we are a people who spend unprecedented amounts of time passively watching actors pretending to be going through the motions of real lives. But there is a lot more to this thing. The actors we see who are below the real movie star level, are commonly called character actors. Through the countless actors in the countless movie plots we have come to know and share a whole catalogue of character types. I am not saying that people haven't always tended to classify the people they came to know by some reference to their character or even character type. It is just that movies, and later the plots and commercials of television have given us all colorful yet rather extensive visual language of character types. Because of the world-wide distribution of much of this material, this visual language of character types now should qualify as a kind of international language. And most of us have come to use this language in our daily lives without thinking very much about it.

THE CONTEMPORARY POLITICAL SCENE

I'll give you a couple of silly examples. Maybe it's not you that does this, but for instance, you probably have a friend who thinks he knows a "drama queen," and another friend who's told you her dad is the "strong but silent type." One reason for bringing up these silly examples is that apart from the world of movie casting these character types don't have to have names. All the same, if we were to scan a list of casting calls, most of us would have no difficulty visualizing, "an innocent girl," "a con artist," " a grizzled old man."[10] I am sure you can visualize others that you might not be able to name so easily. It is important to acknowledge that the currency of these character types has no necessary connection with reality outside of TV and movies. Why should real con artists have to resemble their like in TV and the movies. But that doesn't stop us from using this visual language we get from movies and TV as we "profile" the people daily in our real lives and react to them. Lots of people take it even further. Recall the discussion of branding in the last chapter. These folks go to considerable lengths to dress and act so as to type-cast themselves for both friends and strangers.

One last feature of this that should be mentioned: though this visual language I am describing here probably emerged in the movies, we rely more upon television and other live sources for the confidence that we are getting to know real characters, real people. The point for us to take away from this is that it is now commonly assumed that live TV can get us to really know the people we see; give us that sense that we have some kind of intimate personal knowledge of them. To think about it, this might seem strange when you also consider that, what we have come to call the "reality television" format, is for most of us far from it. We are intuitively aware that there is very little reality to be found in this reality television. Amazingly though, we rely on TV and other live video to get to know people we have no other chance of coming into contact with. Next time you see the array of magazines that confront you at the food store checkout, just think, you know all these people almost as though you spend face time with them in a daily or at least a weekly basis.

Just to point out the irony of this world of media celebrity, live, face to face encounters with the noteworthy can take on a secondary character when compared with the vivid presence that media-sourced contacts bring us. If you have taken pleasure in seeing your favorite entertainer face-to-face, 100 yards distant, at a stadium positioned just under a massive stadium screen, you probably know the feeling. It is not like you can say that the two of you got together and hung out, there and then. Led Zeppelin guitarist, Jimmy Page, has an interesting slant on the thousands to one concert encounters he's had. He suggests that people swarming to see Led Zeppelin at live concerts were there mainly to *make live witness* to the things that were primarily understood and experienced elsewhere (the recorded music and videos).[11] In other words, the fan's experiences remained first and foremost an electronic media experience. But isn't it nice to be able to say, "I saw Zeppelin live"?

A Glance behind the Lens: This makes it worthwhile to, zoom in on the video process, so to speak. I'm not going to get into the science and the literature of television. While that might be interesting, it will be enough for us to simply consider some of the most apparent ingredients of this televised personhood:

Recall for example, the last time you stood in line at the bank or at the fast food place and gazed around the room in your boredom. As your gaze comes to a stop on the overhead security camera's screen, it takes a few moments before you concluded that the person next to the guy with the dumb-looking hat (just like that man in front of you is wearing) is you! So for starters then, let's just note that your own TV image can, at least sometimes, be a barely recognizable abstraction. This is true for most of us.

Then add to that the common observation that, at least for the people we know, they are never quite "themselves" when behaving in front of a cell phone or video camera lens. They "play" for the camera.

THE CONTEMPORARY POLITICAL SCENE

Admittedly, some do it better than others. Some are quite awkward but others seem to take to it. There are some people whose video images seem nothing less than projections of their true personality and character. Movie directors and cinematographers tell us of the screen legends who have that ability to magically transform themselves in front of a lens and become more genuine, and more attractive than they seem face to face. Whether smooth, awkward, in either case, people don't just exist in front of video cameras, it is more like they are behaving so as to manage, not their live present selves, but the image being produced by the photographic process. All this is part of common knowledge about what goes on in front of cameras. But here's the kicker. As soon as we take on the role of the viewer, awareness of this common knowledge all but evaporates. We view these video media images of people more or less uncritically, as instances of the same single reality that we inhabit live and face to face.

That's enough! Let's zoom back out and try to add up this accumulating set of weird observations and contradictions. Because "we" and "us" are shorter words than "people" and "they," I'll use them here, even though you and I know, we don't fall for this media way of knowing people and connecting with them emotionally:

1. With the invention and technological perfection of movies, we discovered they have a startling potential for creating the feeling of intimate and deeply emotional connections with people we will never come in actual contact with.

2. While we prioritize TV and other live video as more real compared to movies and drama, at the same time, we rely on a visual language of character types which developed in movies and drama to help us make sense of our lives and the lives of the people in them.

3. We carefully ignore what is perhaps the most striking difference between video and face-to-face knowing: our video knowing is absolutely one sided and allows for no active expression or inquiring on our parts.

4. We contradictorily accept that TV faithfully represents reality while at the same time we acknowledge that reality TV is poorly scripted, contrived, and phony.

5. We value television and other live video because it brings us into genuine acquaintance with people distant from us in space, and position in society, people who we would otherwise never know or even encounter in our lives.

6. When we see ourselves in videos it gives us a certain feeling of estrangement from those selves we are seeing.

7. And finally, though when we see that people in front of cameras, they seem to act differently, when we only see the resulting videos, we tend to forget this and accept the video as completely equivalent to the reality of face to face observation.

If this section serves its purpose, we can proceed with, at least, the understanding that live encounters with people are far more direct and straight forward than video encounters, especially when in video, we encounter somebody with the facilities that accompany high quality technical expertise, the teams of producers, directors, writers, and technical specialists schooled in their various trades. Even if you take away all this expert support, video yields a whole different sense of familiarity when compared with the familiarity that can occur in unmediated face to face encounters. An entire genre of TV drama which includes "House of Cards," "Scandal," "The Good Wife," and "Brotherhood," consists of behind the scenes spying on the sordid face to face lives of fictional political media celebrities. (And these shows don't seem to have much trouble getting real TV news people to join their casts and play themselves.) Though we might acknowledge the stark differences between real people and media personas in the context of this discussion, we tend not to place much importance on it or even take account of it in daily lives jam-packed with video representations of people we'll never meet.

THE CONTEMPORARY POLITICAL SCENE

TV Politicians

So far in this chapter, we've seen the drift away face to face socializing that has been happening at the same time the politicians and their handlers have been harnessing the tools of video technology. It remains for us to track that one other trend we set out to come to terms with: how contemporary politics has come to focus on personalities and trust. As I have suggested, these developments were accompanied by a turning away from the details of issues, and policies. I also said that voters had turned away from the proxy holder idea of representation which required them to know the details of issues and demand politicians who did their bidding on those issues. It is time we addressed the actual role of the politicians and office holders in all this, in the sense of, "What do they do for a living." Let's just look at three important aspects of their jobs, the laws they make and administer, their public presentation of themselves, and finally a few words about how this politics of trust pushes real issues into two deep groves of those economic and moral divides.

The Laws: What's so different today about the laws for politicians and office holders? After all, don't politicians still speak about issues and laws that will address them? We have yet to reach a point when a believable leader has emerged with only the promise that he/she is wise, and we should trust her/him. Right? So how can it be that issues and policies are receding from politics? I will start with an example that I think might be helpful. Actually it would be more accurate to call it a video demonstration. It is just a small detail that in itself is not important, however, it lays out my little thesis here in graphic detail. You might want to look it up on C–Span, though I can describe it for you well enough to get to the point of it.[12]

Here goes: In the highly contentious run-up to the passage of The Patient Protection and Affordable Care Act (PPACA or more commonly ACA), President Obama summonsed top congressional leaders to a gathering at the White House. In the jargon of international diplomacy, they called a "summit." The ostensible purpose was to iron out some of their differences and in the interests of getting health care legislation passed. I say ostensible because the partisan differences about health care legislation were then, and remain, so rancorous that only a delusional optimist could hope for cooperation and compromise in this matter. But that makes this little detail of the meetings so emblematic of how the partisan divide addresses a whole host of issues.

Anyway, as the partisans met at this televised White House summit, seated around a large rectangle of conference tables, one of them in particular caught my attention. He was Eric Cantor, then House of Representatives Minority Whip, from the Richmond Virginia area. Cantor was opposed to the legislation and he probably expressed that opposition far more effectively in gesture than in word. He sat at his place, sort of crouched behind a stack at least four bound volumes, each maybe 2 inches thick, and made up of 8 and 1/2 by 11 inch sheets of paper. We were given to understand that this stack was the several thousand pages of the health care bill, the proposed law. It would be exaggerating only slightly to say that he appeared to be almost hidden behind its immensity.

That's it. That's my idea of a helpful video illustration. OK, so what's the point? It's not really about Eric Cantor. He was a skillful and popular politician, at least until his constituents voted him out in a primary. It's not about the Republicans. When the Democrats are against something, it is not surprising for one of them to try their own video stunts. No, it is all about that stack of 8 and 1/2 by 11 inch sheets of paper, the take away image from the meeting. Using this pile of papers to represent what might become a law, Cantor and others in opposition were making the beautifully salient point that this proposed law was far too complicated and wide-ranging to be trusted or even explained in simple terms that average citizens might understand. And though there were, at the time, some false claims made about what those thousands of pages contained, Cantor's point was certainly correct. Maybe not as elegant as some might like, but nonetheless, well worth making. How can we trust bills like this one that are too immense and jargon filled for us to comprehend? The answer he was presenting to us was that we cannot analyze, and make judgments and trust the actual bills and the laws which follow. It is far too complicated, even if we had the time. But the politicians we trust are there to make these judgments for us. And in this instance Cantor was telling those supporters who trusted him that he'd done the homework, made the call and condemned the bill.

Folks on the right are forever loudly complaining that our government is too big. What is odd is that nobody from the left is arguing with them about that. In its totality, our governing apparatus is so enormous and shows up in so many places, that in its totality, it is literally incomprehensible. This is true, not only to the average person but for every one of us. Sticking with the PPACA for the moment, some of its impacts are clear and direct, as for example, the ending of pre-existing condition exclusions from health insurance policies. Other of its impacts are vague and reveal themselves, if at all, over years and decades, as for example future health care cost increases as compared to what they might have been without the PPACA. Partisans will be arguing about that one for decades to come.

If you were expecting your little primer to make sense of this gigantic complex entity, please lower those expectations immediately. From President to the least engaged nonvoter, we, each of us, lives with this incomprehensibility to one degree or another. For most of us, government reveals itself to us when it gets in our way, violates our sense of reasonableness or our sense of justice, and even occasionally when it facilitates attaining some objective we approve of. That is to say we experience it not in its totality, but on its margins.

Consider the sheer magnitude of existing laws and regulations at just the Federal level. As new laws take effect, if they are to be considered "general and permanent,"(like for instance, Eric Cantor's stacks of papers later became), they are entered into the volumes of what's called The United States Code (USC) and later published both in print and on line. It is like the one and only law book of the Federal government, only it currently runs to about 35 volumes. Another publication of the Federal Government is the Code of Federal Regulations (CFR). One of the many websites that despise government regulation has counted them up and reports that the CFR contains over a million of them.[13] The Federal Register, a journal of federal government agency rules, new proposed rules and other public notices has been running over 70,000 pages in recent years. And this is just the federal government. In practical terms this points to the fact that the entire spectrum of law and regulation is quite objectively beyond the grasp of any one individual. So how do we manage to function at all? The answer, of course, is that we divide up the whole and specialize. There are multitudes of attorneys, accountants, researchers, and other subject experts who make their careers both within and outside of government by addressing every tiny aspect of this totality. And if it is in their area of expertise, they know the Code, the regulations, and whatever shows up in the Federal Register.

All this is to emphasize that I support Eric Cantor's little demo and even applaud his theatricality. These days, laws are often huge and hugely complicated. They must be integrated into the complex of exiting law and regulations. At the beginning of this discussion, I mentioned the proxy holder and the wise leader as two theoretical varieties of representation, and I said that we are trending toward the latter. It is time that we refine that wise leader notion and bring in line with the scale of actual contemporary laws and governing.

In their every aspect politicians and office holders are now group projects. Our wise leader is merely the face, the main spokesperson, for the combined efforts of his or her staffs, supporting organizations, allied politicians and their staffs and supporting organizations. Everybody knows this at some level but it really should change the way we need to view representation. Our politicians don't just compete by taking positions on a range of issues which are familiar to a knowledgeable electorate. Those days are long gone. Our politicians compete for a generalized voter trust. Voters are seeking politicians who will take our government in the right direction by heading up effective staffs and maintaining the alliances essential to sort through those pages and pages of facts and spin to get to the heart of matters for us. If they are to be considered wise, it is because they select superior staffs and advisors, and broker effectively with other politicians and the myriad of organized interests out there.

We can spot this theme of trust in every phase of governing. In lawmaking, the media might focus on the vote count. In truth, this is a simpleminded approach. At best, the vote can be seen as the resultant force that has emerged among all the political forces that have come to the table, the committee, and subcommittees and their staffs, the drafters, technical experts, legal experts in the field, the lobbyists, the donors, and last but not least, the vocal supporters the vocal opposition, the detractors, the press and the rest of the background noise. What would it look like if we were to be able to watch them "run the credits" movie style, on the passage of a single law?

> **Gloss Note:** Lobbyists, among these subject experts are a controversial bunch. They are employed by interest groups and corporations expressly to maintain access, and hopefully influence with law-makers and government administrators, on behalf of their clients. Since many lobbying firms have their offices on K Street in Washington, D.C., K Street has become a political slang term for lobbying in general. Under the Lobbying Disclosure Act (LDA) lobbyists are supposed to register with the government to make what and for whom they are working known to the public. There are currently around 12,000 registered lobbyists. However, this understates their ranks because of a trend in recent years to avoid registration by

conducting these persuasive activities through trade associations and other "independent" policy advisory organizations. Registered or not, these groups quite often offer their assistance by drafting actual language for proposed legislation.

After a law is passed, its implementation is shaped by the agency staffs and bureaucrats who are to administer it. These might be career civil service types or members of our politician's opposing party. In addition, as proposed implementation and regulations are published in The Federal Register, there is input from many of the same organizations that were in on its passage. And finally the whole law or parts of it can be challenged in the courts.

We are not through yet. Tradition in this country has it that even though a law is passed and implemented, it can fall by the way-side if it is not funded. At local and state levels, the budget process is absolute: at least in the long run, local and state governments can spend no more than they take in taxes. At the federal level this isn't so. The Federal government can print more money as needed, with the risk being inflation and loss of faith in the value of the dollar. As a result, Federal Government debt has long been a partisan issue. But also, as a result of the budgeting process, a law which is passed and implemented can have no effect if the agencies charged with carrying out that law don't get the money necessary to carry it out.

> **Gloss Note:** The Federal government regularly spends more than it takes in taxes. Politicians and their spokespersons talk about this fact in two very different ways, and it can be confusing. If they want to brag that they are spending less, they talk in terms of the annual budget deficit. They will tell us that the overspending for that year was reduced from that of previous years. If the spending is actually less than the taxes taken in, they can brag about a budget surplus. If, on the other hand, they want to criticize the people in office, they will talk about the annual deficits that have accumulated over the years under the leadership of both parties. This accumulated deficit,

(along with all "supplemental appropriations" outside the budget process), is referred to as the national debt. As a rule, in recent years, the left emphasizes their record on the deficit and the right emphasizes the national debt. While both the debt and deficits result from a mismatch between tax revenue and spending, attacking these problems with tax increases is a topic that both sides try to avoid talking about.

24 Hour a Day Know-it-alls: In their roles as trusted participants, it is thus that our representatives in politics and government have come to be expected to be able to respond to anything that comes up in the supercharged 24/7 world of current events. We expect them to sort through the mountains of information and have a ready opinion on everything. The revised wise leader idea of representation now has cast our politicians as the trusted heads of political teams in business to digest the complexity of these times and get things done.

What qualifies as the news each day, the headline items and the stuff just below that in significance, is generated by actual events that are selected and covered by news organizations, internet sources, and sometimes pushed forward by politically motivated organizations attempting to sway public opinion. From the President down to the lowliest of the political office holder and want-a-bees, we expect these people to have opinions about anything in the news. Furthermore, we expect their opinions to be consistent with their established media character, their brand, whether the news is about an earthquake, a war, a developing scandal, a tick in some arcane economic index, a crime, the death of somebody famous, a heroic act, a pop cultural happening, literally anything that shows up in the news. There are, in fact, politicians who would otherwise be relatively unknown, who seem to make it their core mission to jump into the headlines of the news cycle by making statements that are very likely to seem outrageous to most of us. Other politicians get contacted, "Politician A said such in such. What do you think, and what do you think of a person who would say something like that?" A kind of echo chamber sets in motion that keeps the story referring back to the politician who made the outrageous comment in the first place.

A lot of this kind of thing seems neither important nor even news, but maybe I should approach it with a little less sarcasm. If the arena of politics is a place where politicians present a video persona to the public in an effort to get folks to feel that she or he is a trusted leader, these expressions of opinion on anything and everything are some of the critical bits with which they build and maintain their brand. Consider for instance the 2013 outbreak of ebola virus disease in West Africa. Until a single case showed up in a Texas hospital almost a year later, this serious epidemic was outside of the 24 hour news cycle. With the single reported case in the US ebola became the top news item, as politicians high and low offered their emphatic and seemingly expert medical opinions on what must be done, and done immediately, to protect us all from this threat. As the politician's statements swirled to the headlines, the actual medical authorities, the professionals who we depend upon every day for our extraordinary levels of public health, were put on the defensive. Quite apart from the effectiveness of the various proposals being argued about by the politicians, the entire episode can better be understood as being about who we should trust. This news event became an irresistible opportunity for politicians to ply their trade, that is to say, marketing their media persona as one worthy of trust and the political support that can follow that trust.

The Collapse of Issues: The ebola crisis presents a good segway into our thus-far neglected topic of issues. I've been asserting that issues have given way to a politics of personality and trust. To this you might say, nonsense, politicians are talking about issues every day. I grant you that this is so, but only in a limited way. The issues that arise are most often really stand-ins that refer to the larger political differences that we've explored back in Parts II and III. In the end, the ebola crisis turned out mainly to be about two things:

1. The political discussion began and remained primarily within the great moral divide focusing on immigration which revolves around the

questions of, who "we," the Americans are and what separates us from everybody else? The progressive view of that glorious expanding "We." And the conservative counter to this, that the exceptional character of our nation is in part results from the fact that as Americans we have carefully guarded against a wholesale expansion of that "We" to just anybody who wants to come here any time. The progressive politicians saw the Ebola crisis as a struggle against a virus, a struggle to be fought on behalf of all the people in the world with all that medical science could bring to bear. The conservative politicians called for a quarantine to separate us from those who by the way they live can contract this disease. Note that this was not even racial distinction. The opposition to people entering the country targeted non-Africans who'd been administering to the victims.

2. As the crisis continued the political discussion seemed to morph into an argument within the great economic divide about the economy and big government. Progressives view many of the expansions in the size and scope of government as necessary correctives for things that free markets do not accomplish to their satisfaction. Conservatives, on the other hand, see most expansions in their government as relinquishments of their personal liberty. As progressive politicians viewed the ebola crisis took great pride in the medical intelligence and guidance offered by the Centers for Disease Control (CDC), while their conservative opponents viewed CDC pronouncements with suspicion and saw potential and real threats to their personal health emanating from just another bunch of detached, overpaid welfare state government bureaucrats.

With the passage of time, and the successes of those working in West Africa, at the sight of the outbreak it difficult to recapture the intensity of the debate and the fear it generated among us. Nor is it easy to recall just how the crisis devolved into a media debate among a small number of health officials and government and those "24 Hour a Day Know-it-alls" our TV politics has created.

What I am suggesting is that these days you can boil down almost all the debates about issues into instances of the two great divides we took up in Parts II and III. It's not that narrow issues don't reach the level of political debate. It is that issues, large and small, are so consistently captured and placed into one or the other of the great divides we've been looking at. If you are having difficulty accepting this, why not go back to Chapter 3 and go over some of the issues which appear there and work them over like we did with the Broken Windows/Community Policing issue, or like I just did with the ebola crisis.

Summary

Our contemporary politics has been transformed over the past several decades. The customs of lively socializing that America was once famous for had eroded as people have taken on more jobs, longer commutes and a tendency to stare at video screens a lot. As photographic technology progressed, this technology revealed, first in the magic of movies, and later in live TV, that people used it to experience extraordinary feelings of intimate acquaintance which they could not easily distinguish from those same feelings in real face to face relationships. As our self-governing process was expanding in size and complexity to dizzying proportions, this technology and its power of video familiarity became the mainstay of our politics.

I am contending that in combination these developments have relocated the focus of our politics from the many problems and issues that must be confronted as we proceed in governing ourselves to a concentration on media characters who vie for our trust in terms of a couple deep unresolvable divides that separate the right and the left. When, in recent history, this transformation actually solidified is an interesting question. I am reminded of an article I once came across about when the Civil War ended. It had nothing to do with Appomattox and the actual combatants. As I recall, the article reminisced over a series of post-Civil War events extending from the 1870s through to the 1960s that

THE CONTEMPORARY POLITICAL SCENE

were, at the time they happened, each taken up in the press, as historic, symbolic, unifying events that fully and finally ended the Civil War and got us back together as a single nation. Events like when so and so shook hands with so and so, or remarks about the attendees at the funerals of some of the last vets. Needless to say, most turning points in history are not that simple. We can still, several generations hence, see tensions that remain from that bloody war. Well it is much the same with trying to come up with a precise date when print and diverse issues gave way to the video star we trust as the predominating focus of our politics. Having said that, I will firmly assert that it seems to me that the transition was about complete by the early 1980s. OMG! How peculiar. As it happens, by sheer coincidence, a former professional movie star took over the presidency at about this point in time.

I'm not knocking the Presidency of Ronald Reagan here. He is just about universally hailed as a transforming president who saw us almost to the end of the Cold War and redirected our politics considerably to the right. He was a unifying force in times of trouble. He took office after one president had resigned, the next had ended the Viet Nam war in defeat, and the next had watched with us in humiliation as 52 Americans were paraded in front of the cameras as hostages in Iran for 444 days.

Nonetheless, it is a fact that voters had acquired their familiarity with Reagan as a public figure, first from his movies and later from his appearances in TV commercials, and this swing from print to video is our subject. Whether Ronald Reagan would have had a chance of becoming president without this video background is an open question. Whether he could have done it before the 1980s is a little less open; he'd tried and failed. The real reason I brought him up is that I am trying get you thinking about the unique characteristics associated with knowing public figures through video technology as distinguished from the old ways of word of mouth, print, and face to face contacts. The old ways are gone but not forgotten. If you crave word of mouth, and face to face contacts, you can at least passively watch as people are paid to do it for you on TV. Tune in to Morning Joe, or Fox and friends, as you rise, then later you can hang with yer buds at the Cycle or The Five. For better or worse, the transformation to video production in our political discussion is hard to deny. But what about the rest of it? Has our discussion of issues collapsed into a confusion that leaves us only the option of picking leaders we feel we can trust to carry us forward?

Earlier when we took up the topic of ideologies I referred to extreme ideologies as "The Gift of Absolute Clarity." I did this to call attention to the fact that an orientation to politics that explains everything as having one or a couple of causes might be kind of ridiculous. Unfortunately this is how the politicians, the media, and the legions of political pros have been trending. The deep economic and moral divisions they present, resonate with and activate the people who support them and vote for them. But they are only a minority among us. This stuff doesn't work with you and millions of other Americans. My objective in these pages has been to give you just enough of an understanding of our politics so that you could make sense of it and follow the game as I called it. At times I even went so far as to encourage you to experiment with passing as somebody who is politically active. If your time has been at all worthwhile, you are now probably thinking this politics thing is a lot more complicated and depressing than you imagined. I wish this were not so. Sorry, but sophistication typically brings some disillusionment along with it.

Having said all this, I insist that our politics is only hopelessly messed up as long as you and others among the 50% stay out of it. In the space remaining I want to try to show that there are places for you to engage and even make a contribution to our 200 plus year run with self-governing.

Concluding Thoughts

CONCLUDING THOUGHTS

Chapter 12 Where Are We Going From Here?

"Man...feels that he is a participator in the government of affairs not merely at an election one day in the year, but every day."

Thomas Jefferson (1743-1826)[1]

"It is in the voting booth, not on the presidential desk, that the buck finally stops."

Arthur M. Schlesinger (1888-1965)[2]

"In the...disputes of a democratic public, only moral propositions [which are] neutral with respect to various worldviews... claim to be, for good reasons, acceptable for all."

Jürgen Habermas [1]

"If voting changed anything, they'd make it illegal."

Emma Goldman (1869-1940)[4]

Political Cynicism VS Realism

We have covered quite a bit of ground. As you reflect on the preceding chapters, I wouldn't be at all surprised if you are coming to the conclusion that I have failed to charm you into an avid interest in the existing political scene. I am pretty certain that those who were craving some kind of slick persuasive sales job about how fun and profitable politics can be, stopped reading and left us, way back there some place. That's OK, I wasn't writing to them. I readily admit that this accounting of the people who do our politics, and many of the ways the whole process operates, falls short of the way things are supposed to be, but I stand by it. From the start, I aimed to tell you, not what our politics ought to be, or could be, but how our politics is. It is what it is, and our objective here, my readers, was to get to know our politics as it actually is. By the same token, just because it is this way now, is no reason that it must always remain this way.

The two previous chapters might have seemed particularly tough when it comes to hope for the current political scene. The public face of politics, the office holders and the other politicians have taken on the stale numbness of reality TV. Issues die in the deep valleys of the economic and moral divides that separate increasingly uncompromising partisans. Maybe you were right to be put off by politics in the first place. Then again, does all this mean that the media personalities and images that we get from politicians can never be trusted? No. The point is that knowing how this stuff is produced and presented can make us more skillful as we sort through all the information put out there and make up our minds as to what the choices really are. With this knowledge we can be more skeptical about the carefully managed public personalities that politicians and their handlers keep pushing at us. Just because one politician's team may be better financed and more accomplished at publicly presenting her or him, or more adapt at combating the blight of scandal, doesn't mean that we are required to accept their hype, their performances, and trust them.

It is not unreasonable to expect that the current round of nation-wide elections brings campaign spending in at 7 to 9 billion dollars. The census bureau estimates that the voting age citizens numbered 220 million in 2014. Presidential elections tend to bring more people out. However, if as many as 50% or 110 million are active in the election,

CONCLUDING THOUGHTS

this would mean that each one of them accounted for up to around 75 bucks in campaign funding. I'd imagine that you could buy a lot of votes at $75 each. Of course, it doesn't get spent that way. The bulk of it goes to TV ads and on-the-ground get out the vote people; propaganda and personal contact to help you know who you should vote for. If you find this stuff irritating and consider it a threat to true representative government, just wait a minute. Don't forget. We all swim in a sea of ads, and hype, and promotions every day. If you are reading this on a video screen, there is a good chance that there are ads on that screen. Only in sleep do we escape the din of it all. And most of us still manage to sort through the crap and, when we shop, we make market choices that suit us just fine. Most of us are pretty good at separating the preposterous exaggerations and outright lies from the truth as we shop. What is more, we are used to getting our way there in the marketplace, at least to the extent we can afford it. Is there some reason why we can't use this same trusted BS radar for politics? Of course not.

As you look back on the preceding chapters, push this comparison between shopping and political choices for a moment. The similarities are striking. In both politics and shopping, we are warned by *Caveat Emptor* to be wary and face the task of searching for what is true and genuine in that sea of deception, hype, and spin. Beyond that, there is another similarity that should stick with us. If you were to go out to buy a used car, would your primary concern be to search for the most trustworthy used car salesperson you could find? Of course not, you'd sort through the hype and the spin and look for the goods, the car, and figure out how to get it delivered. You might even buy a car from somebody you don't particularly even trust, if the facts are on your side. One of the most disappointing aspects of our politicians both left and right is that they dependably back away from the bold promises they run on. We need to evaluate our politicians, not on what they say they are going to do, but on what they actually accomplish. Politicians who make a career of blaming others for how terrible things are and how different things would be, if they had their way, can be entertaining and inspiring, but if they are elected, they are elected to deliver the goods. Failing to accomplish something in politics is all too often looked upon as heroic, when it is first and foremost just failure.

Deemphasizing the personalities and concentrating on the goods that are important to us is just the start. At the same time, we have been getting pounded with this personality based politics, the issues themselves are being squeezed into that grand ideological debate. Once more I'm using the term ideological to emphasize the way the slightest difference in political views is now taken as a litmus test for loyalty to one side or the other of the great economic and moral divides that dominate our political scene.

The puzzling thing for me is that after all the hype and spin, after recognizing the irreconcilable assumptions about the economy and about morality that keep the partisans fighting mad, I, myself, am still fascinated and energized by politics. This is mainly because even with all its flaws, it works. Ours is one of the best huge scale instance of self-governing around, ever. Maybe we are at a stand-off on a lot of things, but at least we are still talking and trying to avoid political coercion and violence a lot of the time. This being the final chapter, I guess it's where I am supposed to make a pitch. I am expected to recommend that you get involved. With this in mind, I feel obliged to give it a shot. I'll leave you with some closing thoughts. First, a look at the some of the reality that doesn't quite square with the positions the partisans have taken in those economic and moral divides we encountered earlier. Then we need to at least consider whether you can justify continuing not to participate or if you have come to the place where you can imagine some kind of political participation that might suit you and other current non-participants. So now, first to the economy.

CONCLUDING THOUGHTS

Free Markets

Talk of our free market economy is at best nostalgia. For better or worse, taken as a whole, the US economy is, strictly speaking, not a free market economy; not even close. In normal times the various levels of government are now employing almost 15% of the workforce directly (and this doesn't include all the suppliers and contractors. Over one hundred years of layer upon layer of tax penalties, tax subsidies, material and service contracting, and regulation have resulted in a considerable restructuring of the economy with the government favoring, and even subsidizing, some economic players and whole industries and penalizing others. From bottom to the top, there are countless individuals and corporations who depend on government for at least a part of their very economic existence. Regulations and outright restrictions, such as those on food and drugs, distort the market place in ways that consumers have come to rely upon. Intellectual property rights and professional licensing laws intended to protect individual's rights now distort market pricing by offering significant added advantages to giant corporations who possess them. In bad times government comes to the aid of both businesses and individuals with substantial benefits, interest rate relief and massive cash infusions.

Small and medium sized businesses still do operate within a realm where market pricing and the risk/rewards of limited liability investment are the main determinants of success. And while these economic activities involve large numbers of people, the huge corporations often exist in a very different realm where the market power of small numbers of sellers addressing hundreds of millions of buyers upsets the dynamics of market pricing. In addition, their lobbying and other political activities create a very different kind of investment risks.

Everybody now agrees that free markets are far better at producing wealth than any other economic arrangements. But the extreme activists, left and right, are forever spinning their cases all out of proportion. To actually appreciate how silly the extreme rhetoric of the right can be when it comes to the superiority of an absence of government regulation, we need only go to some Latin American countries and witness the economic wonders of the totally unregulated drug cartels have emerged, where competitor status, or even a bad performance appraisal, often means certain death. These intensely competitive criminal enterprises have easily found friendly business connections and migrated out into a world-wide banking system. For the extreme left's goals of an economy managed solely for the good of all, we need to reflect on the numerous failed attempts at planned economies and the coercion they visit on participants. For there to be effective centralized economic planning, the first requirement seems to be an authoritarian government. Then later down the line there comes the requirement that 19% of the population may sometimes have to be wearing size 11 brown shoes because of a mistake in production quotas, or how about driving around in 1957 Pontiacs for lack of any market place alternatives. The fact that free markets are valued by virtually all Americans when combined with the fact that the governments in the US account for such an enormous proportion of all economic activity, should tip us off that the US economy is never going to be transformed into either a completely free market or a completely planned economy.

With this in mind, can't we let go of this, all or nothing, argument about what kind of economy the United States is to have, and pay closer attention to the real economic consequences of government actions past and future? Ours is a mixed economy where regulations and taxes are governing tools that apply to the economy. Sometimes they are implemented to favor certain industries, at other times to protect citizens against extreme poverty and predatory corporate practices, and at still other times to help actually encourage the competition. (Thankfully, our economic players don't compete with automatic weapons. They compete under rule of law.) What needs to be kept front and center is the fact that our governments, federal, state, and local, can and do sometimes deliver huge cash and regulatory gifts both to individuals and businesses. When a law is proposed that will affect the economy, we and our representatives are faced with a cost/benefit business decision. Will the proposal improve the way the market operates and the way of life it supports? Will it result in unreasonable risks or burdens for certain businesses or for others? And we must always be aware that government gifts that make little economic sense can also be great vote getters. So when government action on the economy is contemplated our question can be a simple one: Who actually benefits? Who actually pays? What, if any, are the side effects?

Viewed this way laws and regulations are hard economic issues. Issues like these matter. Sure there will be hype and spin, but economic issues are understandable in terms of good hard numbers both before and after implementation. As time passes, after a law takes effect, were these predictions correct? Does the law/regulation need tweaking? Does it need to be reversed? When it doesn't work right it's not time to blame. it's time to fix. And when candidates and office holders face issues armed with facts, we are faithfully represented in the complex intersection of economy and government.

Morality

It is clear that its authors wrote a US Constitution consistent with a belief in God and the moral teaching of religion. The First Amendment clearly states that Congress shall make no law prohibiting the free exercise of religion. However, it also states that Congress shall make no law "respecting an establishment of religion…" Was this some kind of double-talk cop-out.? This seeming contradiction is endlessly argued at the extremes of our politics. "As a Christian nation we must…" "My daughter cannot be required to pray in public school." However, this no prohibition/no respect pronouncement can seem sensible when placed in the context of politics as we have been considering it here, that is to say, a politics devoted to peacefully resolving our differences. After all, the authors of the U S constitution were the historical survivors of centuries of religious war and bloodshed. It should not be surprising that they charged us with the task of working through our religious differences without hurting one another.

They never said it was going to be easy, but they did say that you can't expect to use the law to beat up on folks who don't have religious beliefs like yours. On the other hand, they left morality out there as a proper subject in our laws. When we are convinced that something is wrong, we can and should recognize this in our laws. Not only that, but it has been our practice to discover new things that are wrong as we went along, and act to make these things illegal. Today we are faced with moral questions that would make no sense in the late 1700s; questions like for example, genetic modification of things like food crops, and even human embryos. Questions of right and wrong remain central to our politics. But morality must be handled carefully in representative governments lest it become an overwhelming destructive force. Let me explain what I mean by introducing an expert on government administered morality. Adam Michnik is a person with a fascinating biography that puts him in kind of a unique position to give us advice on morality in politics. As a Polish citizen he witnessed the oppressive domination of communist government in the days of the Soviet Union. But Adam Michnik is far more than a witness. He was a significant participant in the rise of the anti-Soviet opposition movement. As a journalist and activist, he was imprisoned, released and later imprisoned again. Still he managed to take part in the opposition's negotiations with the communist government which eventually resulted in elections in June of 1989. These elections brought members of the Solidarity movement into the Polish government and turned out to be the beginning of the end of Communist Party rule in that country, and in turn, one of the first events that together resulted in the demise of the entire Soviet Union.

Following the collapse of Soviet dominance there, he became editor of a major Polish newspaper, Gazeta Wyborcza. In the post-Soviet era Michnik became concerned when some political partisans in Poland took up a decidedly anti-communist tact which included, among other

CONCLUDING THOUGHTS

things, glowing recollections of the anti-communist hearings of US Senator Joseph McCarthy in the early 1950s. It seemed that some of Michnik's fellow citizens might be about to trade the decades long practice of persecuting non-communists for a turnover in which it would be appropriate to persecute communists with equal intensity. His reflections on this and other purge oriented political impulses appear in his book, *The Trouble with History: Morality, Revolution, and Counterrevolution*.[5] At length, he reaches back to the origins of the right and the left in the events and characters of the French Revolution.[6] Michnik's life experiences are politically heroic. He's been awarded the title "European of the Year," and with this anti-communist reaction going on there in Poland one might say he's been through the left/right gauntlet in both directions. He makes two points that put our examinations of morality in politics in sharp relief. First, attempts to practice politics on moral grounds lead to the necessity to purge out those who do not share our moral beliefs. Once underway, the morality campaign, which he likens to a virus, destroys the very idea of the citizen. It divides the population into the "sinless" and the "sinful," and pits the two against each other. To do their duty the sinless have to take over the government, the schools, the police and all other points of power. What makes his virus analogy so striking is the list of the names of parties and movements both of the left and the right that have become home to the self-proclaimed sinless from time to time. Of course his underlying point is that none of us are sinless. Here are just few actual names the sinless have come to be known by historically: the Inquisitors, the Jacobins, the Hutu, the Bolsheviks, the Nazis, the Khmer Rouge, the Taliban and now ISIS and Boko Haram. If any 10 of us sat down together, we could easily triple this list in just a few minutes.

Michnik speaks to us both from history and from personal experience when he cautions us about the risks of letting morality override citizenship. The second point he makes for us is that one of the markers that defines those infected by the virus of sinlessness is that they are completely uncompromising. Using this marker, I bet we could come up with a potential list of the sinless in our contemporary political scene. The question of whether or under what circumstances uncompromising politics leads to purges is certainly a separate one. There is probably no iron law of politics that goes from uncompromising stand-off, to vilification, and then on to oppression and purges. However, the potential should not be taken too lightly. Once again, political issues naturally come in all sizes, and we should always be on the lookout for those issues that clearly put the moral people in opposition to the immoral people. While this might seem obvious to you and me, there are many politicians both left and right who seem to miss this point repeatedly. As we examined morality in Part III, when we compare it with the kind of political morality that can get to be viral in Michnik's sen of the term, the skepticism about absolutes and all-encompassing explanations that we saw in postmodernism seems downright safe and appealing.

We got to Michnik and his warnings about the sinless as we were trying to figure out what the authors of the US Constitution thought about the place of religion. Ghita Ionescu (1913-1996) took on this church/state question from quite a different point of view. Like Michnik, Ionescu lived and wrote in the shadows cast by the Soviet Communist government in his homeland, Romania. But unlike Michnik, he got out and settled in the UK and the United States where he studied and wrote about government. In 1965, he even launched a non-communist Romanian government in exile. In his book, *Politics and the Pursuit of Happiness*, Ionescu considers politics in modern industrial societies.[7] Once again this takes him back to the events of the French Revolution and the writings that inspired its participants. Here he shows us that a flawed way of thinking, on both the right and the left, entered politics back then and has remained with us ever since. Put simply, it is the thought, the belief, that politics and government can deliver happiness. The power of government can dispense comforts, it can also dispense pains, but happiness is and remains something in the realm of individual existence. It is a quest that you and I must face on our own and with those we know and love. Politics can only address the context of that quest. Attempts of governments to deliver happiness bring either coercion and repression on the one hand or a permissiveness that threatens the social bonds that permit us to coexist peacefully. Thus, for Ionescu, happiness is not something government can ever provide.

But you already know that. Come to think of it, that is probably part of why you find extreme political activists hard to take. Well, just so you know, according to Ionescu, this would make you politically correct. Once again the political absolutists are the ones we are being warned against. The very diversity of our nation and its many cultural traditions fits the postmodern perspective as well. If there is a single characteristic that makes the United States different from the rest, it is our incredible cultural, racial and ethnic diversity. However, these same cultural, racial and ethnic differences are the raw materials for political appeals that turn citizens against one another. If a majority of political activists had the more postmodern outlook that we explored in Chapter 8, we'd have a moral climate that not only tolerates diversity but excites in its possibilities.

Before going on we should place these political morality concerns in the context of the international scene. There we confront what is surely one of the most striking political issues that we have ever faced. And I say we, because, whether we are political zealots or nonvoters, all of us face this new violent threat to peaceful dispute resolutions. International terrorist groups and those heavily armed and very disturbed individual citizens that dwell among us have become a new and distinctly different enemy. From the school shooters to the organized and heavily armed Jihadists forces, this latest enemy has created a brand new kind of violent confrontation. Their power is in their leverage. But their leverage is not in their numbers. Nor is it in their organization. Whether isolated individuals at home or collectivities abroad, these people are disgustingly preoccupied with cruelty and death. So what's new? There have always been people like that in the variety that comprises us as humans. What sets these people apart is the intersection of their obvious violent and suicidal impulses and the instantaneous global fame that contemporary media offers. Whatever the outcome, they can be sure that their threats will be exhaustively featured in the media and confronted in the political arena. Should you be weighing in on this? War, crime, national sovereignty, press freedom, the arms trade, human trafficking, religious freedom, travel restrictions, government surveillance, mental illness, are just some of the areas affected.

Government Growth

Along with economics and morality there is a third subject that we have bumped up against several times in the preceding pages. As all the rest of this goes on, the government continues to grow. This might seem to be a small point, but it is important. It is already the biggest player in our market economy by far. We know that both the right and the left see this as a problem. Their arguments about what parts of this monster they would like to do without don't acknowledge a central truth about large organizations. Large organizations, including government organizations, don't shrink. They grow. Walmart got bigger and bigger. It carried more and more lines of merchandise. It began to control its suppliers. It went international, planting stores all over the globe. Large organizations including governments keep getting bigger, not smaller. Over time they take on new tasks and new people to do them. And old tasks get bigger. The Interstate Highway system never stops growing. The FBI's criminal registry, for example, now grows at the rate of 11,000 names per day. Nineteen September 11 terrorists brought the Department of Homeland Security into being. Growth for organizations is easy and natural. This is why, with minor blips, and periods where more things are farmed out to contractors, the size of government increases pretty much regardless of whether conservatives or progressives are in power. Politicians may campaign on smaller government but they never really deliver results on these promises. Budgeting restrictions seldom do more than create deceptions, contracting out and new problems.

CONCLUDING THOUGHTS

As each of us contemplates politics and how we relate to it, this natural growing tendency should get our attention. Only an active and critical electorate that is concerned about government growth can really resist an ever-intrusive expanding government and maintain a relationship between government and the citizens that complements our way of life.

Where do You go From Here?

What if you do Nothing?

Without new input from folks like you who don't now participate, one current trend is not about to reverse itself or slow down. The stand-off of the left and right will likely remain. Not only will the partisans of the left and the right continue to dominate our politics, but in their zeal to oppose and obliterate one another, less and less that is important will get done. The polarization might dissipate by itself. However, without a broader participation beyond the extremes, this is not likely. At several points I asked you to stand back and try to think about things from a different perspective. If we do this and reflect on all we have been considering, we can behold something quite amazing: the longest running and certainly one of the most impressive instance of a self-governing republic so far anywhere. Lots of people have been thriving in this rich land for more than a couple of centuries now, and they have been settling a lot of major differences short of violence. Some, among us, have started in obscurity and reached the heights in their chosen pursuits. Sometimes the more typical woman or man did pretty well, sometimes, not so well. The flaws are glaring and the retreats back into violence are far too many. As impressive as our self-governing might seem, it has not, for example, been able to deal peacefully with the challenges that were and are presented by the continent's indigenous peoples or the millions of forced immigrants from the African continent and their descendants. But for most of the rest of the people, our institutions of self governing have brought an unprecedented way of life that has been the envy of most of the rest of the world.

As a consequence of the polarization and distrust that now characterizes our elected officials and the people who vote for them, things of urgent consequence don't get done. At the same time politicians and their supporters openly malign whole segments of our citizenry. As this goes on, organized interests can influence policy in the absence of any concern for what used to be called the public interest. Our Congress vilifies foreign enemies and funds combat against them, but refuses to declare wars. Major decisions about the political direction of the country are made by the courts. The decline in mutual trust and respect among our elected officials leads away from compromise and allows disputes to simmer for decades.

It has been said that with representative government the people get precisely the government they deserve. To this many might say, "fine, OK, it may be a mess, but it isn't really a problem for me, and the way I am spending my life." Though I have tried to make this way of thinking more difficult for you, readers, some of you might still be inclined to think this way. Don't forget, the actions taken today by government have implications far beyond the present. Things can get worse. You not only have to be comfortable with the way things are now but also with the directions that government is taking us. This concern for the subtle unfolding of a bleak future is sometimes argued with the illustration of the frog in the pot of water on the stove. The frog is having a great time swimming around, and a rising temperature can even be stimulating. Bet a lot of frogs could do worse than that. But as things continue to slowly heat up, we end up with a boiled frog. Early in the last century totalitarian dictatorships emerged in several countries. The violent and oppressive regimes in both Germany and Russia, for example emerged out of functioning democratic governments where things kind of went beyond the boiling point. If these pages do nothing more than increase your appreciation of how our governing works short of coercion and violence, then at very least, you might be on the lookout for real threats out there.

CONCLUDING THOUGHTS

While this state of affairs may seem discouraging, I once more remind you that there is an enormous untapped resource out there that could completely reorient our politics. After all, if we consider only the people now active and motivated, this stale political confrontation involves far less than half of us. And of course you, my readers, are a part of that untapped resource. Ask yourself, has this intense polarization taken you in? Are there actions that we can take through self-government that improve on the present but do not send us tripping and falling into those moral and economic terrors that the extreme partisans constantly warn us about? Are there regulations that could be dispensed with that could increase our liberty without doing harm? Are there international agreements that might make life better and war less likely? Has modern technology enabled people to do new kinds of harm which new laws should prohibit? Are there problems and issues that confront your nation, your state, or your community which you might want to weigh in on?

Earlier, in this chapter, I compared sorting through all the hype and nonsense of our politics with the kind of thing you do every day as you interpret all the claims and spin and make your choices in the marketplace. Yet, if we belabor this consumer analogy a bit more, we come upon a couple of important differences that politics presents us with. The first difference is that we cannot take our business elsewhere. The governments we live with are quite literally a monopoly, the only game in town. Second, after we cut through hype in politics (unless we are among the multi-billionaires) we cannot make individual purchases in this market place. At best we can only "chip in" with other people to get things we want. We chip in with all kinds of things: things like votes, contributions, door to door canvassing, contacts with those who are supposed to represent us, even running for office. It might be helpful to dwell for a moment on these two characteristics upon which the shopping analogy breaks down.

Since this self-governing thing is an ongoing process which only involves those who participate, this brings us back to you, the non-participant. You may have thought that you have been ignoring or even rejecting our political system, but by now, I hope that you can see that in an even greater sense our political system is rejecting you. It was designed to settle differences people have without resorting to violence, and low and behold, since you are not included among those people, any differences you might have don't matter. Our government not only neglects those who don't participate, it often harms them. So your primary concern should not be that you reject our politics, it should be a concern for you and the millions of other Americans whose opinions, wishes, and hopes are being completely ignored. If our government does things you think are outrageous, if it coerces you into doing things you don't think are just or right, see if it helps if you remind yourself of the fact that, in a real sense, it isn't your government.

For you it is government that serves the wishes of others; others who probably don't care about you, who probably don't agree with you, and others you quite possibly wouldn't like very much. It is almost funny. Trust me, I participate and follow this stuff, some of these real active folks strike me as just plain selfish, others seem just plain crazy. Oh, but they have a voice in your government, whereas, you do not.

Thus the answer to the question of whose government it is, is clear. It is not yours. And even though you may not find things personally oppressive and hurtful at the moment, that could change at any time without your permission. Sorry, but I will obviously never be a preacher or a salesman. If that's the best I can do at trying to scare you or shame you, I probably didn't get much more than a yawn. In the end, you'll make up your own mind.

Do You See a Part for Yourself?

At the very start I singled out my intended audience as the people who choose not to vote. OK, so what if voting actually is not the end-all for you. What we have gone over in the intervening pages may have

CONCLUDING THOUGHTS

enabled you to glean more than a few new reasons to keep on not voting. Full disclosure: a lot of times, I myself think the quote above from Emma Goldman rings true. But voting or not voting is not quite the central point. Instead, I think the quote from Thomas Jefferson comes closer to the mark. By contemporary standards it might seem to be a statement that is ridiculously optimistic about the prospects of effective self government. However, he is speaking for your government when he says that governing here assumes that, as citizens, we are all engaged in it. And whether it was true in his time or not, it is demonstrably false in these times we live in. Nevertheless, his point is still valid in one important sense. You are assumed to be a part of our governing process. It is depending on you to meet its very definition as self-government. What part have you played thus far? Aside from voting, what part might you take on in the future?

The governments, federal, state and local, that each of us live under will continue to interface with the economy that we rely upon. They will continue to elaborate and enforce rule of law which encourages some things as morally right and discourage some things as morally wrong. And unless action is taken, they will follow their inherent tendency to grow and take on new activities. If you did not fully sense it as you started this little book, you no doubt now realize that you have the knowledge and some tools to enable you to take on this thing, US politics, on your own terms. I am confident that you can deal comfortably with those on the extremes of our economic and moral debates, and find your own way.

Look at you. Maybe you are not politically engaged. But if this book's done anything, I hope it allows you to see the bright side of this. As a non-participant, at least you are far less likely than the partisans to be whacked out with uncompromising political beliefs. And given the numbers, you and the rest of the nonparticipants hold the leverage to control the extremes and keep them in check. Peaceful dispute resolution needs the calming influence of people like you. Its survival in this country demands that we confront issues with mutual respect and reasoned debate. Just having the extremes suspecting that you might weigh in at any time would caution them. You could get up for that, couldn't you? You wouldn't have to have an interest in everything that comes along. In fact, you might think that you'd rather ignore a whole lot of it. However, if you and a lot more of the currently non-participating folks started talking and acting on your political preferences, this all-or-nothing kind of politics might give way to the kind of practical, compromising , problem-solving politics that a self-governing people deserve.

With the politics of trust that these TV personalities are hawking at us, we are allowing real political issues, and relevant choices about how things are here and now, to recede into the deep grooves of the polarized economic and moral divides that have been dominating the scene for too long. You've probably guessed already that I am getting into that pitch I promised. Here it is. Issue based politics doesn't necessarily have to work that way. Issues can stand alone. Solutions to the problems we face can be considered on their merits alone. We are not somehow required to classify each proposed solution as an element irrevocable drift to the left or the right.

Could regulating Uber make the service more reliable? Should we be able to pass and enforce zoning laws? Should we lower school area speed limits? Should we enforce better standards for agricultural produce sold as "organic?" Are there gun purchases that should be prevented by law? Should the proliferation of renewable energy sources be encouraged by tax breaks or even industry subsidies? Should we facilitate the building of the pipeline from Canada to the Gulf of Mexico? Should the stock markets have special tax rules for income from hedge funds or from enormous computer-executed securities trades that are held for only seconds and then sold? Should laws encourage or discourage employees from forming unions? Should we have laws which encourage more privately operated schools? Should we attempt to reduce the prison population? Should we sign the treaty? Should we go to war? These and countless other questions can be

CONCLUDING THOUGHTS

confronted as issues onto themselves in present time. It is not necessary, nor is it effective, to insist that they each be addressed as mere details of an historically predictable and inescapable descent down a slippery slope to complete disaster at the hands of sinister forces on the left or the right.

Unfortunately, reasoned discussion of the issues that confront us here and now has become a rare occurrence in our politics. Most every time that partisans engage on an issue the discourse is quickly reduced, distilled would be a better word, into something very close to the following exchange: "You conservatives are seriously paranoid." As against, "You progressives are hopelessly naive." The issues and the facts, which could be authenticated and brought to bear on them, are lost like the steam as this distillation takes place. To put this in terms of the political divisions we encountered in Parts II and III, government measures that improve the quality of life for many Americans can accomplish their goals without disastrous consequences for free markets. Problems can be addressed in the spirit of genuine human progress with a sober recognition that we humans must be on guard against the flaws and weaknesses that all of us harbor in our characters.

Think of it this way, as someone who hasn't been caught up in this stuff, you don't have to take part in this particular ritual of our contemporary politics. Because you are not trapped in the stand-off, you are prepared for a genuine consideration of each issue by testing the facts and seeking that path which seems likely to do the most good and least harm so far as we can see things ahead of us. And when the doctrinaire bullies try to put you in line, their arguments will only reveal the weakness of the assumptions they begin with.

Your political perspective should enable you to objectively follow the implementation of laws that get passed just as researchers monitor the progress of their experiments. And as laws are implemented frequently, they reveal shortcomings for which corrections can be legislated, rather than simply using any shortcomings to attack those who proposed the law in the first place. If this way of thinking suits you, you are not alone. What is amazing is that there are millions of people who would like our politics to be like that, and there are a whole lot of good, dedicated, politicians and even some of those political pros among these millions.

Maybe you live in a place that is so blue or so red that your vote doesn't seem to matter at all. So what? Voting is only one of the ways to make a difference politically. As I mentioned earlier, there are lots of ways to do politics. Could you volunteer for campaigns, work in person, or on the internet (as of 2015 Facebook alone was getting 160 million US visitors per month), volunteer for community service, write letters, blog posts and comments, put bumper stickers on your vehicle, or signs on your lawn, sign petitions, write articles or books, to publicize your concerns, (Alexander Hamilton and British citizen, John Maynard Keynes, never got themselves elected to high office in this country but their writings still influence on our economy)? You might decide to pick a single issue. Study that one issue enough and yours might be the decisive expert opinion. Maybe you'll just talk to family and friends, or make contributions, or even write a song (like Francis Scott Key, or Woody Guthrie), or join in on political party activities, run for office, start your own party, blog about your views, or hit the streets to protest and maybe get arrested, (on the left, the anti-war movement in the 60s and 70s, on the right, the more recent Tea Party movement, both emerged as a series of rallies and street demonstrations, and both came to exercise serious constraints on what our elected officials might do.) By all means, pick your preference and volunteer for an issue or even a candidate. At very least you will get a sense of the pleasure of socializing with folks you can talk with and relate to. You could end up at work for an organization devoted to your most important issue. And don't sell voting short. As the price of elections goes up, close elections are more likely. You might someday be a part of that small margin that decides an election. It was none other than the father of John F. Kennedy who is supposed to have reminded his son in a 1958 telegram. "Dear Jack, Don't buy a single vote more than is necessary. I'll be damned if I'm going to pay for a landslide."[8]

CONCLUDING THOUGHTS

It has been my aim to fill you in on enough about how this political game is going, to allow you to, at very least, begin to recognize where you fit into it. Need I remind you at this point? There are lots of your fellow citizens who don't buy this peaceful dispute resolution stuff at all. We have already considered the chilling thought that some such folks even have the arms, the ammo, and the expressed intent to defend themselves against our government and anybody else they differ with politically--like maybe even you. Ooops, I just did it again. I started sounding like Chicken Little, screaming my inane, "the political sky is falling" chant. I've said enough. You've endured enough. Now, it's your turn to talk politics.

Notes

Introduction

1. From his movie *Husbands and Wives*, http://en.wikiquote.org/wiki/Talk:Woody_Allen.

2. Orwell, George. Politics and the English Language,1946, P. 8, see, https://www.mtholyoke.edu/acad/intrel/orwell46.htm.

3. The Federalist Papers, http://thomas.loc.gov/home/histdox/fed_10.html.

4. Boston Globe, September 21, 2003.

5. http://usgovinfo.about.com/od/thepoliticalsystem/a/whynotvote.htm.

6. Lemann, Nicholas, The New Deal We Didn't Know, New York Review of Books, September, 26, 2013, Pp. 85-92.

7. Littman, Margaret, Women fans have gridiron pros grinning, Marketing News, February 2, 1998. Also http://www.forbes.com/sites/aliciajessop/2012/11/26/how-new-marketing-approaches-helped-the-nfl-achieve-triple-digit-growth-in-womens-apparel-sales/.

8. The Internet Classics Archive | Politics by Aristotle https://www.google.com/search?q=Politics+by+Aristotle+classics.mit.edu%2FAristotle%2Fpolitics.htm%2F&ie=utf-8&oe=utf-8.

NOTES

Chapter 1

1. http://www.brainyquote.com/quotes/topics/topic_politics3.html#L0igMkuoUBTRpYqS.99.

2. http://dictionary.kids.net.au/word/politics.

3. Mao Tse-Tung, Quotations from the Chairman, Peking, Foreign Languages Press, 1996, P. 117.

4. Hobbes, Thomas, Leviathan, chapter XIII, https://www.gutenberg.org/files/3207/3207-h/3207-h.htm.

5. http://www.youtube.com/watch?v=4xGpDvWeUik, one of several sites.

6. Golding, William, Lord of the Flies, New York, Penguin Putnam Inc., 1954.

7. Birke, Sarah, How ISIS Rules, New York Review of Books, February 5, 2015, Pp. 26-28.

8. Veblen, Thorstein, Theory of the Leisure Class, chapter six, http://www.gutenberg.org/files/833/833-h/833-h.htm.

Chapter 2

1. Gustave Le Bon, The Crowd; A Study of the Popular Mind, A public Domain Book, donated by Caere Corporation, P. 6.

2. Russell Kirk, ED. The Portable Conservative Reader, New York, Penguin, 1982. p. xxiii.

3. From, Declaration of the Rights of Man, http://avalon.law.yale.edu/18th_century/rightsof.asp.

NOTES

4. Chernow, Ron, Washington: A life, New York, The Penguin Press, 2010, P. 658.

5. Schama, Simon, Citizens, A Chronicle of the French Revolution, New York, Alfred A. Knopf, 1989, P. 778.

6. Nussbaum, Martha C., Political Emotions, Why Love Matters for Justice, Cambridge, MA, The Belknap Press, 2013, Pp. 58-65.

7. http://www.studyplace.org/w/images/3/38/Orwell-1938-homage-to-catalonia.pdf.

8. Manufactured Consent, Zeitgeist Videos catalog.

9. Mill, John Stuart, On Liberty, http://www.gutenberg.org/files/34901/34901-h/34901-h.htm.

10. http://en.wikipedia.org/wiki/Jeremy Bentham.

11. Nussbaum, Political Emotions, Pp. 70-73.

12. Burke, Edmund, Reflections on the Revolution in France, New York, Bartleby, 2001, http://www.bartleby.com/24/3/.

Chapter 3

1. Quoted in Russell Kirk, ED. The Portable Conservative Reader, New York Penguin, 1982. p. xi.

2. Locke, John, Second Treatise of Government, Chapter II, Sec. 6. http://www.constitution.org/jl/2ndtreat.htm.

3. http://briandeer.com/social/thatcher-society.htm.

4. Baer, John, The Pledge of Allegiance, A revised History and Analysis, 2007, http://oldtimeislands.org/pledge/pledge.htm.

NOTES

Chapter 4

1. Smith, Adam, The Wealth of Nations, New York, Modern Library, 1994, P. 15.

2. Karl Marx, "The Critique of the Gotha Program, Part I, https://www.marxists.org/archive/marx/works/1875/gotha/ch01.htm.

3. The New Testament, Mathew Chapter 16, verse 26.

4. Porter, Eduardo, The Price of Everything, New York, Portfolio/Penguin, 2011, Pp. 22-23.

5. Ranson, David, Monetary Policy, Market Prices, and Supply-side Forecasting, Cato Journal, Spring/Summer, 192, Pp. 197-229.

6. https://www.youtube.com/watch?v=4vuW6tQ0218.

7. Melville, Herman, Moby Dick, chapter 16, http://www.gutenberg.org/files/2701/2701-h/2701-h.htm#2HCH0013.

8. http://www.pbs.org/wgbh/americanexperience/features/timeline/crash/.

9 The Key to Industrial Capitalism: Limited Liability, The Economist, December 23, 1999.

10. http://www.theonlineinvestor.com/large_caps/.

11. Hitchens, Christopher "Jefferson Versus the Muslim Pirates" in Arguably, Essays by Christopher Hitchens, New York, Twelve, 2011, Pp. 12-20.

12. Chorney, Harold R. , The theory of the business cycle in the work of Keynes, Hayek and Schumpeter: What do we know in the age of globalization? 2001, http://haroldchorneyeconomist.com/2011/09/13/the-theory-of-the-business-cycle-in-hayek-keynes-and-schumpeter/.

NOTES

13. Coll, Steve, Private Empire: Exxonmobil and American Power, New York, Penguin, 2013, Pp. 54 – 57.

Chapter 5

1. Keynes, J. M., A Tract on Monetary Reform (1923) Ch. 3, http://delong.typepad.com/keynes-1923-a-tract-on-monetary-reform.pdf.

2. Schumpeter, Joseph, Capitalism, Socialism, and Democracy, New York, Harper Torchbooks, 1976, P. 364.

3. Collapse, directed by Chris Smith, https://www.youtube.com/watch?v=IVd-zAXACrU&feature=youtu.be%20%C2%B7.

4. http://www.cbpp.org/cms/?fa=view&id=1258, http://www.usgovernmentspending.com/breakdown, http://www.heritage.org/research/reports/2013/08/federal-spending-by-the-numbers-2013, https://www.census.gov/govs/cog/, http://www.cato.org/publications/congressional-testimony/challenges-us-economic-recovery-federal-state-spending, http://www.forbes.com/sites/joshbarro/2012/04/16/lessons-from-the-decades-long-upward-march-of-government-spending/.

5. http://www.theamericanconservative.com/the-norquist-anti-tax-pledge-is-cracking-and-thats-a-good-thing/.

6. Schumpeter, Joseph, Capitalism, Socialism, and Democracy, New York, Harper Torchbooks, 1976, P. 364

7. Adams, David, Cuba's leaders see private farmers as key to saving socialism, Tampa Bay Times, 08-16-2009.

8. Orwell, George, Animal Farm, New York, Holt, Rinehart And Winston, 2009, chapter 9.

NOTES

9. Quoted in, Howard S. Becker, Tricks of the Trade, How to Think About Your Research While You Are Doing It, Chicago, University of Chicago Press, 1998, P. 2.

10. Bobbio, Norberto, Left and Right The Significance of a Political Distinction, Chicago, University of Chicago Press, 1996, Pp. 20-21 http://cnqzu.com/library/Politics/Bobbio-Norberto-Left-and-Right-Significance-Political-Distinction.pdf.

11. Thompson, John A, Woodrow Wilson: Profiles in Power, London, Longman, 2002, P. 164.

12. Lemann, Nicholas, The New Deal We Didn't Know, New York Review of Books, September, 26, 2013, Pp. 85-92.

13. Bobbio, Left and Right, P. 19.

14. Behnegar, Nasser, Leo Strauss, Max Weber, and the Scientific Study of Politics, Chicago, University of Chicago Press, 2003, P. 43

15. Quoted by Paul Krugman, "The Mellon Doctrine," New York Times, 03/31/2011.

16. Roosevelt. F.D., Address at the Democratic State Convention, Syracuse, N.Y., September 29, 1936, two final paragraphs, http://www.presidency.ucsb.edu/ws/index.php?pid=15142.

17. Friedman, Milton, and Anna J. Schwartz, A Monetary History of the United States, Princeton, NJ, Princeton University Press, 1963

18. https://mises.org.

19. laffercenter.com/the-laffer-center-2/the-laffer-curve/.

Chapter 6

1. Berlin, Isaiah, A Message to the 20th Century, New York Review of Books, October 23, 2014, P. 37.

NOTES

2. From "The Last Word," MSNBC, 06/12/2013.

3. Edmond, David, Would You Kill the Fat Man: The Trolley Problem and What your Answer Tells us About Right and Wrong, Princeton, NJ, Princeton University Press, 2014, Chapters 3 and 5.

4. http://moral.wjh.harvard.edu/.

5. Westen, Drew, The Political Brain: The Role of Emotion in Deciding the Fate of the Nation, New York, Public Affairs, 2007.

6. Solomon, Andrew, The Reckoning, The New Yorker, 03-14-2014, Pp. 36-45.

7. Diagnostic and Statistical Manuel of Mental Disorders Third Edition, Washington, D.C. American Psychiatric Association, 1987, Pp. 342-346.

8. http://www.pewsocialtrends.org/2008/10/23/republicans-still-happy-campers/.

9. http://www.reuters.com/article/2012/05/01/us-mayancalendar-poll-idUSBRE8400XH20120501.

10. Gallup 2009, http://en.wikipedia.org/wiki/Importance_of_religion_by_country.

11. Dennett, Daniel, Breaking the Spell, New York, Viking, 2006 P. 222ff.

12. http://www1.umn.edu/news/news-releases/2006/UR_RELEASE_MIG_2816.html.

13. http://www.pewglobal.org/2014/03/13/worldwide-many-see-belief-in-god-as-essential-to-morality/.

14. Edmond, David, Would You Kill The Fat Man, P. 170.

NOTES

15. Haidt, Jonathan, THE RIGHTEOUS MIND: Why Good People Are Divided by Politics and Religion, New York, Pantheon Books, 2012, chapter 11.

16. http://www.compilerpress.ca/Competitiveness/Anno/Anno%20Cranston%20Ideology%20EB%202003.htm.

17. Weber, Max, From Max Weber: Essays in Sociology, New York, Oxford University Press, 1946, Pp. 59-60.

18. Wilson, Edward O, The Meaning of Human Existence, New York, Liveright Publishing, 2014, Pp. 86-88.

Chapter 7

1. S. Jackson, http://www.freerepublic.com/focus/f-news/924558/posts A clever paraphrase of Leo Strauss, Natural Right and History, University of Chicago Press, Chicago, IL, 1965, P. 3.

2. Paine, Thomas, Common Sense, in Paine, Collected Writings, New York, The Library of America, Literary Classics of the United States, Inc., 1955, P. 6.

3. Quoted by Richard Rorty, Contingency, Irony, and Solidarity, Cambridge, UK, Cambridge University Press, 1989, P. xv.

4. Lakoff, George, and Moral Politics, What Liberals and Conservatives Think, 2nd Edition, Chicago, University of Chicago Press, 2002.

5. Hibbing, John R, Kevin B. Smith, and John R. Alford, Differences in Negativity Bias Underlie Variations in Political Ideology, Behavioral & Brain Sciences, June 2014, Vol. 37 Issue 3, P. 297.

6. http://www.libertylawsite.org/liberty-forum/natural-law-natural-rights-and-private-property/.

7. The New Testament, Romans, Chapter 2, verses 14 -15.

NOTES

8. http://www.aquinasonline.com/Topics/natlaw.html.

9. Strauss, Leo, Natural Right in History, Chicago, University of Chicago Press, 1965, Chapter V.

10. Locke, John, Second Treatise Concerning Civil Government, Chapters 5, 9, and 19,http://www.gutenberg.org/files/7370/7370-h/7370-h.htm.

11. Finnis, John, Natural Law and Natural Rights, Oxford, UK, Clarendon Press, 1992, P. 23.

12. Thompson, E.P., Witness Against the Beast: William Blake and the Moral Law, New York, The New Press, 1993, Chapters I and 2.

13. Lanchester, John, "Money Talks," The New Yorker, August 4, 2014, Pp. 30-33.

14. Benjamin, Andrew, Ed. The Lyotard Reader, Oxford, UK, Blackwell, 1989, P. 316

15.Leviticus Chapter 20, verse 10; Deuteronomy Chapter 21, verses 18 – 21; and, 1 Kings Chapter 11, verses 1 – 3.

16. http://www.peta.org/.

17. http://americanhumanist.org/Humanism/Definitions_of_Humanism.

18. Wilson, David Sloan, Does Altruism Exist, Culture Genes and the Welfare of Others, New Haven, CT, Yale University Press, 2015, Pp. 113-114.

Chapter 8

1. Didion, Joan, We Tell Ourselves Stories in Order to Live: Collected Nonfiction, New York, Everyman's Library, 2006, p. 185

2. Coen, Ethan, and Joel Coen, *The Big Lebowsky*, 1998, http://www.imdb.com/title/tt0118715/ .

NOTES

3. Dennet, Daniel C, Darwin's Dangerous Idea, New York, Simon and Schuster Paperbacks, 1995, P. 59

4. Ewen, Stuart, PR! A Social History of Spin, New York, Basic Books, 1996, Pp. 3-18

5. Malinowski, Bronisław, Argonauts of the Western Pacific, London, Routledge & Kegan Paul LTD, 1922, Made available by the internet archive, Pp. 1-26.

6. Nietzsche, Friedrich The Will to Power, (Nov. 1887-March 1888), P. 2 https://ia700508.us.archive.org/6/items/TheWillToPower-Nietzsche/will_to_power-nietzsche.pdf.

7. http://www.academia.edu/201465/Heidegger_on_Philosophy_and_Language, P.8.

8. http://www.pg.com/en_US/brands/all_brands.shtml.

9. Bedbury, Scott with Stephen Fenichell, A New Brand World, New York, The Penguin Group, Pp. 13-14

10. Nobokov, Vladimir, Lolita, New York, Everyman's Library, 1955, P. 330

11. http://www.imdb.com/list/ls051370237/.

12. Benjamin, Andrew, Ed. The Lyotard Reader, Oxford, UK, Blackwell, 1989, P.xvi.

13. https://www.youtube.com/watch?v=s_c3cNG5ttk&list=PLZ9xwy-OlUxWOBQvn4WSKivKFET3-LxCk.

Chapter 9

1. http://www.vanityfair.com/news/2010/11/moynihan-letters-201011.

2.. Sinclair, Upton, I, Candidate for Governor: And How I Got Licked, Los Angeles, University of California Press, 1994, P. 109.

NOTES

3. Offerman, Nick, Gumption, New York, Dutton, 2015, Pp. 99-100.

4. http://www.foia.gov/how-to.html.

5. https://www.opm.gov/policy-data-oversight/data-analysis-documentation/federal-employment-reports/historical-tables/total-government-employment-since-1962/.

6 Ewen, Stuart, PR! A Social History of Spin, New York, Basic Books, 1996, P. 48.

7. http://www.businessinsider.com/largest-ethnic-groups-in-america-2013-8.

8. http://www.irs.gov/pub/irs-pdf/p4220.pdf.

9. http://definitions.uslegal.com/e/equal-time-doctrine/.

10. https://en.wikipedia.org/wiki/Fairness_Doctrine.

11. https://en.wikipedia.org/wiki/List_of_think_tanks_in_the_United_States.

12. Coll, Steve, Private Empire: Exxon Mobil and American Power, New York, Penguin Press, 2012, Pp. 335-347.

13. http://users.clas.ufl.edu/ufhatch/pages/01-Courses/current-courses/08sr-newton.htm?utm_source=lasindias.info/blog.

Chapter 10

1. Hitler, Adolf, Mein Kampf, Pp.135-137. http://www.angelfire.com/folk/bigbaldbob88/MeinKampf.pdf.

2. Suskind, Ron, "Faith, Certainty and the Presidency of George W. Bush," The New York Times Magazine, October 17, 2004.

3. http://www.thenation.com/article/170841/exclusive-lee-atwaters-infamous-1981-interview-southern-strategy.

NOTES

4. http://www.afirstlook.com/edition_9/theory_list, Click on: " Spiral of Silence (PDF) Elisabeth Noelle-Nuemann."

5. Shermer, Michael, The Believing Brain, New York, Times Books, 2011, P. 5.

6. Luntz, Frank, Words that Work: It's Not What You Say, It's What People Hear, New York, Hyperion, 2007, Pp. 72-80.

7. http://www.completecampaigns.com/article.asp?articleid=8.

8. http://www.annenbergpublicpolicycenter.org/new-annenberg-survey-asks-how-well-do-americans-understand-the-constitution/.

9. http://www.npr.org/blogs/itsallpolitics/2012/05/21/153024432/sophomoric-members-of-congress-talk-like-10th-graders-analysis-shows.

10. https://www.youtube.com/watch?v=lstA7j5fmio.

11. Brock, David, Blinded By the Right, New York, Three Rivers Press, 2003

Chapter 11

1. Darnton, Robert, "How to Become a Celebrity," New York Review of Books, May 21, 2015, P. 8-10.

2. Quoted in Lewis H. Lapham, "Ignorance of Things Past," Harper's Magazine, May 2012.

3. De Tochville, Democracy in America, translated by George Lawrence, New York, Harper & Row, 1966, Pp. 223-4.

4. Putnam, Robert D., Bowling A: The Collapse and Revival of American Community, New York, Touchstone, Simon & Schuster, 2001.

5. www.c-span.org/video/?157570-1/book-discussion-bowling-alone-collapse-american-community.

NOTES

6. https://www.google.com/search?q=mckinley+front+porch+campaign&tbm=isch&tbo=u&source=univ&sa=X&ved=0CCYQsARqFQoTCLja-6m6q8cCFYLPgAodhRgMDw&biw=839&bih=633.

7. Fowles, Jib, Starstruck, Celebrity Performers and the American Public, Washington D.C., Smithsonian Institution Press, P. 14.

8. Wills, Garry, The Politics of Celebrity: John Wayne's America, New York, Simon and Schuster, 1997, Pp. 107-110.

9. Becker, Howard S, Art Worlds, Berkeley and Los Angeles, University of California Press, 2008, Pp. 7-9.

10. Hershenson, Janet and Jane Jenkins, A Star is Found, New York, Harcourt, 2006, P.46.

11. https://www.youtube.com/watch?v=XIeQWy2SR9s.

12. At two hours 35 minutes into a C-Span video of the meeting, http://www.c-span.org/video/?292260-1/white-house-health-care-summit-part-1.

13. http://finance.townhall.com/columnists/politicalcalculations/2012/10/21/counting_all_the_us_governments_regulations.

Chapter 12

1. Meacham, Jon, Thomas Jefferson: The Art of Power, New York, Random House, 2012, P. 499.

2. Wills, Garry, James Madison, New York, Times Books Henry Holt Company, 2002, P. xviii.

3. Habermas, Jürgen, The Future of Human Nature, Malden, MA, Polity Press, 2003, P. 32.

4. https://www.lewrockwell.com/2013/07/butler-shaffer/the-democracy-illusion/.

NOTES

5. Michnik, Adam, The Trouble with History: Morality, Revolution, and Counterrevolution, New Haven, Yale University Press, 2014. Pp. 31-35.

6. Ibid, Pp. 55-98.

7. Ionescu, Ghita, Politics and the Pursuit of Happiness, New York, Longman Group Limited, 1984, Introduction and chapter 9.

8. http://www.esquire.com/news-politics/interviews/a6770/kennedy-family-history-0110/.

www.ingramcontent.com/pod-product-compliance
Lightning Source LLC
Chambersburg PA
CBHW020931180426
43192CB00035B/185